Reasonableness in Liberal Political Philosophy

This collection offers a thought-provoking critique of the role of the concept of reasonableness in liberal political philosophy, focusing on the proposed relationship between reasonableness and the establishment and preservation of a just and stable liberal polity. The chapters explore the explicit and implicit use of the idea of reasonableness, presenting an analysis that both incorporates normative and empirical observations and employs a number of different analytical approaches, including liberalism, feminism, environmentalism, Marxism, and communitarianism.

This book is unique in providing in a single volume a critique that engages not only a vast array of issues but also a diversity of critical perspectives. In the course of doing so, it not only rectifies a deficiency in the existing scholarship, it also addresses the issues of sociopolitical justice and stability, offering new, insightful critiques that respond to the increasingly complex circumstances and conflicts that confront life in contemporary pluralistic societies. This book will be a valuable resource for those interested in liberal political philosophy and its potential usefulness in helping to secure a just and stable polity.

This book was previously published as a special issue of the *Critical Review of Social and Political Philosophy*.

Shaun P. Young is an Instructor in the Department of Political Science at Carleton University (Canada). His publications include *Beyond Rawls: An Analysis of the Concept of Political Liberalism* (Rowman and Littlefield Publishing Group, 2002); and *Political Liberalism: Varations on a Theme* (State University of New York Press, 2004), editor. He has also published a number of articles examining various aspects of liberal political philosophy. Forthcoming works include a book entitled *John Rawls: The Search for Justice and Stability in a Plural World* (under contract with the State University of New York Press). He is a member of the editorial board of *Minerva – An Internet Journal of Philosophy*.

Reasonableness in Liberal Political Philosophy

Edited by Shaun P. Young

Routledge
Taylor & Francis Group

LONDON AND NEW YORK

Published 2009 by Routledge
2 Park Square, Milton Park, Abingdon, Oxon OX14 4RN
52 Vanderbilt Avenue, New York, NY 10017

First issued in paperback 2018

Routledge is an imprint of the Taylor & Francis Group, an informa business

Copyright © 2009 Edited by Shaun P. Young

British Library Cataloguing in Publication Data
A catalogue record for this book is available from the British Library

Typeset in Times by Value Chain, India

ISBN 13: 978-1-138-88232-4 (pbk)
ISBN 13: 978-0-415-37178-0 (hbk)

CONTENTS

*This book is dedicated to my daughter Faith.
I hope that she may know only love and
reasonableness in her life.*

Preface

Words can be a very powerful tool for conveying thoughts and emotions; however, they can also prove an extremely problematic mechanism for accomplishing such a task. Arguably, the latter situation is often true with respect to the term *reasonableness*. Though used pervasively to explain and/or justify arguments and behaviour, its malleability renders it vulnerable to misunderstanding, manipulation and, subsequently, conflicting interpretations among its different proponents. Hence, when one speaks of "reasonableness" it is dangerous to assume that all those listening will know precisely what is intended by reference to that term. Yet, its heterogeneous character also makes it a very interesting topic for examination.

I would like to take this opportunity to express my immense gratitude to the contributors to this volume for agreeing to engage such a challenging subject and for doing so in such a thoughtful and often provocative manner. I believe that the chapters that occupy the following pages very ably help to demonstrate both the complexity and the importance of the topic under investigation. Susan Dimock deserves a special note of thanks for accepting my last-minute request to contribute to the collection, which I know is much better for her involvement. I would also like to extend my utmost appreciation to Richard Bellamy, for his support and extremely helpful guidance.

Finally – and, as always – I would like to thank my wife, Kate, and our two daughters, Amy and Faith, who have always been more than reasonable in enduring the demands necessitated by my research and writing.

Notes on Contributors

Edward Andrew is Professor Emeritus of Political Science at the University of Toronto. His publications include *Closing the Iron Cage: The Scientific Management of Leisure* (Black Rose, 1981); *Shylock's Rights: A Grammar of Lockian Claims* (University of Toronto Press, 1988); *The Genealogy of Values: The Aesthetic Economy of Nietzsche and Proust* (Rowman and Littlefield, 1995); and *Conscience and its Critics: Protestant Conscience, Enlightenment Reason and Modern Subjectivity* (University of Toronto Press, 2001). He has also published numerous articles and chapters on various themes and thinkers, including Plato, Machiavelli, Locke, Marx, Nietzsche, Weil, Heidegger, Robert Nozick and George Grant. He is currently working on a book on Patrons of Enlightenment.

Terrell Carver is Professor of Political Science at the University of Bristol. His publications include *Karl Marx: Texts on Method* (1975); *The Logic of Marx* (ed.) (1980); *Engels* (1981; reissued as *Engels: A Very Short Introduction*, 2003); *Marx's Social Theory* (1982); *Marx and Engels: The Intellectual Relationship* (1983); *Marx and Engels: A Conceptual Concordance* (ed.) (1983); *A Marx Dictionary* (1987); *Marx's 'Grundrisse' and Hegel's 'Logic'* (ed.) (1988); *Friedrich Engels: His Life and Thought* (1989, repr. 1991); *Cambridge Companions to Philosophy: Marx* (ed.) (1991); *Rational Choice Marxism: Assessments* (ed.) (1995); *Cambridge Texts in the History of Political Thought: Marx, Later Political Writings* (ed.) (1996); *Gender is not a Synonym for Women* (1996); *Interpreting the Political: New Methodologies* (ed.) (1997); *The Politics of Sexuality* (ed.) (1998); *The Postmodern Marx* (1998); *Engels After Marx* (ed.) (1999); *Men in Political Theory* (2004); and *Palgrave Advances in Continental Political Thought* (2006). He has also published articles in numerous journals, including *Inquiry, Political Studies, Political Theory, History of Political Thought, Economy and Society, The Pacific Review, International Political Science Review, Journal of Political Science, Studies in Political Thought, Journal of the History of European Ideas, Marx-Engels-Marxism Quarterly of Japan, Alternatives, Review of International Studies, European Journal of Political Research, Strategies, European Political Science, New Political Science, International Studies Review,* and *International Affairs.*

Susan Dimock is Professor of Philosophy and Director of the York Centre for Practical Ethics at York University (Canada). Her publications include *Classic Readings and Canadian Cases in the Philosophy of Law* (Toronto: Prentice Hall, 2002), editor; *Classic Readings and Cases in Philosophy of Law* (NY: Longman, 2006), editor; *Applied Ethics: Reflective Moral Reasoning* (Toronto: Nelson, 2004), co-edited with Christopher Tucker; and *Liberalism* (Dordrecht, Netherlands: Kluwer, 2000), co-edited with Jan Narveson. Her areas of research and teaching are philosophy of law, ethical theory and political philosophy.

Gerald F. Gaus is James E. Rogers Professor of Philosophy at the University of Arizona; in 2005-2006 he was Distinguished Visiting Professor of Philosophy at the University of North Carolina, Chapel Hill. His publications include *Value and Justification* (Cambridge University Press, 1990); *Justificatory Liberalism* (Oxford University Press, 1996); *Public Reason*

(Ashgate, 1998), co-edited with Fred D'Agostino; *Social Philosophy* (M.E. Sharpe, 1999); *Political Concepts and Political Theories* (Westview, 2000); *Contemporary Theories of Liberalism: Public Reason as a Post-Enlightenment Project* (Sage, 2003); *The Handbook of Political Theory* (Sage, 2004), co-edited with Chandran Kukathas, and *On Philosophy and Economics* (Wadsworth, 2007). Forthcoming works include *Values, Justice and Economics*, co-edited with J. Lamont and C. Favor (Rodopi). His research interests include moral theory, liberal political theory, and the nature of rational action. He is currently completing a book on principled liberalism to be published by Cambridge University Press. He is co-editor of the journal *Politics, Philosophy, and Economics*.

Mathew Humphrey is Reader in Political Philosophy at the University of Nottingham. His principal area of research is environmental political theory, and his publications include *Ecological Politics and Democratic Theory: the Challenge to the Deliberative Ideal* (Routledge, 2007) and *Preservation versus the People?* (Oxford University Press, 2002). He has also published a number of articles in various referred scholarly journals.

Peter Lindsay is an Associate Professor of Political Science and Philosophy at Georgia State University. His previous publications include *Creative Individualism: The Democratic Vision of C. B. Macpherson* (State University of New York Press, 1996), and articles in various journals, including *History of Political Thought, Polity*, and *Social Theory and Practice*. He is currently writing on issues of just property rights.

Patrick Neal is Associate Professor of Political Science at the University of Vermont. His publications include *Liberalism and its Discontents* (New York University Press, 1997), as well as numerous articles on various aspects of liberal political theory. Recently his research and writing have focused on the relationship between religion and liberal-democracy.

Thomas A. Spragens, Jr is Professor of Political Science at Duke University. His publications include *The Dilemma of Contemporary Political Theory: Toward a Post-Behavioral Science of Politics* (Dunellen, 1973); *The Politics of Motion: The World of Thomas Hobbes* (University Press of Kentucky, 1973); *Understanding Political Theory* (St. Martin's Press, 1976); *The Irony of Liberal Reason* (University of Chicago Press, 1981); *Reason and Democracy* (Duke University Press, 1990); and *Civic Liberalism: Reflections on Our Democratic Ideals* (Rowman and Littlefield, 1999). His current research examines changes in American liberalism over the past several decades.

Shaun P. Young is an Instructor in the Department of Political Science at Carleton University (Canada). His publications include *Beyond Rawls: An Analysis of the Concept of Political Liberalism* (Rowman and Littlefield Publishing Group, 2002); and *Political Liberalism: Variations on a Theme* (State University of New York Press, 2004), editor. He has also published a number of articles examining various aspects of liberal political philosophy. Forthcoming works include a book entitled *John Rawls: The Search for Justice and Stability in a Plural World* (under contract with the State University of New York Press). He is a member of the editorial board of *Minerva – An Internet Journal of Philosophy*.

Introduction

Shaun P. Young

What does it mean to act 'reasonably' and why is it important (or necessary) to behave in such a manner? Though such questions have for centuries captured the attention and exercised the energies of philosophers, they have possessed particular importance for liberal philosophers. Indeed, it has been argued that the idea of 'public reasonableness is at the centre of liberalism' (Moore 1996, p. 167; see also, for example, Macedo 2000). Liberals' fascination with reasonableness is a consequence of their desire to establish and sustain the socio-political conditions essential to a just and stable society. Liberalism was originally developed as a means by which to secure political stability in societies in which the presence of religious pluralism had produced years of repression, persecution, and civil war. The violent, deadly, and destabilising conflict that arose in sixteenth- and seventeenth-century Europe as a result of the public intolerance of religious diversity brought with it the realisation that a new approach to responding to doctrinal disagreement was necessary if one wished to avoid such conflict in the future and provide for the type of peaceful coexistence needed to ensure political stability in pluralistic societies.

Early liberal philosophers recognised that the ability of liberalism to achieve its goals was itself a function of its capacity to provide a *just* governance framework. If liberalism was to reduce to an unproblematic or manageable level the likelihood of divisive, destabilising conflict among the members of pluralistic societies, then it would need to offer a governance framework that was perceived to treat all competing interests 'justly'. In other words, liberalism would need to secure justice in order to achieve the desired (and necessary) political stability. In turn, realising justice would require that all citizens be treated 'fairly', which they are to the extent that the governance framework places only 'reasonable' demands upon them. Consequently, for early liberals, there was a fundamental interdependency between reasonableness, justice, political stability, liberalism, and the achievement of what John Rawls labelled a 'well-ordered' society: reasonableness was understood to be a critical component of the project of liberalism.

Perhaps unsurprisingly, liberal philosophers' understanding of the specific character of 'reasonableness' has evolved with the passage of time. As the socio-political circumstances confronting the inhabitants of 'liberal' societies have changed, so too has philosophers' understanding of the precise demands that a liberal governance framework must satisfy if it is to secure and sustain justice and, by extension, political stability. Thus, for example, the criteria for satisfying Hobbesian reasonableness differ drastically from those generated by Humboldt's definition of reasonableness, which, in turn, is significantly different from that of Rawls. However, despite such periodic metamorphoses, liberal theories of justice have continued to embrace the belief that the realisation of a well-ordered polity (however that might be defined) requires that reason(ableness) guide – indeed, regulate – behaviour in the public realm. Given that liberalism is a child of the 'age of reason', such a fact should not be surprising.

Purpose of book

The purpose of this book is to offer a critical examination of the role of the concept of reasonableness in liberal political philosophy, with a particular focus on the proposed relationship between reasonableness and the opportunity for individuals to pursue and realise a plurality of competing, conflicting and often irreconcilable interests and ends. Even within the sphere of liberal political philosophy, reasonableness is an essentially contested concept, a quality the specifics of which have been understood in a number of different and, at times, competing ways. Of course, despite the heterogeneous manner in which it has been represented and assessed, all understandings of reasonableness possess certain fundamental similarities. For example, reasonableness is typically understood to demand toleration and reciprocity (though the degree to which it does so has certainly varied).

A prominent feature of many of the chapters contained in this book is a reference to the work of Rawls: for many of the contributions, Rawls's arguments serve as the principal focus of analysis and critique. Though some may believe such a situation regrettable, arguably, it is quite understandable given Rawls's indisputable role in bringing the issue of 'reasonableness' to the fore of contemporary political philosophy.[1] That is not to suggest (nor do any of the contributors claim) either that Rawls is the only philosopher with anything noteworthy to say on the matter or even that he has developed a conception of reasonableness that is in some sense(s) superior to all others. Rather, the prominence of Rawls's arguments should be understood only as a reflection of his significant contribution to recent scholarship that engages the topic of socio-political 'reasonableness'.

In turn, it is possible to identify in the contributions responses to a number of the prominent and persistent questions that have been generated by Rawls's arguments (and, more generally, liberals' use of the notion of reasonableness). In particular, each of the chapters addresses one or more of the following questions: Is liberal reasonableness problematically exclusionary? Is it suitably democratic in character? And is it a practical and sufficient guide for public behaviour? The first question has been a prominent component of not only the lengthy (and ongoing) debate between Marxists and liberals, but also the more newly emergent critiques of liberalism offered by feminists and multiculturalists. The second question has been an animating source of the continually increasing volume of contemporary discourse surrounding the idea of deliberative democracy. Finally, the third question is one that has occupied (in particular) those who have analyzed the significance of the modifications that Rawls has made to his arguments between the publication of *A theory of justice* (1971) and the appearance of *Political liberalism* (1993).

Using Marxism, religion, and jurisprudence (respectively), Terrell Carver, Patrick Neal, and Susan Dimock engage a number of concerns surrounding the question of the exclusionary character of liberal reasonableness, and essentially conclude that, though it is certainly not unproblematic, reasonableness need not necessarily be as exclusionary as many have suggested. In 'Liberalism, reason(ableness), and the politicization of truth: Marx's critique and the ironies of Marxism', Carver argues that there is notably less hostility and, subsequently, incompatibility, between (genuine) Marxism and liberal reason(ableness) than is typically conceded either by Marxists or liberals. He suggests that while Marx rejected a number of liberal propositions, such as the superiority of a self-regulating market or the inescapability or 'good' of the 'outrageous but predictable inequalities of outcome' (p. 123) , he was certainly not 'illiberal'. Indeed, in certain respects – for example, his support for equality of outcome and universal (male) suffrage – Marx was 'more liberal than most' (p. 122). Similarly, in 'Is public reason innocuous?', Neal contends that the apparent and commonly accepted antagonism between the consistent and meaningful observance of religious beliefs/values and the demands of liberal public reason is more a matter of an exaggerated understanding of the latter than an actual conflict. Once one considers the numerous qualifications that accompany Rawls' conception of public reason, its *prima facie* daunting character proves to be more chimera than reality, and the actual constraints it imposes do not render it irresolvably incompatible with the personal obligations that typically accompany the affirmation of any of the established religions. In 'Reasonable women in the law', Dimock notes that, as manifested in the 'reasonable (wo)man' standard that has emerged in the US and other countries that practice a common law approach to jurisprudence, the liberal understanding of reasonableness has often functioned to the detriment of women, failing to recognize crucial differences between men and women. Nevertheless, it has been and can continue to be a progressive concept if properly understood and employed.

Related to the question of exclusion is that of the democratic character of liberal reasonableness, the degree to which it supports and enables (or frustrates) the realization of democratic practices as such are generally understood. In 'Environmentalism, fairness, and public reasons', Mathew Humphrey suggests that liberal public reason legitimises a problematically limited understanding of what constitutes a valid public justification for activities whose goal is to alter the political landscape; in so doing, liberal public reason leaves environmentalists (among others) lacking the political means required to challenge the entrenched political morality effectively. If it is to offer the necessary 'transformative' opportunity, liberal public reason must, Humphrey contends, embrace 'a more contextual understanding of political justification' that differentiates between 'various levels and forms of coercion in political life and appl[ies] different standards of justification between them' (p. 188). In 'Democratic reasonableness', Thomas Spragens, Jr argues that liberal public reason(ableness) is an essential component of a democratic system of governance. It is the liberal notion of political reasonableness that rendered illegitimate the elitist, aristocratic understanding of political reason that initially reigned supreme, and, instead, required a belief both in human equality and the capacity of the demos to be reasonable in its attitudes, conduct, and judgment (p. 195) – i.e., an affirmation of the notion of *democratic reasonableness*. However, Spragens cautions that, even when such reasonableness prevails, there remain 'irremovable impediments to the power of democratic reasonableness to produce determinate substantive convergence – a rational consensus – on social policy or principles of justice' (p. 211).

The chapters by Gerald Gaus, Ed Andrew and Peter Lindsay, and Shaun Young confront in different ways the question of the sufficiency and practicality of reasonableness as a guide for public behaviour. In 'Reasonable utility functions and playing the cooperative way', Gaus uses game theory (in particular, the prisoners' dilemma scenario) in order to demonstrate that, contrary to popular belief, considerations of reasonableness – understood as 'a desire to engage in fair cooperation as such' – can be effectively and productively incorporated into theories of rational decision-making concerning the collective good. He suggests, however, that it would be mistake to conclude, as some have, that reasonableness can essentially eliminate the challenges associated with cooperative decision-making. Though reasonable people would be 'more successful' at avoiding situations such as a prisoners' dilemma, all people – whether purely rational or also reasonable – would behave similarly if entangled in such a situation. In 'Are the judgments of conscience unreasonable?', Andrew and Lindsay also argue that reasonableness alone cannot prevent irrational or unreasonable behaviour. In particular, despite the contemporary inclination to believe otherwise, reasonableness is unable to 'mediate the conflicts that exist between the individual and society' (p. 237) and, consequently, by itself reasonableness is an inadequate guide for public behaviour. A possible source of assistance, it is suggested, is the notion of conscience. Though essentially dismissed as an unacceptably private and subjective mechanism for guiding *public* behaviour, Andrew and Lindsay contend that conscience, too, can offer a means for resolving difficult moral questions that concern public affairs. Finally, in 'Exercising political power reasonably', Young questions the ability of the notion of reasonableness to protect adequately against the abuse of political power. In particular, in demanding that the governance framework assign primacy to reasonableness, Young suggests that political liberalism generates what he labels the 'paradox of reasonableness': making reasonableness the 'final court of appeal' with respect to 'public' matters 'facilitates the emergence of unreasonableness (i.e., abusive behaviour) to a degree that critically enfeebles the former's capacity to sustain the political justice and stability deemed necessary to establish and preserve a well-ordered polity' (p. 257).

Though the above description associates each of the contributions with a particular question related to the validity and acceptability of the liberal understanding and use of reasonableness, such a categorization is incomplete, especially insofar as it neglects to examine the possible overlap among the identified categories. For example, in important respects, a concern with the democratic character of liberal reasonableness seems unavoidably to also involve a broader concern with its exclusionary qualities. Similarly, any assessment of the sufficiency and practicality of liberal reasonableness as a guide for public behaviour would also seem to encompass the issue of democratic character, at least insofar as one's focus is liberal-democratic polities. Thus, a number of the chapters actually respond (directly or indirectly) to all of the abovementioned concerns. In confronting such concerns, the contributions also engage and contribute to debates that have long occupied political philosophers and, more immediately, have served as the focus for a significant work of provocative and influential scholarship.

Some parting observations

As both a philosophical approach to life and a practical political project, liberalism has achieved a global ascendancy in the marketplace of ideas; so much so, that toward the end of the twentieth century at least one celebrated commentator (Fukuyama 1992, p. xi) heralded the 'end of history', insofar as liberalism had, it was suggested, 'conquered' all of its notable ideological rivals and in so doing had achieved an unquestionable and irrevocable legitimacy as the appropriate framework for personal and political relations. Somewhat paradoxically, however, liberalism's ascendancy has been accompanied by an ever greater scepticism concerning its continued capacity to respond effectively to the problems of tolerance and accommodation confronting increasingly complex and diverse contemporary societies. Indeed, perhaps more so than ever before, political philosophers have been questioning the ability of liberalism to offer a viable solution to the dilemmas of justice and stability posed by pluralism. Arguably, liberals' ability to rebut the arguments of their critics persuasively will to a significant degree be determined by the manner in which they define and employ the concept of reasonableness.

The chapters that occupy the proceeding pages survey some of the prominent ways in which the notion of 'reason(ableness)' has been understood and employed by liberal political philosophers and note various criticisms that have been levelled against those understandings. It is hoped that the analyses offered therein will not only prove interesting, but also meaningfully expand the discourse surrounding the notion of reasonableness and help to identify some of the difficulties that continue to impede the realisation of an ideally reasonable liberal polity.

Notes

1. Whether one agrees or disagrees with Rawls's conclusions, it is difficult to deny his influence. To a degree that is relatively unique among individual philosophers, he helped define the theoretical framework and vernacular in which his contemporaries theorized.

References

Fukuyama, F., 1992. *The end of history and the last man.* New York: Avon Books.

Macedo, S., 2000. In defense of liberal public reason: are slavery and abortion hard cases? *In*: R. George and C. Wolfe, eds. *Natural law and public reason.* Washington, DC: Georgetown University Press, 11–49.

Moore, M., 1996. On reasonableness. *Journal of applied philosophy,* 13(2), 167–178.

Rawls, J., 1971. *A theory of justice.* Cambridge, MA: Harvard University Press.

Rawls, J., 1993. *Political liberalism.* New York: Columbia University Press.

Liberalism, reason(ableness) and the politicization of truth: Marx's critique and the ironies of Marxism

Terrell Carver

Liberalism was self-identified with reason from the outset. However, it is also worth reviewing what exactly in the liberal view was reason's 'other' – the intellectual and practical targets of the liberal critique – in order to assess how reasonable or unreasonable liberal reason really is (Hampsher-Monk 1992, pp. 153–154; Eccleshall *et al.* 1994, p. 32). Marx self-identified as a critic of liberalism, but also as a proponent and associate, both in theory and in practice (Carver 1998, pp. 119–145). The latter aspect of his thought and practice has been distinctly undervalued in all traditions of commentary, and he has been categorized much too readily as non-liberal. This sometimes happens because he was a revolutionary and advocated violence, both of which are erroneously taken to be alien to the liberal tradition, its institutions and practice (McLellan 1980a). In other commentary his views on rights, justice, dictatorship, class and democracy are taken simplistically, so that they fit the given presumption that he was non-liberal to the core (Popper 2003, Kolakowski 1978, cf. Levin 1989). Liberals and Marxists alike have had a stake in making Marx non-liberal for political purposes, finding distance between his views and liberalism, emphasizing contradiction between his theory and liberal ideals, and even giving him a personality at odds with the supposed virtues in character and conduct that liberals like to think they exemplify, namely respect for others' views, willingness to compromise, acknowledgement of value-pluralism, and the like (Berlin 1996).

My purpose here is to make this situation much more complex on all sides, that is, to re-read Marx in a way that draws out the links and continuities between his views and those that were identified as liberal in his time and ours. This will enable me to construct a more subtle reading of his critique of liberalism, one that I hope liberals will take rather more seriously and rather less dismissively than virtually all the literature on Marx has encouraged them to do. A corollary to this will be an encouragement to liberals to consider the disjunction between their idealized liberalism and some three centuries or so of liberal theory and practice rather more carefully than is usually the case. Lastly, I consider the irony in the foundational rationalism ('scientific socialism') through which Engels and others interpreted Marx's ideas, given that Marx's critique of liberalism politicized reason(ableness), and that this happened long before post-Marxists began to cope with 'anti-foundational' redefinitions of democracy and 'the political' (Carver 1983, 2000, 2003a; Laclau and Mouffe 2001; Mouffe 1993).

Liberal politics and Marx

Commentary on Marx begins with biography, and biography is a genre. It comes with an almost ready-made template through which a chronologically ordered account of anyone's life and times can be rendered intelligible and interesting. Typically this involves periodization into 'stages' (e.g., early, middle, late), and an apparatus of mind-changes, breaks or distinct phases of development (towards what we – supposedly – already know to be the case about the subject's ideas, fame, influence, major works, etc.). Marx is no exception, and he is conventionally portrayed as evolving through Hegelian romanticism, liberalism, Young Hegelian radicalism, revolutionary communism or non-utopian socialism and – in a way that was supposedly though problematically consistent – positivism or determinism (Carver 1983, pp. 11–12; Carver 1992).

The Althusserian *coupure épistemologique* was the most famous of these periodizations, precisely because it proposed such a clean break between an early and a late Marx, and precisely because the philosophical presumptions behind the two Marxes were so sharply delineated. Dramaturgically it was superb since it proposed an almost Pauline moment of conversion from 'Hegelianism' to 'science' and attempted to locate this in terms of space and time, as it were, in a text (initially *The German ideology*). As a way of interpreting Marx, it failed, all the more so because the date of the break kept slipping to a point later and later in his career, until it became apparent that he was himself going to be judged radically deficient in his own mind for failing to meet a criterion of scientificity. This was presumed by Althusser and his readers to guarantee (had Marx achieved this) his wholehearted reception into modern intellectual life and politics (Arditti 2006). Only very backward and unprogressive minds, in thrall to ignorance and superstition, unreasonableness and Hegelian vagueness, could resist the congruence of science and reason, or so the supposition went.

Marx's 'break' with liberalism – according to the interpretive tradition – was very nearly as sharp, but unlike the Althusserian *coupure*, it has stuck in the literature without much question. While the debate over Marx as Hegelian vs. Marx as scientist had a certain philosophical liveliness (because neither Hegelian thought nor science enjoys much fixity of definition and evaluation amongst philosophers), the liberal–radical break was much easier to defend and indeed never much challenged. This is because liberals and Marxists are happiest with Marx as he (supposedly) became, i.e., the revolutionary (and therefore supposedly non-liberal) communist, and because most liberals have therefore not been keen to rescue this (supposed and exclusively) liberal period of his for their own purposes. For liberals it was tinged with unwelcome criticism, and derived from an obvious turncoat. J.S. Mill, by contrast, was a much safer pair of hands, deriving from an impeccably liberal family, maturing into a form of radicalism, including works that even put him on the right side of the 'woman question'. Most liberals could at least understand (if not wholly accept) this, and he seemed to evolve in himself without any whiff of revolution, violence or warfare (except against the most flagrant reactionaries abroad) (Duncan 1973). Marx's (supposed) liberalism has therefore been isolated as 'early' in his periodization, rejected most notably by himself (supposedly), and therefore dismissed as having little or no continuity in his thought or otherwise.

Liberalism and liberal politics, though, need some introduction. The 'others' to liberal ideas – things, of course, that make liberalism 'liberal' by contrast – include worshipful and uncritical, indeed censoring, constraining and constricting, ideas and institutions, typically identified with religious establishments and practices which reject criticism, debate, enquiry, innovation and experiment. Reason is thus typically, for liberals, the exercise of scrutiny by individuals, who have as much chance of being right as institutions, which are themselves in a position to invoke tradition, received opinion, authorised texts and views, and generally presume an overall superiority over and beyond what any individual can muster. Reasonableness is a manner of pursuing this, that is, calmly and objectively, dispassionately and tolerantly, allowing the give and take of speech, and admitting no practices of intimidation, general claims to superiority or authoritarian closures. While experiential, evidential, mathematical, experimental and therefore scientific enquirers were often held up as liberal models, most liberals were not scientists, and indeed, scientific enquiry was always something of a liberal ideal, rather than a model derived from, or directed at, practising scientists.

Politically liberals were therefore opposed to authoritarian regimes, which, in any case, usually derived some of their authority via religious establishments as described above. Liberals thus rejected (at least in their theory) natural hierarchies of ruler and ruled, the subjection of civil rulers to ecclesiastical authority, manifestations of absolute and arbitrary power (rather than legislation impartially administered), the hereditary principle in rulership and office-holding (notwithstanding numerous compromises), and undue interference with market relationships (though by no means was 'free trade' as such a catechistic article of faith). While liberal regimes were virtually all born through armed struggle, violence and civil war, liberals generally prefer to forget this, or at least sanitize and memorialize the details in ways that create distance between the (presumed) peacefulness of their own order, and those who are said to advocate otherwise, namely revolutionaries, terrorists, insurgents and the like, despite the fact that in many cases they had themselves occupied these roles or supported those who did or in any case benefited from such actions in crucial ways.

Despite the historical record, liberals like to see themselves as inherently peaceful, excluding force through rule of law, reluctant to go to war, and then doing so only for the most noble of reasons, namely fine-grained concepts of justice and criminality, and certainly not for the glories of conquest or empire (see Locke [1689] 1988 for foundational discussions). Imperial, aristocratic and more recently fascist regimes have glorified war, conquest and violence, which are certainly in contrast with liberal ideals. The extent to which self-styled liberal practice, or indeed liberal principles themselves, actually allow or encourage many of the same phenomena is not an issue at this point in my argument, though it should be flagged that Marx's critique of liberalism points in just this direction. Nor is it my point that liberals are as bad as those they criticize; mostly they are not. Rather my point is that liberals do not merely fail sometimes to live up to their own ideals, but indeed are prone to idealize themselves and sanitize their history to the point where forgetting (an active process) and erasure (more serious forms of cover up) are pertinent issues (Klein 1997). To their credit, liberals and their regimes mostly allow this kind of critique free rein, even if they do not propose very often to change very much in response.

Marx's 'early' liberalism was undoubtedly of the classic variety. Hardly anyone then was a completely radical democrat (one person/one vote, with no sexual, class or racial discrimination), precisely because the prior question was any form of constitutional rule at all. Authoritarian and monarchical rulers were the norm, their personal power generally blessed by religious hierarchies, and they were obviously above the law by their own definition, because their will was the law. The more enlightened ones had mechanisms of consultation in the form of advisory assemblies, diets, dumas and the like, which did not challenge their principle of ultimate authority. Indeed, challenges to this principle, such as had strikingly and widely occurred during the French Revolution and the aftermath of liberatory wars and struggles across Europe, were precisely discouraged, most notably during the Carlsbad era of the 1820s, when leftover constitutions from the Napoleonic era were summarily revoked in Germany, and authoritarianism re-established in the Austrian Empire and surrounding states.

Liberals then, as occasionally now, are democrats only to a degree, which is not necessarily all that radical. Liberal constitutions may indeed include institutions and practices that involve appointment rather than election (typically second chambers or supreme courts), and numerous other devices (from electoral colleges to party lists to quangos) that quietly but effectively ensure limited and elite patterns of participation. Of course, liberals have also variously favoured progressive agendas that expand democratic participation, ranging from referendum and recall to primary elections and gender quotas. My point is that there is a huge range of liberal views about involving individuals within a polity in a myriad of practices commonly associated with democracy, and that the liberal agenda has changed not just with the predilections of individual liberals but also with the state of play in revolutionary politics as liberals struggle with authoritarians. Marx's liberalism arose in a situation where the idea of representative and responsible government was itself a revolutionary sentiment, and freedom of expression a matter of grudging and very brief bouts of tolerance. Repression was very real, taking the form of prosecution and imprisonment, expulsion, loss of civil rights, blacklisting and other forms of social and economic discrimination (Breckman 1999).

Marx was always a mainstream liberal in his opposition to non-constitutional regimes whose (mistaken) claim to legitimacy was derived from mystical beliefs and the support of religious hierarchies. He was always in favour of a politics of, by and for the people, objectively and dispassionately administered. Passionate advocacy and heated disagreement were not foreign to his nature, but those who suffered from this and complained about it were perhaps not seeing his point. They might have done better to defend to the death his right to say what he said in the way that he said it. Liberals are not always scrupulously polite, and plenty have endured their time 'in the wilderness' because they saw no need to compromise, and indeed were determined not to. Marx may have lacked some political skills, but then he did not have many public offices to run for or hold, given his position in exile in England after 1849. He was never anywhere near advocating specific acts of violence, other than in defence of liberal gains in the democratic revolutions of 1848, which had indeed instituted representative and responsible governments, much to the fury of monarchists and reactionaries. He was notably against *coups d'état*, *agents provocateurs*, terrorism and mayhem just for the sake of disruption (Thomas 1980).

Far from being illiberal and an enemy, Marx was a victim of liberalism's erasure of its revolutionary record, other than in sanitized and memorialized terms that take the violence and indeed aggression out of its heroic struggles. Marx was there in the struggles that themselves became violent, and in that way extracted concessions (even if not abdication) from authoritarian rulers and generally made their cause look beleaguered and pre-modern. By the late 1860s and the 1870s, constitutional rulership was on the way in, and authoritarian rulers on the way out in Europe. He advocated revolution to the extent that it appeared to be the only practical way forward to liberal goals, just as many liberals did, and he advocated violence only to the degree that it was goal-driven and directed at enemy forces, and then, so far as we can tell, in appropriately proportional ways. It is not the case that he advocated violence based on sweeping judgements of class (or any other) form of guilt-by-association; this was precisely what he accused 'the enemy' of doing, notably when the communards were massacred by occupying (supposedly) liberal forces in Paris in 1871 (Marx [1871] 1986). *The communist manifesto* explicitly acknowledges that individuals have a choice to forsake their class backgrounds (as Marx and Engels had done), and that some have made and will be making that very choice. It is hard to be more liberal about 'the individual' than that. While Marx was certainly in favour of tough measures of self-defence for liberal gains, he was also certainly more honest than most liberals about what was entailed in those tough measures, which was not just a simple recourse to violence. This would, of course, be organised violence, which entails authoritarian structures such as armies, though the authoritarianism does not extend in theory to absolute and arbitrary power (even if in wartime or terrorist emergencies compromises are notoriously made in that direction) (Marx and Engels [1848] 1976).

Class dictatorship is taken to be a watershed dividing Marx's outlook from that of liberalism. What divides Marx from liberalism, however, is class, not dictatorship (McLellan 1980b, pp. 229–230). Liberal regimes under threat, and in wartime, resolve themselves into dictatorships (or near dictatorships) with little difficulty, and indeed even in (so-called) peacetime, apparatuses of national defence and security are in normal liberal practice allowed to insulate themselves from public and judicial scrutiny to some extent (liberal principles notwithstanding). Marx's differences with liberals were therefore early and acute. I do not actually see him as having a liberal 'phase', precisely because I think his ideals remained largely the same and were largely derived from liberalism (and certainly not from its authoritarian 'others'). Moreover I think that his class perspective arrives very early in his life, doubtless as a matter of sentiment rather than exposure to anything dogmatic or even very intellectual (Lubasz 1976).

This is a hard claim to substantiate, given that he had few opportunities to demonstrate any inclinations in this regard. Engels made opportunities for himself to do this from the time that he was 18 years old, so in a sense Marx could have taken some chances in that direction, and did not. Marx evidently preferred the more coded politics of university intellectuals, and did not seem to have the kind of journalistic connections and ambitions that the young Engels very ably demonstrated (Carver 1989). Be that as it may, by the time of Marx's first-ever publications, his newspaper articles of 1842, his sympathies were clearly with the working class, even if they were peasants and wine-growers. Here is where he parts company with liberals even today. Marx did not blame their plight (unemployment and severe economic hardship) simply on government irresponsibility and inaction; rather he blamed it on a coalition of interests, in effect, between the non-constitutional regime and modernizing property holders who were prepared to sacrifice liberal principles of participation (i.e., their own) for advantages that an authoritarian regime could deliver. These were summary alterations to the property system, ending medieval rights to forage on the one hand, and steering clear of any notion, on the other, that rulers had immediate responsibilities to the poor, whether as victims of social change or bad harvests.

In that way Marx crossed a number of liberal boundary lines early on. He did not buy the idea that the market is a self-regulating, autonomous entity outside of, or indeed superior to, governmental control. Nor did he buy the liberal doctrine that the state must itself be minimal precisely for this reason. Nor did he buy the nuanced liberal doctrines of equality that legitimated economic inequality as either inescapable or good. Nor did he buy the liberal exclusions on political participation that rather similarly transformed a principle of equality into a justification for regular and persisting patterns of inequality, this time in terms of political rather than economic power. He was, conversely, notably suspicious of regimes where the coincidence of political and economic power was celebrated as the evident goal of liberal struggles, even if this were dignified by free speech and contested elections. Marx would certainly have enjoyed Will Rogers's quip, 'We have the best Congress money can buy' (http://chatna.com/author/rogers.htm).

In certain obvious senses, Marx was more liberal than many or indeed most liberals of his time in that he took equality of outcome to be important to actual individuals, and in no sense something that could be traded off against ringing statements that endorsed equality as a general principle of mere procedure. He was thus never prone to the implied social Darwinism that afflicts market theorists, against which equality of opportunity is either a contradiction or a rather vain hope (unless expanding economies and technological change together make substantial relative alterations in class structures in favour of the worse-off). Marx was certainly against market relations in principle, even if programmatically he was quite prepared to compromise with them in practice (Marx [1875] 1989). Market relations were not a realm of freedom and choice, but rather one through which power and wealth, on the one hand, and exploitation and relative disadvantage, on the other hand, tended to accumulate and persist, for no reason that he ever found justifiable. That is, he never found convincing the moral defences that liberals offer for market outcomes, namely, that those who are well rewarded work harder than those who are not, and that those who are not are only deserving of charity (or the most minimal, non-dependency-creating support) to stave off starvation. In a sense he was more generous to the human spirit than liberals often are, arguing that if work were a self-consciously social contribution, people would find personal satisfaction in making it, and that indeed, work did not have to be something merely to be endured for the sake of other goods (Marx [1867] 1996). Unlike liberals, he had little to say about those who might not respond to this idealization in practice; whereas liberals are not necessarily all that unhappy in presuming that those who are feckless and lazy deserve very little, if anything.

Marx's post-liberalism is thus a view that takes social class seriously, precisely because it takes individuals seriously. Economic relations and outcomes in the present are the concerns of real individuals, as opposed to liberal promises of inter-generational mobility for anyone's offspring. It was the reality of inter-generational disadvantage that interested him, and he was acutely conscious of the way that mythologies, even liberal ones, could take people's minds off their current working conditions, wages and wealth, and children's likely prospects. Whether he was right to pin his political strategy on reason and reasonableness in this way seems a moot point, but his strategy does begin to reveal the extent to which liberal reason, reasonableness and reasoning rests uneasily with, and indeed arguably meshes with, the structures of property and power in constitutional regimes, even in ones with present-day mass suffrage.

Marx and reason(ableness)

On the one hand Marx argued that political ideas were inescapably class-related, and that ruling ideas and class dominance had a certain obvious relationship (Marx and Engels [1848] 1976, Marx [1859] 1987). There was no doubt that he saw his ideas as linked to the interests of the modern industrial working class, and indeed to the longer-term interests of humanity in some larger sense, i.e., its potential for some uniquely human form of emancipation (Marx [1844] 1975a). However, why was he arguing about ideas in this way in the first place? This goes back to his rejection of liberal (and other) universalisms which he saw as false and excluding in various respects. Any universalism deriving from religious sources was *ipso facto* rejected by Marx, on grounds that these were projections of human qualities onto imaginary beings. Some qualities could certainly be partial to some classes or interests, but even if this were not true, Marx would have had no time for the exercise, which he deemed mystificatory and enslaving (Marx [1844] 1975a). Reason(ableness), for Marx, excluded the supernatural, though this development was in any case a historical, intellectual and social development.

Other more secular forms of universalism could not be dismissed quite so easily. The rationalism propounded by liberals had a progressive historical justification for Marx, not least for its role in debunking authoritarian pretensions, especially in politics, but also in intellectual enquiry and interchange. Marx supported a free press and indeed ran one on a number of occasions, and he had no recorded sympathies with censorship or intimidation (Marx [1842] 1975). He clearly wanted to expand the circle of the enfranchised citizenry, and consistently supported the struggles for universal (male) suffrage (Marx [1852] 1979). This was more liberal than most, as most liberals favoured property and educational requirements so that reason(ableness) in politics would not be swamped by those who were ignorant, lacking time, resources or abilities for education. J.S. Mill himself argued against universal education at public expense (Riley 1998). The list of demands in *The communist manifesto* of 1848 is an unobjectionably liberal set of demands, including progressive taxation, an independent central bank, representative and responsible government, etc. (Marx and Engels [1848] 1976). No doubt many liberals viewed this programme as 'socialist' precisely because it burst the bounds of liberal reason(ableness) in terms of the powers it awarded to (male) humanity in a universalistic way (i.e., across the whole population of a nation-state), rather than adhering to the liberal view (albeit one that was oftentimes not explicitly acknowledged) that reason(ableness) is not, or probably can never be, universally distributed internationally throughout (even) male minds (Tunick 2005, Prokhovnik 2002).

Marx's real complaint about liberals is that they were 'bourgeois', and in that way necessarily allied to capitalists. He saw their liberalism as falsely inclusive and hypocritical, that is, their principles of equality (say, in terms of voting) were never completely and straightforwardly delivered in practice, and they had no real intention, so he observed, of doing this. History bore Marx out on this as indeed suffrage reform was never an easy struggle. Moreover, their principle of equality licensed outrageous but predictable inequalities of outcome, which at that time were not mitigated by any (supposedly) countervailing practices to realize an 'equality of opportunity'. Again, these were not easy practices to institutionalize, and in recent years, they have been rather easily 'rolled back' in the US and other 'market' economies. From the liberal perspective, as it appeared to Marx (and which is by no means out of style), inequalities were either natural and therefore inescapable in some biological or social way, or, alternatively, positively to be encouraged as 'just rewards' to individuals. Hence inequalities would be the source of economic benefits (such as employment) for those who were (for whatever reason) less entrepreneurial or risk-taking or self-denying of present gratification.

In his own opinion, Marx's greatest discovery was itself a resolution of an equality question, namely how does an apparently equal exchange of values result in profits for one party, and subsistence wages for the other? (Marx [1867] 1996). This is in part a general equivalence problem about the origin of profit from equal exchanges, which he solved by conceptualizing capital as self-expanding value, and in part it is an analytical justification of a theory of exploitation, which he resolved by linking self-expanding value solely to inputs of human labour-power in the production process. His result, so he claimed, put (liberal) economists to right in resolving the formal paradox with which they had been wrestling, and it gave the lie to the commonplace view (and political message) that workers were in fact receiving a fair day's wage for a fair day's work through market exchange.

While there are numerous objections to the theory, the outlines are impeccably liberal in origin, because equality and individuals are the issue. Liberals tended to naturalize the property system and governmental systems through which market exchanges are possible, whereas Marx responded by historicizing these as political constructs wrenched from feudalism or worse (Wolff 2003). Moreover, he took liberal doctrines of the public good more seriously and inclusively than they did, without evidently obligating individuals to anything more than they did (viz., rule by a majority of 'the people') (Marx [1875] 1989). While at the time industrial workers were never the majority in any community where the liberal–reactionary battle-lines were drawn, and while Marx was notably disappointed with peasant voters (when in France they voted for Louis Bonaparte and his plebiscites), it is clear that he had a more universalistic and inclusive idea of 'majority' than most liberals of his time, certainly the respectable ones (and even given his notable lack of interest in the 'woman question', on which male liberals did not have a very good record either) (Marx [1852] 1979, Carver 1998, pp. 206–233).

In sum, Marx's complaint about liberals was that liberal political economy either naturalized the class structure or justified it as in some sense in the common interest. In both cases his critique is an immanent one, in that liberalism espouses individual equality as a principle of some sort, but endorses unequal market outcomes as a practice, linking the two with arguments, whether about individual creation of property, or of procedural justice in its transfer, that make the two consistent. Marx's version of liberalism, where it takes on board inequalities, goes for inequalities of need, rather than inequalities of effort and desert (Marx [1875] 1989). His version of freedom was not the freedom to trade, but to contribute, and his version of work was not one of minimizing unwanted effort but of maximizing contributory satisfactions (Marx [1844] 1975b, [1875] 1989). Marx's position is incompatible with liberal economics, but not necessarily with liberalism, shorn of its investment in the 'bourgeoisie', or as Locke put it, 'the industrious and rational' (Locke [1689] 1988: II.34).

What, then, can we say about Marx's rationalism, and his evident use of, and belief in, reason, and appeals to reasonableness? The universalism here seems to lie in his historicization of human species-activity as self-making through processes that themselves define what is reasonable, and produce the reason/ unreason binary line. The universalism, then, is in the process, rather than in the content, and the historicization makes it the opposite of timeless (Marx and Engels [1845–1846] 1976). However, the globalization of industry and trade that he foresaw by 1848 promises a more substantial universalization of content as humanity becomes universally interconnected, and as common processes then produce a common form of human self-creation. While on one level the bourgeoisie is remaking the entire world in its own image, on another level, in Marx's view, the industrial proletariat lives – more and more – in radical disjuncture (Marx and Engels [1848] 1976). At this point in the story Marx wants two things: firstly, the proletariat to generate forms of reasonableness that subvert 'bourgeois' justifications of inequality, such that equality principles generate outcomes that are defensibly equal, rather than inequalities that require defences; and secondly, the proletariat to emerge as in some sense an emanation of the human potential, rather than just a majority group or coalition of interests, or even embodiment of a common good or general will. The link between Marx's own use of reason in his work and commonsensical proletarian rationality is clearly asserted by Marx, though famously it was somewhat less than obvious in his own political encounters, or those conducted after his death under the sign of Marxism (Marx [1865] 1985).

Ironically, Engels's presentation of Marx as a system-builder on the Hegelian model, beginning with a review in 1859, worked against Marx's own model as outlined here, precisely because it appeared to locate the source of historical change and development in a concept of 'materialism', rather than in the specifics of human social production in material settings. It occluded Marx's universalizing link between globalizing economic practices and the development of proletarian/pan-human rationality and reason(ableness), because it located rationality and reason(ableness) in 'science', which Engels took to be a set of fixed principles (the famous three laws of 'dialectics') through which nature, history and thought (i.e., logic) could all be understood, explained and reconciled. Engels's Marxism thus had its roots in a timeless certainty of truth, rather than a historical and therefore social process of (highly uneven) development; it had the grandiosity of a universal and trans-historical 'key' to everything (something which Marx specifically disavowed); and it generated an easy confusion between 'matter' as an object of scientific (and therefore incontrovertible) study, and economics or economic activity as the crucial (though hardly the only) element in the ongoing process of human self-creation. Engels's reading of Hegel was really a characterization, rather than a reading, and his presentation of Marx 'spun' him in certain directions that were fashionable at the time (mainly the 1870s and early 1880s).

While many Marxists did not completely substitute Engels for Marx (as Engels somewhat coyly advised, on occasion), Engels's legacy is an extremely weighty one, and has been for more than a century the 'standard' interpretative frame for Marx (Carver 2003b). While some 'Hegelian' Marxists ('Hegelian' in a sense radically different from what Engels had in mind) began to question Engels's timeless notions of causality, determinism and certainty, it is only recently that post-Marxists have shaken the Marxist interpretation of Marx to its roots by severing the link between class consciousness and material conditions (Laclau and Mouffe 2001). Most post-Marxists, though, do this without separating Marx from Engels with any particular rigour, and tend to think therefore that they are necessarily departing from Marx. On my reading of Marx, this is not at all true, but the point at issue in this discussion should now be clear: a historicizing account of reason(ableness) plays a crucial role in Marx's thought, and is in no way inconsistent with what he has to say about the socio-economic processes of change and development that he thinks are so important, and indeed increasingly so in an era of accelerating globalization. His universalism is not one of timeless truths delivered to those of less rationality (an intellectual authoritarianism that he despised), but is rather something altogether more political and clearly linked to large-scale changes in power-relations. This is the Foucauldian dimension of power/knowledge through which post-Marxists approach the process of political change, and while it lacks Marx's specific prioritization of industrial production, and his emancipatory universalization of the proletariat, the form through which social change is conceptualized – an ongoing formation of power/ knowledge configurations – is very similar, not least because Marx's works were available to Foucault, and not the reverse (Barry 2006).

Where, then, does this leave reason(ableness)? After all, Marx's version of historicized humanity allows for any amount of species-malleability (and even biological self-creation of the human senses), but this is in any case itself a kind of universalization (Marx [1844] 1975c). The question is not so much the famous one, 'Did Marx have a conception of human nature?', as 'What does a conception of human nature actually commit anyone to?' (Geras 1983). The thrust of Marx's views on humanity (which are consistent across his career) is to avoid any supposed knowledge of some truth or standard to which humanity must trans-historically conform, and rather to see what can be generalized about humanity as deriving from an ongoing historical process of rather unpredictable (or rather only somewhat predictable) self-change. His claim is that humanity has reached the point where it could itself control its own development in self-set ways (which is quite different from predicting it, or determining somehow that this development had an inherent direction or limits), and his choice of methods was a profoundly thorough rationalism (Marx [1859] 1987). Marx writes as if he has discerned humanity's potential for rational control of itself, as if collective means could be found for implementing this, and as if these means would necessarily have to be democratic (Marx [1875] 1989). Whether he is discerning this as some truth, or recommending it in some normative way, is not really clear. No doubt these positions could be consistent with sufficient reflexivity, viz. when enough people accept a recommendation then it is in a sense true of humanity, understood as remaking itself through historical processes of development. Of course, Marx insisted that ideas alone could not do this work, or rather that ideas have their importance as causal factors in social change when economic systems are in place, or can be forged, to sustain them (Marx [1859] 1987). And of course he also espoused the converse: high technology is of little use without educational and economic systems of 'social capital' to make it work.

Turning Marx's argument around (as Foucault did) shows us that he was more right than he knew. The power/knowledge systems of liberal economics have produced bourgeoisification on a global scale, and created, as it were, the disciplinary mechanisms that reward consumer consciousness and individual aggrandizement (rather than contributory producer-consciousness directed to collective benefits). As Marx said, the cheap prices of commodities are battering down the Chinese walls of traditional cultures everywhere, and presenting a counter-model to his own of both human individuality and collective good (Marx and Engels [1848] 1976). One area where neither he nor liberals were very keen to tread is in the connection between international trade, globalized warfare, and various forms of imperialism, or rather this could all have come up in the volume of *Capital* that Marx never got to: *The world market* (Barkawi 2006, Carver 1975). Perhaps his message is that reason(ableness) is very much what humanity makes it, and that the 'economic rationality' of global trade is not in theory the only candidate.

Marx is liberalism's gadfly on that point, and his critique will not go away. There may be ways (more or less persuasive) of rationalizing individual and class inequalities as just outcomes of liberal principles, but the war-factor needs much closer attention than Marx managed, though he did his best on the colonial wars in India and the Middle East. Much as liberalism has been inclined to bracket off a pre-political sphere of 'private' relations between individuals (and their cipher-like children or dependents), so it is inclined to bracket off war as an anomaly for which some 'outside' agents are to blame, and to see imperialism as a problematic episode for which liberalism itself provided a 'successful' conclusion. However, few anti-imperialistic struggles were fuelled by free-market liberalism as an ideology, and it is not at all clear that Marx is ruled out in current protests and struggles over human rights. Typically these are for rights that Marx himself defended and from which he himself benefited, depending on where he was at the time: free speech, free association, free elections, representative and responsible government, etc. As he pointed out in his political journalism, even the well-off in class-divided societies should fear those elements who drum up hysteria in order to curtail rights, flout the law and rule by decree and thuggery (Marx [1852] 1979). Crucially this happens in defence of 'order' and 'property', precisely the twin benefits that liberalism aims to deliver (Carver 2004). Does it? Perhaps in many cases it delivers more of the latter than the former, and it does so inter-generationally with predictable selectivity. That, I think, is Marx's point, and the nub of his critique of the reason(ableness) invoked by liberals and referenced in liberalism. These conceptions are not timeless and apolitical, so he argued, and neither perforce were his. He presents his readers, therefore, with an explicit political choice.

References

Arditti, B., 2006. Louis Althusser. *In:* T. Carver and J. Martin, eds. *Palgrave advances in continental political thought.* Basingstoke: Palgrave Macmillan, 182–195.

Barkawi, T., 2006. *Globalization and war.* Lanham, MD: Rowman & Littlefield.

Barry, A., 2006. Foucault. *In:* T. Carver and J. Martin, eds. *Palgrave advances in continental political thought.* Basingstoke: Palgrave Macmillan, 244–259.

Berlin, I., 1996. *Karl Marx: his life and environment,* 4th ed. Oxford: Oxford University Press.

Breckman, W., 1999. *Marx, the young Hegelians, and the origins of radical social theory.* Cambridge: Cambridge University Press.

Carver, T., 1975. *Karl Marx: texts on method.* Oxford: Blackwell.

Carver, T., 1983. *Marx and Engels: the intellectual relationship.* Brighton: Harvester/Wheatsheaf.

Carver, T., 1989. *Friedrich Engels: his life and thought.* Basingstoke: Macmillan.

Carver, T., 1992. Methodological issues in writing a political biography. *Journal of political science,* 20, 3–13.

Carver, T., 1998. *The postmodern Marx.* Manchester: Manchester University Press.

Carver, T., 2000. Post-Marxism. *In:* G. Browning, A. Halcli, and F. Webster, eds. *Understanding contemporary society.* London: Sage, 71–83.

Carver, T., 2003a. Marxisms and post-Marxisms. *In:* A. Finlayson, ed. *Contemporary political thought.* Edinburgh: Edinburgh University Press, 198–208.

Carver, T., 2003b. *Engels.* Oxford: Oxford University Press.

Carver, T., 2004. Marx's *Eighteenth Brumaire of Louis Bonaparte*: democracy, dictatorship and the politics of class struggle. *In:* P. Baehr, and M. Richter, eds. *Dictatorship in history and theory.* Cambridge: Cambridge University Press, 103–128.

Duncan, G., 1973. *Marx and Mill.* Cambridge: Cambridge University Press.

Eccleshall, R., Geoghegan, V., Jay, R., Kenny, M., MacKenzie, I., and Wilford, R., 1994. *Political ideologies,* 2nd ed. London: Routledge.

Geras, N., 1983. *Marx and human nature.* London: Verso.

Hampsher-Monk, I., 1992. *A history of modern political thought.* Oxford: Blackwell.

Klein, N., 1997. *The history of forgetting.* London: Verso.

Kolakowski, L., 1978. *Main currents of Marxism.* Vol. 1. *The founders.* Oxford: Oxford University Press.

Laclau, E. and Mouffe, C., 2001. *Hegemony and socialist strategy,* 2nd ed. London: Verso.

Levin, M., 1989. *Marx, Engels and liberal democracy.* Basingstoke: Macmillan.

Locke, J., [1689] 1988. *Two treatises of government.* ed. P. Laslett. Cambridge: Cambridge University Press.

Lubasz, H., 1976. Marx's initial problematic: the problem of poverty. *Political studies,* 24(1), 24–42.

McLellan, D., 1980a. *Marx before Marxism,* 2nd ed. London: Macmillan.

McLellan, D., 1980b. *The thought of Karl Marx,* 2nd ed. London: Macmillan.

Marx, K., [1842] 1975. Proceedings of the sixth Rhine Province Assembly. *In:* K. Marx and F. Engels, *Collected works.* Vol. 1. London: Lawrence & Wishart, 132–181.

Marx, K., [1844] 1975a. Contribution to the critique of Hegel's *Philosophy of law.* Introduction. *In:* K. Marx, and F. Engels, *Collected works.* Vol. 3. London: Lawrence & Wishart, 175–87.

Marx, K., [1844] 1975b. Comments on James Mill. *In:* K. Marx, and F. Engels, *Collected works.* Vol. 3. London: Lawrence & Wishart, 211–228.

Marx, K., [1844] 1975c. Economic and philosophical manuscripts of 1844. *In:* K. Marx and F. Engels, *Collected works.* Vol. 3. London: Lawrence & Wishart, 229–346.

Marx, K., [1852] 1979. *The eighteenth Brumaire of Louis Bonaparte. In:* K. Marx and F. Engels, *Collected works.* Vol. 11. London: Lawrence & Wishart, 99–97.

Marx, K., [1859] 1987. Preface to *A contribution to the critique of political economy. In:* K. Marx and F. Engels, *Collected works.* Vol. 29. London: Lawrence & Wishart, 261–265.

Marx, K., [1865] 1985. *Value, price and profit. In:* K. Marx and F. Engels, *Collected works.* Vol. 20. London: Lawrence & Wishart, 101–149.

Marx, K., [1867] 1996. *Capital.* Vol. 1. *In:* K. Marx and F. Engels, *Collected works.* Vol. 35. London: Lawrence & Wishart.

Marx, K., [1871] 1986. *The civil war in France. In:* K. Marx and F. Engels, *Collected works.* Vol. 22. London: Lawrence & Wishart, 307–59.

Marx, K., 1875] 1989. *Critique of the Gotha programme. In:* K. Marx and F. Engels, *Collected works.* Vol. 24. London: Lawrence & Wishart, 75–99.

Marx, K., and Engels, F., [1845–1846] 1976. *The German ideology.* Vol. 1. *In:* K. Marx and F. Engels, *Collected works.* Vol. 5. London: Lawrence & Wishart, 15–452.

Marx, K. and Engels, F., [1848] 1976. *Manifesto of the communist party. In:* K. Marx and F. Engels, *Collected works.* Vol. 6. London: Lawrence & Wishart, 477–519.

Mouffe, C. (Ed) (1993) *The return of the political* (London: Verso).

Popper, K., 2003. *The open society and its enemies,* 5th ed. Vol. 2, *Hegel and Marx.* London: Routledge.

Prokhovnik, R., 2002. *Rational woman,* 2nd ed. Manchester: Manchester University Press.

Riley, J., 1998. *Mill on liberty.* London: Routledge.

Thomas, P., 1980. *Karl Marx and the anarchists.* London: Routledge & Kegan Paul.
Tunick, M., 2005. John Stuart Mill and unassimilated subjects. *Political studies,* 53(4), 833–848.
Wolff, J., 2003. *Why read Marx today?* Oxford: Oxford University Press.

Is public reason innocuous?

Patrick Neal

> I make a point in *Political Liberalism* of really not discussing anything, as far as I can help it, that will put me at odds with any theologian, or any philosopher (Rawls 1999b, p. 622).

The volume of critical literature, not a little of it quite intense in tone, that *Political liberalism* has elicited suggests that in this respect at least, Rawls failed miserably. The doctrine of public reason is perhaps the most controversial and controversy-generating aspect of the work, especially as it bears upon the issue of the appropriate place of religion in liberal-democratic politics. Rawls is commonly portrayed as one of the leading exponents of a political theory of liberal secularism that is hostile, or at least inhospitable, to religion.

I do not attempt here to speak to this issue directly. Instead, I propose to pursue a particular line of thought in regard to the idea of public reason without claiming that it captures, in an 'all things considered' sense, all that we might want to say about it. The line of thought is this: the idea of public reason is largely innocuous in terms of the practical demands it imposes upon citizens. When one adds together the considerable list of qualifications and specifications that attend Rawls's articulation of the idea, there is simply not much of a burden left to bear. A full defense of this claim would require not only the assembling of evidence in support of it (the task of this paper) but also a serious engagement with the evidence from Rawls's ideas that seems to point in the other direction. It would thus require a comprehensive engagement with Rawls' theory considered and judged as a whole, and I do not undertake that task here. I do think that this exercise can usefully contribute to that kind of engagement insofar as it succeeds in bringing vividly before the mind's eye the character of Rawls's theory when viewed through (the admittedly) partial lens here adopted.

I stress this methodological point so the purpose of my effort here will not be misunderstood. In pursuing the hypothesis that the idea of public reason is innocuous, I am not trying to mount a defense of the idea of public reason. I stress this point for two reasons. First, I simply have no interest in defending or criticizing the general idea of public reason on this occasion. My aim, as per above, is to contribute to the process by which a considered judgment about the idea might be pursued. Second, it would not necessarily constitute a defense of Rawlsian public reason even if it should turn out that the idea is, all things considered, largely innocuous. Some sympathetic to the idea of public reason generally will think it a mark against, not for, Rawls's account of it if it should turn out that the portrait I sketch in this essay is an accurate one. They may feel that the powerful ideas animating the idea of public reason demand more of us as citizens than Rawls is willing to ask.

To bring forth clearly the interpretation of public reason as innocuous, I will follow the simple procedure of considering in turn five major aspects of Rawls's theory that constitute considerable qualifications of the idea of public reason with respect to the demands that idea places upon citizens. These aspects are the distinction between Exclusive, Inclusive and Wide accounts of public reason (discussed in part two), the concept of constitutional essentials and basic justice (part three), the idea of the 'completeness' of public reason (part four), the idea of public reason as a moral rather than a legal duty (part five) and the question of the forum to which public reason applies (part six). In the conclusion (part seven), I highlight the manner in which the consideration of these factors collectively yields a portrait of public reason as innocuous.

Inclusive, not Exclusive public reason

The single most important qualification of the idea of public reason is Rawls's decision to endorse the 'inclusive' rather than the 'exclusive' interpretation of it (Rawls 1996, p. 247). To the best of my knowledge, Lawrence Solum was the first scholar to mark this distinction in relation to Rawls's work, and in the original edition of *Political liberalism* Rawls thanks Solum (along with Amy Gutmann) for discussion on this point (Solum 1993). The exclusive view of public reason is a requirement that reasons given in terms of comprehensive moral or religious doctrines be excluded from political justifications offered on constitutional essentials and matters of basic justice. As Rawls puts it, this view would maintain that such comprehensive reasons 'are never to be introduced into public reason' (1996, p. 247). I think that many casual observers of the scholarly literature take this to be Rawls's considered position, and thus he is often lumped into the category of those who allegedly want to 'banish religion from the public square'.

Rawls interestingly says that he was first 'inclined' to the exclusive view, but changed to the inclusive view after becoming convinced that the former was 'too restrictive' (1996, p. 247). The inclusive view allows 'citizens, *in certain situations*, to present what they regard as the basis of political values rooted in their comprehensive doctrine, provided they do so in ways that strengthen the idea of public reason itself'. (1996, p. 247; emphasis added). In effect, the inclusive view allows the expression of reasons based on comprehensive doctrines, including religious views and reasons, if (a) the social situation is such that the idea of public reason itself is supported and strengthened by the introduction of such, and (b) such reasons are accompanied by the expression of what we might call standard public reasons. The inclusive view, considered from a practical point of view, would allow the expression of comprehensive moral and religious views in the public political forum so long as standard public reasons were along to act as a kind of theoretical chaperone. Rawls's reason for finding the exclusive view too restrictive would seem to have been the realization that in a non-well ordered society, the long-range ideal of achieving a regime committed to public reason might be best served by short-term means that would go beyond public reason as understood on the exclusive view. This is the burden of his discussion of the case of Martin Luther King in *Political liberalism* (1996, pp. 247–250). I leave aside the many interesting questions that this view raises in order to stress here the simple point that this qualification renders the idea of public reason much less restrictive than it might first have appeared. Perhaps not entirely innocuous, but surely something short of a secular crusade to remove religion from public life.

In 'The idea of public reason revisited', Rawls moved even farther away from the exclusive interpretation of public reason through the introduction of what he termed 'the Proviso'. The addition of the Proviso to the Inclusive view results in a new interpretation of public reason that Rawls labels 'Wide'. The Proviso instantiates two significant changes from the Inclusive view. The most obvious and commonly noted change is that the usage of comprehensive or religious reasons need no longer be *contemporaneously* accompanied by standard public reasons. Rather, the requirement is now stated in the form that 'in due course, we give properly public reasons to support the principles and policies our comprehensive doctrine is said to support' (1999b, p. 145). This aspect of the Proviso serves to relax the condition described in (b) above. Rawls acknowledges various practical questions that this aspect of the Proviso may provoke,[1] but sensibly avoids any attempt to answer them in advance through appeal to some general rule: 'how they work out is determined by the nature of the public political culture and calls for good sense and understanding' (1999b, p. 153).

The less immediately obvious change constituted by the Proviso may be seen in the following passage announcing it: 'This requirement still allows us to introduce into political discussion *at any time* our comprehensive doctrine, religious or non-religious, provided that, in due course' (1999b, p. 144; emphasis added). Permission to invoke non-public reasons at any time in effect relaxes the condition stated in (a) above. Under that condition, the introduction of non-public reasons was constrained by the requirement that such introduction be for the purpose of strengthening the idea of public reason itself under certain (non-well-ordered) social conditions. The Proviso still retains the idea that the purpose of justifications, even if offered in terms of one's comprehensive view, is to strengthen the ideal of public reason and the general system of political liberalism of which it is part. However, there is no longer the requirement that one can advance such justifications only in a non-well-ordered regime. In effect, the Proviso allows one to make political justifications in terms of one's own comprehensive moral or religious view even in a well-ordered political regime.

In sum, the 'wide' view of public reason is considerably more lax in terms of the practical requirements it would impose upon those citizens who affirm its ethic than is indicated by some of the more heated rhetoric that is often used to describe the 'liberal attack on religion'. To be sure, the wide view of public reason is not equivalent to an ethic of 'anything goes' in political justifications, and there are numerous critical questions that can be raised about it. Still, it is important to realize that it is a position genuinely different from the exclusive view of public reason to which Rawls says he was originally attracted.

Constitutional essentials and basic justice

Another significant qualification of the practical impact of public reason is the limitation of its scope of application to what Rawls calls 'constitutional essentials and questions of basic justice' (1996, p. 214). Rawls says that 'many if not most political questions do not concern these fundamental matters' (1996, p. 214), which would indicate that public reason is similarly not applicable to many, if not most, political questions.

For ease of reference, I am going to refer to the category of questions to which public reason does apply as 'fundamental' questions. One complex issue arising out of Rawls's discussion is that of determining the precise nature of the difference between fundamental and non-fundamental questions. We will obviously not be able to tell just how significant the limitation of public reason to fundamental questions is until we have on hand such a determination.[2] However, for present purposes I want to direct attention to an indirectly related issue that takes us more deeply into the internal logic of Rawls's account of public reason than would a direct discussion of the criteria of separation. This is the issue of the *rationale* for limiting public reason to fundamental questions in the first place.

At first glance, it seems odd that Rawls would propose such a limitation. The duty to employ public reason is not, in Rawls's theory, a grudgingly accepted limitation upon liberty justified by appeal to some notion of unfortunate necessity. It is rather a positive expression of the central ethos of the theory; an instantiation of the willingness of citizens to live together politically as free and equal democrats, manifesting their respect for one another through their commitment to foregoing the use of the coercive power of the state in ways that would override the liberty of action to which they acknowledge their fellows to be entitled. It is not at all immediately clear why one who embraced this understanding of political liberalism would not want public reason to apply throughout the entirety of the public discussion of political issues, at least when this is practically possible.

Let's now examine Rawls's explanations of the qualification with this background in mind. Rawls's first explanation occurs in *Political liberalism*. He writes:

> Some will ask: why not say that all questions in regard to which citizens exercise their final and coercive political power over one another are subject to public reason? Why would it ever be admissible to go outside its range of political values? To answer: my aim is to consider first the strongest case where the political questions concern the most fundamental matters. If we should not honor the limits of public reason here, it would seem we need not honor them anywhere. Should they hold here, we can then proceed to other cases. Still, I grant that it is usually highly desirable to settle political questions by invoking the values of public reason. Yet this may not always be so (1996, p. 215).

This is a curious passage, not so much for what it says as for what it does not say. Granting that it makes sense to examine whether public reason makes sense in the fundamental cases, it still seems surprising that Rawls did not go on to address the issue of non-fundamental questions. Moreover, his statement that it is 'highly desirable' to settle all questions through public reason makes his final, unexplained comment ('Yet this may not always be so') seem especially perplexing. Why might it not always be so?

Speaking of non-fundamental issues later in *Political liberalism*, Rawls says that 'to resolve these more particular and detailed issues it is *often more reasonable* to go beyond the political conception and the values its principles express, and to invoke nonpolitical values that such a view does not include' (1996, p. 230; emphasis added). But again, he does not offer any explanation of why this would be the more reasonable thing to do. Note, though, that the departure from public reason is framed here not as a concession to necessity (on the thought that public reason is too indeterminate to speak to non-fundamental issues) but rather in a positive light. But why exactly it might be reasonable to abandon public reason is not explained.

The issue becomes even more complicated when we turn to *Justice as fairness: a restatement*. There, Rawls remarks that a 'satisfactory account' of public reason would ultimately 'show how these [non-fundamental] questions differ from fundamental questions, and why these restrictions imposed by public reason do not apply to them, or if they do, at least not in the same way or so stringently' (Rawls 2001, p. 91). Rawls does not attempt to fill out the idea of public reason in the way indicated here. That is no ground for criticism of his view, because he acknowledges the missing elaboration. However, he does go on to say, speaking of the difference between achieving justifications based in public reason on fundamental and non-fundamental issues, that 'we should distinguish, then, between these two cases, the first attainable (we hope) and desirable, the second neither attainable *nor desirable* (2001, p. 91; emphasis added). I can find no discussion in Rawls's work that speaks to the issue of why it would be desirable to go beyond public reason on non-fundamental matters, nor am I able to propose a plausible rationale for his position here. The idea that it could be reasonable or desirable (or both) to go outside of public reason on non-fundamental issues seems to fit poorly with the internal logic of the theory of political liberalism and its demanding conception of citizenship. One can understand the sense in which going outside of public reason might be seen as a necessary concession to the fact (if it is one) that public reason is too indeterminate to yield judgments on non-fundamental issues, but that would appear at least to be a far cry from it being 'desirable' to go outside of public reason.[3]

One might be tempted to think that Rawls is simply trying to limit the weight of the duty that public reason imposes by allowing (encouraging?) departures on non-fundamental matters. Put more bluntly, it could be that such a position is part of his general strategy of avoidance of conflict designed to achieve overlapping consensus, the desire not to alienate potential sources of support for political liberalism from (holders of) comprehensive moral views other than his own comprehensive liberalism. It is especially tempting to read him this way if we are thinking of the comprehensive religious views that political liberalism hopes to attract as adherents. Thus it could be that Rawls, aware of the hostility to the idea of public reason that emerged from numerous religious critics, sought to moderate the weight of the yoke that it constitutes for religious citizens (and perhaps thereby increase the degree to which they might participate in an overlapping consensus around the principles of political liberalism) by expressing not only the limitation to fundamental matters but also the positive value of going beyond it on non-fundamental matters.

But this is, admittedly, purely speculative, and perhaps not fair to Rawls in the first place. For on this view, Rawls's position here is ultimately strategic, driven not by the internal logic of the theory but by a kind of *ad hoc* concession designed to elicit support. The only thing that can be said with certainty, I think, is that the ultimate rationale for the reasonableness and desirability of going beyond public reason on non-fundamental matters, assuming it is not necessary to do so, is unclear.

T.M. Scanlon makes an interesting attempt to clarify the matter in his recent contribution to the *Cambridge companion to Rawls*. He gives two reasons for the restriction of public reason to fundamental matters. We can label these the arguments of significance and feasibility. The significance argument refers to the idea that the basic structure of society affects the lives and opportunities of citizens in ways over which they have very little, if any, control. On the other hand, 'in a just political order, while citizens do not consent to every piece of legislation … they do have a fair opportunity to make their opinions heard and affect the outcome through speaking and voting and through their representatives' (Scanlon 2003, p. 163). The idea, then, is that it is most important to employ public reason when determining the basic structure (fundamental issues) because these issues are more significant in that they have deep and less easily changed effects upon us as citizens.

This argument does not seem persuasive to me. Even if we accept the difference in significance that Scanlon identifies, it still does not seem to provide a justification for departing from public reason on the non-fundamental matters. Even if it is true that we have more control over how these issues affect us, and therefore a greater ability to change them if they affect us negatively, it is not clear why any of this makes it acceptable to depart from public reason. It may provide a reason for thinking that the costs of departing from public reason will not be as great here as they are with regard to fundamental issues; but that is not the same as a reason for departing from public reason in the first place, and it is certainly not a reason that would explain why it is positively desirable to depart from public reason on these issues.

Scanlon's second argument is the feasibility argument. The argument here is similar to those considered in the following section on completeness. The idea is that 'it does not seem plausible that a political conception – which must refrain from taking sides on issues on which reasonable comprehensive views may disagree – could provide the basis for answering all questions that arise in the course of legislation' (Scanlon 2003, p. 163). Thus we must allow citizens to go outside of public reason if decisions are to be reached. For reasons that are explained in the following section, I do not think that Rawls's idea of public reason will be incomplete in the sense worried about here. However, even if it is, the feasibility argument seems to me to provide an ultimately unsatisfying account of the restriction of public reason to fundamental issues. It is, in essence, a concession to necessity, not a statement of a positive reason for the restriction. Moreover, it seems that if Rawls had intended the restriction to be understood in this way, he could certainly have made that clear. However, he did not. And, as we have seen, he chose to portray the allowance of non-public reasons on non-fundamental issues as something that was reasonable and desirable, rather than framing it as a concession to necessity. Now I suppose one could say that the allowance is reasonable and desirable just exactly because it is unfeasible to not allow it, and so there is no difference between the two explanations. But that seems an unlikely coincidence. If that is what Rawls intended, he certainly took a circuitous route to saying it. I do not think it is what he intended, and perhaps Scanlon does not either, for, after all, he thought to provide the significance argument in addition to the feasibility argument when seeking to explain Rawls's position sympathetically.

These issues cannot be resolved here. They leave open the issue of what constitutes the best systematic account of the restriction of public reason to fundamental questions from within the perspective of political liberalism, assuming the restriction is not simply a concession to necessity. However, it is clear that this restriction constitutes a significant restraint upon the duty of public reason considered as a practical requirement.

Completeness

Rawls has consistently expressed the view that an adequate conception of public reason must be 'complete'. Before unpacking the rather complex idea of what it means for public reason to be complete, it will help to set the discussion against a more general background. At first glance, it might seem odd to characterize the requirement of completeness as one of the factors that functions to push the doctrine of public reason in the direction of being innocuous. The demand for completeness appears to require specific, substantive answers to questions concerning constitutional essentials and matters of basic justice. Rawls does say things that support this understanding of the completeness requirement, and one charge that is often leveled at Rawls's idea of public reason so understood is that it is fundamentally anti-political. The charge is that the doctrine of public reason functions so as to fix the results of fundamental political questions in advance of these questions becoming open in a practical sense to actual citizens. The force of the charge derives from the claim that Rawls, while championing political debate at one (surface) level, tries to limit or remove it at another (deeper) level by proposing rules (the doctrine of public reason) that function so as to ensure that the outcomes of political debate are 'always already' largely determined. From this point of view, his doctrine of public reason is seen as something that indirectly shuts down and dampens political contestation (for example, see Mouffe 1990).

However, Rawls also says a number of things about public reason that incline toward a quite different, more open and flexible understanding of the requirement of completeness. We might call the first inclination the 'closed' conception of completeness and this latter one the 'open' conception. Insofar as the 'open' conception is correctly seen as the proper interpretation of the idea of completeness, the general requirement of public reason will again turn out to be more innocuous than it might have first appeared to one who supposed the 'closed' conception to be the correct one. In this section, I want to briefly sketch each of these interpretations through consideration of their textual basis.

The closed interpretation of completeness

To understand why public reason must be complete, we must first recall why a conception of political justice needs an account of public reason in the first place. Rawls says that 'it is *essential* that a liberal political conception include, besides its principles of justice, guidelines of inquiry that specify ways of reasoning and criteria for the kinds of information relevant for political questions'. These guidelines (i.e., public reason) are seen as essential by Rawls because without them, 'substantive principles cannot be applied and this leaves the political conception incomplete and fragmentary' (1996, pp. 223–224; emphasis added). When Rawls says 'cannot be applied' in this passage, I do not think he means literally 'cannot be applied' as if this were a purely pragmatic problem in the same sense in which one could not, for example, apply the rules of, say, football until one had on hand a statement of what those rules are. Rather, I take him to mean that without public reason the principles of justice 'cannot be applied' in the sense that they cannot be applied in ways that are non-arbitrary and internally coherent. After all, in the case of the political conception of justice, as opposed to my football example, we do have on hand a statement of what the substantive principles of justice are. On Rawls's view these are the 'values of equal and civil liberty; equality of opportunity; the values of social equality and economic reciprocity; and let us add also values of the common good as well as the various necessary conditions for all these values' (1996, p. 224). This statement of political values is, obviously, highly abstract. Affirmation of these values at this level of abstraction is not vacuous; it will serve to demarcate political liberals from, say, monarchists and aristocrats (Rawls 1999b, p. 173), but it will not settle the political disagreements characteristic of the major ideological variants of political liberalism, ranging from libertarian supporters of economic laissez-faire to democratic socialists. Some will maintain that the settling of such disagreements is to be left to the warp and woof of ordinary political contestation; in effect, different parties will compete to 'fill in' the abstract values of political liberalism with their own preferred, more particular, interpretations of what those values mean (or should mean). Rawls would appear to accept this view, with the qualification that the contest be conducted within the bounds of public reason.

The key question, then, is whether a suitably complete public reason would function so as to give unfair advantage to some parties in this contest by deciding questions[4] in advance (of politics). Rawls is certainly aware of this issue. Indeed, he acknowledges that the difference principle is not to be understood as a constitutional essential in political liberalism (1996, p. 229). In other words, Rawls recognizes that the difference principle is not the only reasonable interpretation of the abstract value of 'a social minimum providing for the basic needs of all citizens' (1996, p. 228). The difference principle is a particularly 'demanding' interpretation of that value (1996, p. 229), and does not constitute a constitutional essential in political liberalism. It is a policy that would have to win out over competitors in an ordinary political contest.

Rawls defines 'completeness' most directly when he says in *Political liberalism*:

we want the substantive content and the guidelines of inquiry of a political conception, when taken together, to be complete. This means that the values specified by that conception can be suitably balanced or combined, or otherwise united, as the case may be, so that those values alone give a reasonable public answer to all, or to nearly all, questions involving the constitutional essentials and basic questions of justice. For an account of public reason we must have a reasonable answer, or think we can in due course find one, to all, or nearly all, those cases. I shall say a political conception is complete if it meets this condition (1996, p. 225).

The crucial phrases in this passage, at least for our purposes, are those referring to 'a reasonable public answer' and 'a reasonable answer'. Note that both nouns are singular. It is possible (though mistaken, I think – see below) to read this passage and these phrases as amounting to the view that a suitably complete public reason is one that provides a single 'correct' answer to all or at least most questions of basic justice and constitutional essentials. It can appear that this singularity is the sort of completeness that Rawls is demanding from public reason. This is the closed interpretation of the idea of completeness. It is buttressed by the language Rawls uses that insists upon the 'necessity' of a complete account of public reason, lest the basic political values be left 'incomplete and fragmentary'. On this interpretation, public reason gives particular, substantive answers to foundational questions of basic justice and constitutional essentials, and then sets parameters of legitimacy within which the political contest over non-foundational issues is to take place.

The open interpretation of completeness

The open interpretation sees public reason as constituting a kind of grammar for political debate, without specifying any sentences, as it were. On this view, public reason doesn't actually decide any substantive political question, foundational or otherwise. Without denying that grammar can have an impact upon what is believed and said, and without claiming that it is neutral amongst all possible (substantive) sentences, I nevertheless do want to claim that the open interpretation would render the idea of completeness in public reason far more innocuous than would the closed interpretation. Let's first examine some of Rawls's statements that support the open interpretation, and I will then return to the 'singular answer' passages above that seem to support the closed interpretation.

Rawls's most explicit statements in support of the open interpretation came in his last works, where he tried to clear up what he saw as misunderstandings of certain ideas originally articulated in *Political liberalism*. In the *Commonweal* interview conducted in 1998, he remarks that 'There are many arguments within public reason, and that's the thing to emphasize. I didn't emphasize it enough, you see' (Rawls 1999a, p. 619). Speaking of arguments about physician-assisted suicide, he says that 'the idea of public reason isn't about the right answers to all these questions, but about the kinds of reasons that they ought to be answered by' (1999a, p. 619). Or in another formulation, he says that public reason 'doesn't answer any particular question, but only says how political questions should be discussed' (1999a, p. 622).

The 'open' quality of these statements is borne out by examples that Rawls discusses in 'The idea of public reason revisited'. He first uses the issue of school prayer to illustrate public reason. He acknowledges that some will think that liberalism will insist upon barring school prayer, but Rawls points out that a case can be made for school prayer that is perfectly legitimate in terms of public reason because it relies on political values. Even religious establishment is entertained by Rawls as a possible candidate for defense within the terms of public reason. Patrick Henry's case for Anglican establishment in Virginia and the teaching of Christianity in public schools is cited by Rawls as a case that was 'argued almost entirely by reference to political values alone' (1999b, p. 164). Henry had argued that 'Christian knowledge hath a natural tendency to correct the morals of men, restrain their vices, and preserve the peace of society, which cannot be effected without a competent provision for learned teachers' (1999b, p. 164). These criteria ('preserve the peace...') do not run afoul of public reason; had Henry argued instead on the grounds of the truth of Christianity and the need to worship God in the (presumably correct) Anglican manner, it would be a different matter. Later in the same essay, Rawls allows that the case against the legalization of abortion articulated by Cardinal Bernadin is one that falls within the scope of public reason (1999b, p. 170). The cardinal's argument is described by Rawls as appealing to a certain balance of the values of 'public peace, essential protections of human rights, and the commonly accepted standards of moral behavior in a community of law' (1999b, p. 170).

The discussion of Bernadin's argument against abortion is particularly relevant here, when it is seen in light of Rawls's discussion of the abortion issue in the original edition of *Political liberalism*. There, after a discussion of the three political values (due respect for human life, ordered reproduction of society over time, equality of women as equal citizens) he saw as most relevant to the issue, Rawls had stated:

> Now I believe any reasonable balance of these three values will give a woman a duly qualified right to decide whether or not to end her pregnancy during the first trimester ... any comprehensive doctrine that leads to a balance of political values excluding that duly qualified right in the first trimester is to that extent unreasonable. ... Thus, assuming that this question is either a constitutional essential or a matter of basic justice, we would go against the ideal of public reason if we voted from a comprehensive doctrine that denied this right (1996, pp. 243–244).

This passage, more than any other in *Political liberalism*, seems to support the closed reading of the idea of completeness. It is often read as saying, in effect, that a right to abortion in the first trimester is a dictate of public reason, and hence not reasonably open to being denied. Note that the upshot of the passage is to suggest not that the position against the right to abortion is *wrong*, but rather that it is *unreasonable*. Not surprisingly, many scholars who do not share Rawls's substantive view about the issue of abortion felt that the doctrine of public reason was functioning here as a way of supporting a substantive judgment surreptitiously by appealing to the allegedly non-substantive category of public reason.

In 'The idea of public reason revisited', Rawls spoke to this issue and said: 'some have quite naturally read [the passage above] as an argument for the right to abortion in the first trimester. I did not intend it to be one. (It does express my opinion, but my opinion is not an argument)' (1999b, p. 169). He goes on to say that the purpose of stating his opinion about the abortion issue was merely one of illustration. He meant, he says, to illustrate the idea that 'the only comprehensive doctrines that run afoul of public reason are those that cannot support a reasonable balance or ordering of political values on the issue' (1999b, p. 169). So, the statement about abortion is intended to be understood hypothetically, in the (tautological) sense that *if* it is true that Rawls's opinion about abortion (i.e., a reasonable balance requires a first trimester right *and* no similarly reasonable case can be made for denying this right) is correct, *then* it follows that a comprehensive view disagreeing with this view must be wrong and hence *must* run afoul of public reason. But as a hypothetical illustration (i.e., not an argument), the same point could be made by saying that *if* it is true that a reasonable case (Cardinal Bernadin's?) can be made against the right to abortion *and* no similarly reasonable case can be made in support of it, *then* it follows that a comprehensive view disagreeing with this must be wrong and hence *must* run afoul of public reason. To see the symmetry between the two 'illustrations' is to see the open conception of completeness. A complete public reason, on this view, functions as a permissive concept, not as a determining one. That is to say, public reason provides for any number of substantive positions on an issue, so long as they utilize the grammar of public reason. Once a position is 'in' beyond this stage of permission, public reason itself cannot tell citizens how to determine the issue – they will have to attend to the substance of the issue and the details of the arguments in reaching a judgment. And so while Rawls's original statements about abortion seemed to incline in the direction of public reason as a closed concept that determines, the later statements instead incline in the direction of public reason as an open concept that permits but does not determine, except in those (rare?) cases where no reasonable case can be made in public reason for more than one particular position on an issue.[5]

I have had to use the language of 'inclination' here because even as Rawls has moved in the direction of the open concept there are counter-tendencies. For example, the burden of his discussion of Cardinal Bernadin's position seems to be to allow that a case can be made against abortion from within the bounds of public reason. Rawls specifies the three political values to which Cardinal Bernadin appeals to deny the right to abortion, and then says 'I don't, of course, assess his argument here, except to say that it is clearly cast in some form of public reason' (1999b, p. 170). Now, if Rawls had stopped here, I think it would be unequivocally clear that he is employing the open concept of complete public reason and is telling us, contrary to his originally expressed illustrative opinion on abortion, that a case against abortion can be made within public reason. Of course, it would not follow that Rawls himself would agree with that case; we know that he would not (unless he changed his mind) because of his originally stated opinion. Yet what Rawls immediately goes on to say after the passage above complicates this understanding. He says: 'Whether it itself is reasonable or not, or more reasonable than the arguments on the other side, is another matter. As with any form of reasoning in public reason, the reasoning may be fallacious or mistaken' (1999b, p. 170). I find it very surprising that Rawls should have used the term 'reasonable' as he does here. We expect him to say, in effect, 'now whether Cardinal Bernadin is right or not is another matter; just because his case is made in public reason doesn't mean it's the right position to hold'. Fair enough – but that isn't what Rawls says. He says that whether Cardinal Bernadin's position is 'reasonable' or not is another matter. But how can Cardinal Bernadin's position be 'unreasonable' if it is made from within public reason? Given the later reference to fallacy or mistake, the charitable reading of Rawls here would be to see him as using 'unreasonable' to refer to things like logical errors, mistakes of inference, or even false premises. But it seems to me that it generates confusion to do this, given the specific way in which Rawls employs the concept of reasonableness in the theory of political liberalism. The core idea is to distinguish legitimacy from truth, and to claim that a person can be politically reasonable without necessarily being correct in his or her political judgments.

Indeed, Rawls himself stresses in 'Public reason revisited' that political liberalism 'does not hold that the ideal of public reason should always lead to a general agreement of views, *nor is it a fault that it does not*' (1999b, p. 170; emphasis added). He says that in the normal case, unanimity of views is not to be expected:

> Reasonable political conceptions of justice do not always lead to the same conclusion; nor do citizens holding the same conception always agree on political issues. Yet the outcome of the vote, as I said before, is to be seen as legitimate provided all government officials, supported by other reasonable citizens, of a reasonably just constitutional regime sincerely vote in accordance with the idea of public reason. This doesn't mean the outcome is true or correct, but that it is reasonable and legitimate law, binding on citizens by the majority principle. (1999b, p. 169)

In light of these comments, it is hard to understand why Rawls would say that it is an open question as to whether Cardinal Bernadin's case against abortion made from within public reason 'is itself reasonable or not'. One might say that using 'reasonable' as a loose synonym for 'correct' is surely understandable, and in many contexts I think this would be true. But in the context of Rawls's theory, where the concept of the reasonable carries enormous argumentative weight, it remains a puzzling usage to me. After drawing the distinction between truth and legitimacy in the passage cited above, Rawls remarks that 'some may, of course, reject a legitimate decision, as Roman Catholics may reject a decision to grant a right to abortion' (1999b, p. 169). The reference to Catholics here is meant to be illustrative of a general point; Rawls could just as well have said 'some may, of course, reject a legitimate decision, as some liberals may reject a decision to disallow a right to abortion'. Perhaps if he had varied his illustrative examples by political profile a little more than he actually did, readers might have been more easily able to see the sense in which completeness is properly understood as open rather than closed.

But what of the 'singular noun' passages considered earlier, which seemed to indicate that Rawls endorsed the closed conception of completeness? In light of the discussion of the abortion example, I think the best way to understand those passages is as follows. When Rawls says we want public reason to yield 'a reasonable answer' lest it fail to be complete, he doesn't mean '*a single* reasonable answer' but rather '*at least one* reasonable answer'. Public reason would be incomplete if no reasonable answer on a particular issue could be reached while obeying its constraints. But it is suitably complete as long as there is one position that emerges from reasoning conducted within those restraints. Moreover, the emergence of more than one reasonable answer does not mean that public reason is incomplete. It simply means that a complete public reason has yielded an array of choices about which political judgment will have to be exercised. Not all of these choices will represent true or ultimately correct judgments; but they will represent legitimate judgments. 'Complete' public reason is oriented toward legitimacy, not toward truth. It is a threshold concept that permits, not a perfectionist concept that determines.

This leaves open the question of how to conceptualize the nature of the contest that goes on between multiple positions within public reason. Rawls often refers to the concept of a 'reasonable balance' among public reasons as a way of modeling this conflict, but says very little about how this idea might be cashed out more specifically. I am skeptical that public reason itself could be a source of determining more and less reasonable 'balances' in any authoritative sense. But that issue is not of concern here, and must be left aside for another occasion.

The key point here is that while the demand that public reason be 'complete' might first appear to make public reason an extremely demanding practical restraint upon a citizen's political views, it turns out to be a much lighter burden once we understand it on the open as opposed to the closed interpretation. So understood, it is not a condition that requires one to affirm a particular answer to political questions, except in those cases, which would seem to be quite rare (if existent at all), where only one answer passes the threshold requirement of public reason.

V. Moral, not legal duty

From the beginning, Rawls has made it clear that the duty to utilize public reason is not to be understood as a legally enforceable duty. He calls it 'the duty of civility – to be able to explain to one another on those fundamental questions how the principles and policies they advocate and vote for can be supported by the political values of public reason' (1996, p. 217). He says that it is 'of course, not a matter of law. As an ideal conception of citizenship for a constitutional democratic regime, it presents how things might be, taking people as a just and well-ordered society would encourage them to be. It describes what is possible and can be, yet may never be, though no less fundamental for that' (1996, p. 216; see also Rawls 2001, p. 115). From a practical point of view, then, it is of considerable importance to realize and remember that on Rawls's own terms, the law should not be used to enforce the duty of civility.

Why is it obvious ('of course') that the duty should not be a legal one? After all, the duty of civility to use public reason appropriately expresses the very essence of Rawls's conception of citizenship. A citizen who fulfills the duty acknowledges the inevitability of reasonable pluralism about the good in a free and democratic society, and hence manifests thereby his willingness to live with his (reasonable) fellow citizens on equal terms. Such a citizen refuses either to seek to use coercive political power to advance his own conception of the good or to use it to advance his own personal interests or preferences. He is (understood to be) neither a moral fanatic nor a selfish consumer. Embodying the high public office of 'citizen', he instead seeks to fulfill his official responsibilities through the practice of public reason. That practice orients his attention toward the question of what best serves the common political good and away from his own interests as a moral and natural person. Rawls himself draws the apt comparison: 'public reason with its duty of civility gives a view about voting on fundamental questions in some ways reminiscent of Rousseau's *Social Contract*' (1996, p. 219).

To say that Rousseau was willing to legally enforce the requirement of political civility would be putting it mildly; the fourth book of the *Social contract* describes the institutional means he is willing to countenance in order to ensure the achievement of this central ideal. A few representative chapter titles will convey the seriousness of his intent: 'On dictatorship'; 'On censorship'; 'On civil religion' (Rousseau 1987). Of course, Rawlsian liberalism is not Rousseauian democracy; still, one wonders why Rawls is so willing to eschew the use of coercive law altogether as a means of pursuing the fulfillment of this important ideal. What is the problem?

One possible answer might be that it would not be practically possible or, more mildly put, not pragmatically advantageous, to attempt to legally enforce the duty. One might imagine a large and dangerous security apparatus being necessary to monitor people's political speech and activity if one were to try to somehow legally enforce the duty. The costs seem likely to be worse than the possible benefits, and one can only imagine the levels of cultural resentment that would be generated by, say, public officials snooping around to make sure that no one mentioned God or religion in an 'uncivil' way. Actually, of course, one need not imagine it at all – such resentment is readily discernible today in the vehement reaction against what is portrayed (rightly or wrongly) as the liberal attempt to attack religion in the name of secularism through theoretical ideas like the duty of civility to employ public reason! In any case, Rawls does not advance such a pragmatic argument, and it is just as well because it would leave untouched the really interesting theoretical issue of whether the duty is justifiable or not.

Before considering the answer Rawls does give to our question, it is worth pointing out that partial legal enforcement of the duty is certainly possible in a practical sense. Leaving aside voters and political speakers generally, consider for a moment only elected legislators. Their law-making activity is subject to review by courts charged with the duty of enforcing constitutional rights, and something quite similar to Rawls's duty of civility has long been legally enforced upon them. Consider, for example, the so-called 'Lemon test' for determining whether legislation violates the Establishment clause of the First Amendment. The Lemon test, formulated by Justice Berger in the 1971 case of *Lemon v. Kurtzman*, requires (among other things), that legislation concerning religion must have a 'legitimate secular purpose' (Fowler and Hertzke 1987, pp. 226–227). In this sense, at least, there is no practical barrier to the legal enforcement of the duty of civility. Indeed, one imagines that Rawls would support the Lemon test (or some more perfect analogue) as a reasonable interpretation of the duty of civility.

Whatever Rawls would have said about the Lemon test, let us turn our attention to what he does actually say by way of explaining why public reason is to be a moral and not a legal duty. As it turns out, he actually says very little about this. In *Political liberalism*, he twice remarks that the duty to follow public reason is to be understood as moral and not legal, but he gives no explanation for or commentary upon the point (1996, pp. 217, 253). In 'The idea of public reason revisited', he explains the point with reference to the value of free speech. He says: 'I emphasize that it is not a legal duty, for in that case it would be incompatible with freedom of speech' (1999b, p. 136). I take it, then, that Rawls is allowing that the right of free speech, correctly understood, allows one to say things that violate one's moral duties as a public official. In one sense, this seems perfectly unobjectionable and straightforward. Rawls's commitment to a robust notion of free speech simply means that he is acknowledging that that freedom will sometimes be abused but that it is not desirable to seek to legally prevent that abuse. Presumably, the good of free speech outweighs whatever benefits would be gained from (trying to) legally enforce the duty of civility.

Still, it is worth remarking that this or some other case would need to be made by Rawls. For it is not simply obvious that free speech is *this* important. Consider, for example, that we do hold public officials responsible for upholding the constitution, and we hold them rightly impeachable for violation of duty if they do not. A public official who has told military secrets to the Russians will not be absolved because he claims to have been exercising his right of free speech. Now, public reason is not a part of the constitution of any actual political regime, but one supposes that in a regime ordered according to Rawls's ideas some 'implications' of public reason would be, or certainly could be, constitutionally required. So, for example, a legislature in Rawlsiana might be constitutionally required to provide a public reason for its proposals. Suppose a legislator said that he was supporting mandatory Christian prayer in schools because, and only because, it was the correct means of properly conveying respect to the one and true God. Granted, it is hard to imagine this being treated as a crime. However, it does seem plausible to claim that it is an impeachable offense by the standards of a Rawlsian constitution. And so it isn't quite the complete opposite of a crime either. The legislator could, arguably, be rightly removed from office for dereliction of his duty, and in that sense the duty would be legally enforceable.

At the least, I want to say that the reason for not making the duty a legal one can't be simply that this makes the duty less taxing, hence more innocuous, and therefore more palatable to those inclined to feel that public reason is too restrictive. The decision to make it legal rather than moral has to be motivated by some consideration internal to the theory of political liberalism, at least insofar as we accept that it is pragmatically possible to legally administer it in at least partial ways. Given how important the idea of public reason and the duty of civility is to Rawls's overall conception of a healthy democratic polity, it seems surprising to me that he so readily and casually allows that it is not a legal duty. Appeals to 'free speech' are not, after all, enough to dissuade him from supporting the public financing of electoral campaigns in the name of democracy.

Again, we see that consideration of Rawls's qualifications lead us into complex and unresolved issues about the internal rationale for them. However, for the moment the point to notice is that once again we have a qualification that constitutes a significant limitation of the practical burden upon citizens imposed by the idea of public reason.

The limited forum of public reason

In laying out the primary characteristics of public reason, Rawls says that it is 'imperative to realize that the idea of public reason does not apply to all political discussions of fundamental questions, but only to discussions of those questions in what I refer to as the public political forum' (1999b, p. 133). The public political forum is only one of three zones of activity in Rawls's general conception of political society. The other two are the 'nonpublic political culture' and the 'background culture' (1999b, p. 134) The background culture is 'the culture of civil society', and it encompasses a very wide array of institutional practices. Rawls mentions 'churches and associations of all kinds, especially universities and professional schools, scientific and other societies' (1999b, p. 134).

The requirement of public reason does not apply to *any* of these activities. It is essential that any judgment of Rawls's idea of public reason in terms of its (alleged) tendency to banish religious argumentation specifically or moral argumentation generally from political life take this limitation into account. Rawls himself notes that 'sometimes those who appear to reject the idea of public reason actually mean to assert the need for a full and open discussion in the background culture. With this political liberalism fully agrees' (1999b, p. 134). Note that the zone of activity referred to here as 'background culture' is non-governmental, but certainly not non-political. Rawls refers to the reasons characteristic of activity in this zone as 'social, and certainly not private' (1996, p. 220). The discussion of issues of politics and policy that goes on through the associations of civil society is (or at least should be) the very life-blood of political democracy, and Rawls's concept of public reason places no restraint whatsoever upon religious or moral argument within this zone.

The other zone of activity to which the duty of public reason does not apply is what Rawls calls the 'nonpublic political culture'. He speaks of this zone as 'mediating' between the public political culture and the background culture (1999b, p. 134). Significantly, this zone 'comprises media – properly so named – of all kinds: newspapers, reviews and magazines, televisions and radio, and much else' (1999b, p. 134). This is another major limitation upon the requirement of public reason. Once one realizes that the activities of the media are not included within the purview of public reason, it is much more difficult to think of public reason as a mechanism for removing religion from the 'public square'.

In the other sections of this essay, we have seen various senses in which the requirement of public reason is qualified and limited. Here, we might pause to reflect upon just how limited the range of applicability of that duty, however understood, turns out to be. To be sure, nothing in the account of public reason that Rawls gives ensures that debate and discussion of politics in the background culture of civil society and through the mass media will be vibrant, robust or enlightening. It is a commonplace of our political culture that it fares poorly by these standards, and it is sometimes suggested that the notion of public reason and similar ideas plays an important role in perpetuating this (alleged) failure. But it is hard to see how that could be so once the idea is understood for what it is. After all, it does not even apply to these realms of activity.

Or does it? If one focuses, as I have above, on the zones of activity to which public reason doesn't apply, the remaining zone to which it does can begin to seem rather limited. Let's return to discuss that zone, the area of 'public political culture'. Rawls first subdivides this zone into three more specific activities: (1) the *discourses of judges* in their decisions, especially the judges of a supreme court; (2) the *discourse of government officials*, especially chief executives and legislators; (3) the *discourse of candidates* for public office and their campaign managers, especially in their public oratory, party platforms and political

Zone of activity	Relevant actors	Duty of public reason applicable?
Public political forum	Judges, legislators, candidates	Yes
Nonpublic political culture	Media	No
Background culture	Civil associations	No

Figure 1. The scope of public reason.

statements (1999b, p. 133; see also Rawls 1996, p. 215). He later adds a fourth, and very important activity, the *activity of citizens* when voting and when engaged in the electoral process. Rawls describes this fourth activity as follows:

> How is the ideal of public reason realized by citizens who are not government officials? ... To answer this question, we say that ideally citizens are to think of themselves *as if* they were legislators and ask themselves what statutes, supported by what reasons satisfying the criterion of reciprocity, they would think it most reasonable to enact. When firm and widespread, the disposition of citizens to view themselves as ideal legislators, and to repudiate government officials and candidates for public office who violate public reason, is one of the political and social roots of democracy, and is vital to its enduring strength and vigor. Thus citizens fulfill their duty of civility and support the idea of public reason by doing what they can to hold government officials to it (1999b, pp. 135–136).

The question of how restrictive public reason is, is complicated by the fact that the offices described above (judge, executive, legislator, candidate, citizen) will be 'occupied' by natural persons who will also occupy various different roles in the background culture and nonpublic political culture. While it seems in principle possible to distinguish these identities clearly, it will be more difficult to do so in actual cases. Everyone will agree that Justice Scalia, for example, as a judge is to enforce the provisions of the constitution, not his religious beliefs. And everyone will agree (I assume) that it is perfectly legitimate for Antonio Scalia to appeal to the whole truth of Catholic doctrine in, say, a parish Sunday school class. But what should we say about a speech by Justice Scalia given to an open audience at a public university? Does he have a blank check with regard to public reason, as presumably he does in the Sunday school class? I raise the issue not to explore it, but to suggest that the doctrine of public reason may not fit very easily with the exigencies of politics as it practiced. Let me explain.

The focal case for public reason is when political power, backed by the coercive force of state sanctions, is being exercised on a fundamental matter ('constitutional essentials and basic justice'). Respecting one another as civic equals requires that we exercise such coercive power in responsible ways. Rawls's doctrine of public reason expresses his understanding of what such responsibility amounts to. The clearest case in support of public reason is the activity of the judge. Rawls calls the judiciary the 'exemplar of public reason' (1996, p. 216) and at one point he says that one way to check whether we are following public reason is to ask ourselves how our own argument 'would strike us presented in the form of a supreme court opinion. Reasonable? Outrageous? (1996, p. 254). It is, I think, easy to see why this is so. In a democracy, there is no legitimate basis for judges to make law upon the basis of their personal moral or religious beliefs. This seems a clear and focal case of the usurpation of rightful, legislative, authority. And as a matter of fact, we go to some length as a matter of habitual practice to avoid the 'role confusion' issues I alluded to above. Judges generally avoid the public, political fray. But what about the case of legislators? They are to stay within the (wide) boundaries of public reason in the legislative chambers, and presumably out on the campaign trail. But what about their appearances on radio and TV shows, or before various civic associations? If they are not 'actively campaigning' (or should we assume that elected officials are always campaigning and so always under the authority of public reason?), are they free to skirt the requirements of public reason?

And what about citizens? It is clear that Rawls expects them to vote from a point of view that respects public reason, but *in the process of arriving at the moment of voting* they are apparently free to go outside the bounds of public reason in their political discussions in the background culture. But this seems to create an odd dynamic. It is legitimate to take the 'whole truth' as the citizen understands it from the point of view of her comprehensive moral or religious view into account as one shapes and forms one's political sensibility, but then one is to switch to the point of view of public reason at, as it were, the moment of publicly declaring one's decision.

I think one can see here the sense in which Rawls means that the judiciary is the exemplar of public reason. We ordinarily think that judges are more constrained than legislators in terms of democratic decision-making. The distinction between making and applying law is partly a distinction about the scope of discretion rightly thought to be available to legislators and judges respectively. Legislators we think of as creating something, and in line with all creative activity (as opposed to administrative activity) we tend to think of it as rightly understood as original and generative, less subject to that which is already in place. With judges it is just the opposite. Creative activity on the part of judges raises issues of legitimacy which we do not apply so readily to legislators. It is possible that this view, which I take to be a relatively accurate account of the conventional view of these matters, is mistaken, and ought to be revised. I take Rawls to be advocating as much, insofar as he is trying to make us attend to the duties of the office of citizenship, to see that office, in its legislative capacity, as similar, rather than deeply different from, the judicial office. And, of course, he does have a telling point on his side – citizens are bound to uphold the constitution, though we often think of this as something that applies only to (other) public officials, or even only to judges.

It may be that to take the idea of citizenship as office fully seriously would push one further in a Rousseauian direction than Rawls was prepared to go. It seems a bit artificial to draw as sharp a separation as Rawls does between the zones of public activity in a democratic polity, and to see the idea of public reason as one that applies in an all-or-nothing fashion in these various zones. It may be, as many critics of Rawls claim, that the ethos of public reason, if not the specific idea of it, would permeate each of these zones of activity and extend even into the 'private' sphere as well. I will not address that issue here. Instead, I will simply point out that considered in terms of what it would amount to as a set of literally practical demands upon citizen behavior, the duty of public reason is substantially qualified by its restriction to what Rawls calls the 'public political culture'.

Conclusion

This survey of five important aspects of Rawls's doctrine of public reason leaves many particular problems of interpretation and application unresolved. Still, it is sufficient to demonstrate that the duty to public reason, considered as a practical requirement incumbent upon individuals, is far less draconian a measure than is often suggested in criticisms of political liberalism. Especially when the five qualifications considered here are seen in combination with one another, the duty to public reason seems largely innocuous in terms of the actual constraint upon behavior it would impose upon a religious citizen who affirmed it. That is the core claim of this essay.

Of course, one could object that there is more to it than this. I have been careful to speak of public reason from the particular angle of considering it as a 'practical requirement', and it might be argued that this is to miss the forest for the trees. However light the literal burden of public reason might be, the deeper point (it may be said) is that in political liberalism it is religious and moral conscience which is measured by the standard of liberal politics, and not the other way around. This is certainly true, and this order of priority raises fundamental questions about the relationship between conscience and political order, especially from the point of view of conscience.

These are questions for another occasion, and are admittedly not directly engaged by the analysis undertaken here. Still, even, or perhaps especially, from the point of view of conscience, it is vital to recognize that when it comes to models of liberal political order, all cows are not grey. Any citizen who, in light of his conscience, discovers himself to be a dissenter from the reigning terms of political order certainly has reason to consider the weight of the yoke he will have to bear.

Notes

1. Rawls is not ordinarily given to sarcastic humor, but I wonder if some bite is not intended for his detailed critics when, speaking of the unanswered questions his Proviso leaves hanging, he writes: 'One is: when does it need to be satisfied? On the same day or some later day?' Am I wrong to read a hint of exasperation in that final question?
2. For definition, see Rawls (1996, p. L); see also Rawls (1999b, p. 133).
3. For an argument in favor of extending public reason to non-fundamental matters, see Thompson (2004).
4. By 'questions' here I mean 'questions open within the framework of political liberalism', not political questions generally. Some of those questions are, indeed, 'closed' from the beginning by political liberalism. For example, monarchy is automatically ruled out by the foundational commitments of political liberalism. I do not view this type of closure as a problem. One can, of course, question the foundational commitments to the ideas of equality and liberty; indeed, I would say that from the point of view of philosophy one should do this, or at least try to intellectually prepare oneself to do it as seriously as one is able. But political liberalism and public reason are not trying to shut down philosophical inquiry; they are political doctrines aimed at making

sense of the practical requirements of constitutional government in a liberal-democracy. The point is to try and understand what institutions and policies are required to fulfill the value of equality; it is not that of trying to assess that value against foundational alternatives.

5. This had been the case supposed in Rawls's original discussion of abortion in *Political liberalism*. The key there was not his position on abortion, but the fact that he supposed that no alternative position could be justified in terms of public reason. In that case, public reason would generate a specific answer, in the sense that only one answer passed the threshold of public reason. The discussion of Cardinal Bernadin in 'The idea of public reason revisited' indicates that while Rawls has not changed his mind about abortion, he does seem to have changed his mind about there being only one position on it that can be justified through public reason.

References

Fowler, R. and Hertzke, A., 1987. *Religion and politics in America.* Boulder, CO: West-view Press.

Freeman, S., ed. 2003. *The Cambridge companion to Rawls.* Cambridge: Cambridge University Press.

Mouffe, C., 1990. Rawls: political philosophy without politics. *In:* D. Rasmussen, ed. *Universalism vs. communitarianism.* Cambridge, MA: MIT Press, 217–236.

Rawls, J., 1996. *Political liberalism.* New York: Columbia University Press.

Rawls, J., 1999a. *Commonweal* interview with John Rawls. *In:* S. Freeman, ed. *Collected papers.* Cambridge, MA: Harvard University Press, 616–623.

Rawls, J., 1999b. The idea of public reason revisited. *In:* J. Rawls, *The law of peoples.* Cambridge, MA: Harvard University Press, 129–180.

Rawls, J., 2001. *Justice as fairness: a restatement,* ed. E. Kelly, Cambridge, MA: Harvard University Press.

Rousseau, J., 1987. *On the social contract.* Indianapolis, IN: Hackett Publishing Company.

Scanlon, T., 2003. Rawls on justification. *In:* S. Freeman, ed. *The Cambridge companion to Rawls.* Cambridge: Cambridge University Press, 139–167.

Solum, L., 1993. Constructing an ideal of public reason. *San Diego law review,* 30(4), 729–762.

Thompson, D., 2003. Public reason and precluded reasons. *Fordham law review,* 72(5), 2068–2087.

Reasonable women in the law

Susan Dimock

Introduction

Use of standards of reasonableness is pervasive in the law: criminal law, tort law, employment law, and others invoke such standards as 'reasonable care', 'reasonable foreseeability', 'reasonable time', 'reasonable fee', 'reasonable force', and 'reasonable belief'. What counts as reasonable in these and many other areas of law is typically conceptualized against a 'reasonable man' or 'reasonable person' standard. A reasonable level of care is the degree of care a reasonable person would have exercised in the circumstances; what is reasonably foreseeable is what a similarly situated reasonable person would have foreseen, etc. Introduced in law in the early eighteenth century, the reasonable man standard quickly became essential to decision-making in almost every area of law. This concept of reasonableness is, moreover, entirely normative: reasonable conduct is acceptable conduct; unreasonable conduct exposes one to legal liability of some kind. It is unsurprising, therefore, that many contemporary political theorists (T.M. Scanlon, John Rawls, Charles Larmore and Brian Barry, among others) have developed conceptions of liberalism with reasonableness at their explanatory and justificatory core.

In this essay I examine the use of reasonableness standards in two areas of law that are of special concern to women, and with respect to which many legal jurisdictions and academic commentators have urged employing a gender-specific conception of reasonableness: workplace sexual harassment and self-defense. In both it has been thought important to replace the (supposedly) universal reasonable person with a gendered reasonable woman. I argue that in both cases the reasonable woman standard violates important norms of legality.

In sexual harassment cases, instead of assessing the liability of respondents by examining their conduct to determine if it was reasonable and lawful, use of the reasonable woman standard focuses on the state of mind and actions of their victims. 'Rather than the harasser... being held to certain standards of behavior, it is the recipient of male actions who is judged according to whether she reacted appropriately' (Cahn 1992, p. 1417) Concomitantly, its use in self-defense converts a traditional legal justification into an excuse. These results are legally untenable and politically pernicious.

Hostile environment sexual harassment

Early reforming liberals sought the inclusion of women within the protections and opportunities afforded by liberalism predicated on the equal moral worth and equal rights of persons. Under the influence of equality theory, anti-discrimination laws were passed, and women were granted access to a range of workplaces that had previously been denied to them on the basis of biological differences. Equality theory was predominant in both the civil rights and women's liberation movements. In the United States, Title VII of the Civil Rights Act (1964), and other civil rights laws prohibiting discrimination on the basis of gender, were first understood and litigated against the backdrop of equality theory. Equality theorists did not deny biological differences between the sexes, but argued that such differences were often unjustly used to block women's access to a wide range of workplaces and to make unjustified assumptions about the unequal capabilities of women compared with men.

The gains achieved under equality theory should not be minimized: they were revolutionary. Nonetheless, most feminists now believe that equality theory is inadequate to comprehensively account for women's experience of gender discrimination and to rectify continuing forms of inequality in the workplace and the home. Although workplaces were opened up to women, they faced continuing discrimination: sexual harassment, stereotyping, entrenched institutional attitudes and measures of competence that were implicitly sexist, and a failure to accommodate parenting responsibilities. In the home, women continued to find themselves enmeshed in a web of normative expectations that placed upon them primary responsibility for child care and domestic management even though they were working outside the home (Hochschild and Machung 1989).

In light of these realities, women working for gender equality within the workplace refocused their efforts from access to genuine inclusion. Inclusion required not only recognition of the ways in which women are equal to men, but the ways in which they are different; those differences had to be accommodated if women were to participate fully in the workplaces to which they had gained access. Accommodation required highlighting women's differences and how those differences required modification of male workplace structures. As Kathryn Abrams has pointed out, however, the push for accommodation required advocates of gender equality to develop 'generalizations' about women.

> Accommodation ... required that advocates propound a series of generalizations about women, so that employers and lawmakers know what has to be accommodated. These generalizations, for example, describe how women's professional life-cycles proceed, how women perceive sexual conduct in the workplace, and how their performance and characteristics are likely to be perceived by others (Abrams 1992, p. 1030).

Highlighting women's differences, and reliance upon generalizations, were not strategies that could be embraced without danger, however, as Abrams fully acknowledges. This danger is dramatically revealed by the use of reasonable woman standards in the law.

The 1980 Equal Employment Opportunity Commission characterized hostile-environment sexual harassment as follows: 'Unwelcome sexual advances, requests for sexual favors, and other verbal or physical conduct of a sexual nature constitute sexual harassment when ... such conduct has the purpose or effect of unreasonably interfering with an individual's work performance or creating an intimidating, hostile, or offensive working environment' (29 C.F.R. § 1604.11(a) [1992]). Considerations of unreasonableness *per se* define the range of actionable unwelcome sexual conduct.

Women have the right to be free from sexual harassment that is so pervasive as to alter the conditions of employment and create an abusive working environment (*Meritor Savings Bank, FSB v. Vinson* 477 U.S. 57 [1986]). In a majority decision penned by then Justice Rehnquist, the US Supreme Court held: 'Without question, when a supervisor sexually harasses a subordinate because of the subordinate's sex, that superior "discriminate[s]" on the basis of sex', in violation of Title VII (*Meritor*, at 64). Further, subjecting an employee to sexually stereotyped insults and demeaning propositions can affect the working environment because of their impact upon the psychological and emotional well-being of the employee, and so can constitute hostile environment sexual harassment (*Bundy v. Jackson* 641 F.2d [D.C. Cir. 1981]).

Findings of sexual harassment creating a hostile environment require a showing of two elements. First, the behavior must consist of unwelcome sexual advances, requests for sexual favors or exposure to other offensive conduct because of one's sex. Whether the behavior is unwelcome is a purely subjective matter. Because different individuals may welcome different kinds of sexual behavior, a complainant must express, in words or actions, that the conduct is unwelcome in order for the behavior to be actionable.[1] Second, 'for sexual harassment to be actionable, it must be sufficiently severe or pervasive "to alter the conditions of [the victim's] employment and create an abusive working environment'" (*Meritor* 67, quoting *Henson v. Dundee*, 682 F.2d 897, 904 [11th Cir. 1982]). The US Supreme Court left open whether this second element should be understood subjectively or objectively, but the lower courts tended initially to interpret it objectively. Thus the determinations as to one of the essential matters of fact involved in assessing whether a respondent's actions have created a hostile environment were made from the perspective of the 'reasonable person' (*Rabidue v. Osceola Ref. Co.* 805 F.2d 611 [6th Cir. 1986]).[2]

Many feminists argued that the gender-neutral perspective reflected in the reasonable 'person' standard was illusory, because women perceive and respond to sexual overture, innuendo and conduct in the workplace differently than do men (Abrams 1989, Gutek 1985, Brenneman 1992). Stereotypes differentially affect men and women; men and women are differentially secure in their workplaces and in society; and women may find sexual advances coercive given differences in experience of sexual violence. Thus assessing claims of sexual harassment on the basis of how a reasonable man or even reasonable person would respond to the totality of the activities and contextual factors involved would simply not be a reliable guide to whether those activities created an environment that was abusive and hostile to women. Similarly, attending to gender differences is important for understanding sexual harassment as more than just offensive. To be called a 'whore', 'cunt', 'pussy', or 'tits' (as the supervisor in *Rabidue* called female employees, for example), is not merely offensive; it is abusive, intimidating, degrading and demeaning. Such behavior defines women by their sex, and degrades them on the same basis. Hence a 'reasonable woman' standard ought to be employed to evaluate conduct alleged to be harassing and to have created a hostile and abusive environment.[3] Circuit courts began adopting a reasonable woman standard as appropriate for such cases in 1987.[4]

While many considered the adoption of a reasonable woman standard progressive, and necessary to reveal the false universality and neutrality that abounds hidden in the law, working to the detriment of many non-dominant groups including women, it is not without danger. As indicated, it relies explicitly not only on differences between men and women, but upon generalizations about women and their experience that may misleadingly suggest that women are a more univocal and homogeneous group than they are. It risks replacing one falsely universalized standard with another.

The danger is well recognized by those who critique difference theory on the ground that it falsely essentializes women and masks power inequalities between different groups of women (Minow 1987 and 1988, Harris 1990, Spelman 1988, Crenshaw 1989). It facilitates the marginalization and exclusion of women who do not fit the generalization, which tends to be of privileged white women (excluding women of color, lesbians, women who are handicapped or poor, etc.). It threatens to replace the false universality of the male perspective with an equally false universality of the privileged woman (Childers 1993, Triades 2002).

Use of the reasonable woman standard is also problematic because it invites and perpetuates institutional reliance on stereotypes about women created by men (Abrams 1992, p. 1033; Blackwood 1992). In sexual harassment law, women must be seen as more chaste and sensitive than their male counterparts in the workplace. In domestic violence law, they must be seen as passive, helpless and dependent. Women's reclamation of these stereotypes for use in certain legal contexts has been moderately successful. Yet, as with all reclamations of male understandings of women, the dangers inherent in such a strategy ought not to be minimized. Insofar as such stereotypes both reflect and reinforce male domination of women, they are dangerous tools indeed.

The strategy of generalizing difference risks allowing its generalizations to be used to stigmatize or limit women, or reintroduce assumptions of biological difference that work to their continuing detriment.

> Decision makers who are unfamiliar with the dynamics of socialization or the complex and variable process of social construction may find it easier to ascribe differences to biology and to present them as universal and noncontingent. Thus the differences in women's perceptions of sexual conduct in the workplace may be ascribed not to the fact that longstanding discrimination has made women less secure in the workplace, nor to the fact that the high incidence of sexual violence against women in our society has made many women see coercion in potential sexual encounters. Instead, differences in perceptions may be described as transcultural, a part of the natural modesty or chastity through which women attempt to conserve their limited reproductive endowment (Abrams 1992, p. 1035).

Generalizing difference, then, may perpetuate and legitimize stereotypes about women that both distort their experience and limit efforts to institute workplace changes eliminating the sources of those experiences.

These are familiar objections to the use of the reasonable woman standard in sexual harassment law. It is another, less commonly raised, objection with which I end. This objection is most important for our purposes, because it alleges that reasonableness standards are *per se* conservative (whether gendered or not). Some feminists allege that reasonableness is inherently conservative because it is always defined relative to a concept of societal consensus. They may think this because they are implicitly working with what Steven Scalet calls 'the empty vessel' account of reasonableness, particularly with some version of it which presupposes that what juries and judges fill the empty vessel with are a community's judgment of 'what is proper' or 'what is socially acceptable' (Scalet 2003, p. 76 and accompanying notes). This is the view of Jane Dolkart, for example, who writes:

> Reasonableness is determined by the trier of fact with reference to community standards. Thus, reasonableness incorporates into the law societal norms of behavior. It is a defender of the status quo as defined by those who dominate majority discourse. This is a uniquely inappropriate standard to use in an antidiscrimination statute, the main purpose of which is to provide protection to minority interests over majoritarian interests (Dolkart 1994, p. 198).

Eileen Blackwood likewise thinks that reasonable conduct is that which most people would find acceptable (Blackwood 1992, p. 1022). If reasonableness standards are simply a reflection of societal norms and expectations, then there is good reason to think they are *per se* conservative.

Lynn Dennisen offers an alternative explanation for the charge of inherent conservatism in reasonableness standards in sexual harassment cases. She argues that the Circuit courts are divided over the interpretation of the prohibition of sexual harassment, some taking it as requiring the complete elimination of harassment, and others requiring only that sexually harassing conduct not exceed the level of harassment generally present, and so reasonably expected, in society at large or within a given workplace. On the latter interpretation, harassment must cross a threshold determined by contemporary societal and workplace attitudes in order to be found unreasonable (Dennisen 1993, pp. 477–478). This interpretation was followed in *Rabidue*, with the predictable result that the court found no breach of Title VII: 'The majority trivialized the harassing conduct and found that the displays of sexual misconduct in *Rabidue* had a "de minimus" effect upon the plaintiff's work environment when considered in light of current societal mores' (Haag 1993, p. 234).

If the charge of inherent conservatism is correct, moreover, it will make no fundamental difference if we move from a 'reasonable person' to a 'reasonable woman' standard, for even the latter will reflect the broader social consensus.[5] That the reasonable woman standard will itself be a conservative standard is the view of some critics, for good reason. For whereas there have been two competing conceptions of the reasonable man in legal history – '(i) an ideal, albeit not perfect, person whose behavior served as an objective measure against which to judge our actions and (ii) an average or typical person possessing all of the shortcomings and weaknesses tolerated by the community' – it is the average or typical woman who provides the standard of reasonableness in sexual harassment law (Adler and Peirce 1993, p. 807). Such women are neither hypersensitive nor indifferent to men's harassing behavior; their reactions are, instead, average reactions, as determined by societal norms and expectations. Insofar as such reactions will reflect the gender inequality against which typical reactions are experienced and expressed, the reasonable woman will tolerate a considerable amount of harassing behavior. Thus, even if we modify the group whose consensus is to be ascertained, so that reasonable conduct is what most women would find acceptable, such a concept remains inherently conservative, infected by the effects of historic and continuing forms of sexual oppression. Such a concept is inherently incompatible with any use of law to change prevailing attitudes or the social consensus. Insofar as genuine sex equality requires a rejection of the prevailing norms of acceptability, any standard of reasonableness will hinder rather than further that goal.

This critique of reasonableness standards depends upon the premise that the content of such standards is to be determined by community consensus, prevailing attitudes and accepted practices. But this interpretation of reasonableness was rejected in tort law as early as 1932 by Judge Learned Hand. In his famous decision in *The T.J. Hooper v. Northern Barge Corp.*, Judge Hand explicitly rejected a social consensus or common practice understanding of reasonableness:

> There are, no doubt, cases where the courts seem to make the general practice of the calling the standard of proper diligence; we have indeed given some currency to the notion ourselves .... Indeed in most cases reasonable prudence is in fact common prudence; but strictly it is never its measure; a whole calling may have unduly lagged in the adoption of new and available devices. It may never set its own tests, however pervasive be its uses. Courts must in the end say what is required; there are precautions so imperative that even their universal disregard will not excuse their omission (60 F.2d 737 [2nd Cir. 1932] at 740).

This raises the possibility that, even if judges have typically relied upon community standards to give content to the reasonable woman standard, they need not do so, and thus the charge of inherent conservatism leveled against reasonableness standards is overstated.

No doubt some feminists have overstated the case against reasonableness standards in the law. But we cannot dismiss the charge of conservatism (perhaps 'conventionalism' would be better) quite so quickly. The problem is that in tort law there is an objective measure of reasonable care (i.e., efficiency), and courts can assess a given defendant's conduct against this measure, thus enabling a finding of negligence even for conventionally established practices; in the case of sexual harassment, by contrast, what is being assessed is not conduct but the effect of conduct on a reasonable person or a reasonable woman. Being assessed is a complainant's reactions to the behavior of others. How can such reactions be assessed as reasonable or unreasonable except by the use of a typical or average person or woman standard? There seems to be no alternative (i.e., ideal) measure of reactions. Thus the charge of conservatism cannot be raised without qualification against all reasonableness standards in the law, but it might nonetheless be inherent in constructions of reasonable reactions to sexual conduct in the workplace.

Some feminists have indeed advocated a kind of ideal reasonable woman standard to correct this problem. They defend a standard designed explicitly to meet the needs of women in litigation, a standard reflecting a clear normative choice with respect to representation. Thus Martha Chamallas has argued for a reasonable woman who is aware of patterns of discrimination in the workplace and committed to eliminating them (Chamallas 1992). Kathryn Abrams prefers to construe the reasonable woman as the 'most vulnerable woman' in the workplace (Abrams 1992, p. 1039). Such a strategy, however, risks privileging the perspective of some women while devaluing that of others; concerns of essentialism that marginalize some in developing generalizations that represent only some and that will result in the reintroduction of limiting stereotypes by decision-makers seem inescapable on this approach.

What we need, instead, is a complete refocusing of the question. Rather than determining whether harassment has occurred by evaluating the responses of its victims to determine whether they were reasonable, we should employ our reasonableness standards in the traditional way: as the demarcation between faulty and faultless conduct. We must, in other words, examine the alleged harasser's behavior. Was his behavior reasonable? Is it reasonable to display graphic or violent pornographic images in a workplace; to refer to female employees or co-workers by sex-specific derogatory names; to continue to ask an employee out socially after she has clearly and repeatedly declined such invitations; to put a gun in the crotch of a co-worker and then sniff it; to fondle an employee at work in the presence of others employees?[6] Such questions must be answered against a backdrop of the values implicit in the law which such actions are alleged to impugn, in this case values of equality and nondiscrimination. Given those values, such conduct cannot be deemed reasonable.

Direct assessment of the reasonableness of the conduct complained of would not require the use of generalizations about differences between men and women, and so would not be open to the objections of essentialism, bias and stereotyping that any particularized standard of reasonableness, drawn on group membership, must involve. It would provide a single standard under which all cases of harassment could be adjudicated (including those involving men as the victims of harassment by woman, same-sex harassment, etc.). A reasonable employer/supervisor/co-worker standard would, furthermore, directly invite consideration of power differentials between the parties to the dispute, which are independent of sex or gender. Unlike a reasonable woman standard, this would not require a continuing recognition of the essential differences between men and women, and thus is less likely to be used as an ongoing justification for differential treatment based on presumed group differences.

Self-defense

To justify the intentional use of deadly force on the grounds of self-defense, defendants typically have to establish four facts: that they believed they were in imminent danger of death or grievous bodily harm from an unlawful attack; that they used a reasonable amount of force to repel the danger, or believed that killing was the only action available to them to repel the threat; that they believed that retreat or legal aid was unavailable; and that they were not the aggressor in creating the danger. In the case of the three beliefs – that one is in imminent danger from unlawful attack, that nothing less than the use of deadly force will repel the attack, and that retreat is not available – defendants must also prove that their beliefs were reasonable in the circumstances. These requirements will be referred to as imminence, necessity or proportionality, and no escape or no alternatives in what follows.

Self-defense claims are especially problematic in a range of cases involving battered woman who kill their batterers. Indeed, the traditional understanding of the conditions under which each of the three beliefs could be reasonable had to be expanded for woman who kill their batterers at times when they are not under immediate attack, when their batterers are sleeping or otherwise acting without overt violence (non-confrontational cases). They kill in response to threats of future violence. The first condition of self-defense, that one must believe oneself to be the victim of an unlawful assault, allows significant latitude for interpretation in most Anglo-American jurisdictions, since assault includes not only actual applications of force but threats of force.[7] The imminence requirement, however, that one must believe oneself to be at imminent risk of suffering serious bodily injury or death, has been most problematic in non-confrontational killings. That the risk of harm be immediate or at least imminent cannot be shown if the threatened violence is to occur in the future. Similarly, it has been difficult for such women to prove that they acted proportionately by killing when faced with threats from unarmed abusers or abusers who threatened less than deadly force, or that killing was necessary to protect themselves. Finally, proving that one has no reasonable alternative to force also seems difficult to establish when the violence is not imminent or on-going, for generally one is required to withdraw or seek assistance from legal authorities if one can rather than use violent self-help. Thus when battered woman kill their batterers in response to threats of future harm, the risk of death or serious bodily harm may not be immediate, and so the apprehension of imminent risk may not be reasonable. If such killings take place when the batterer is otherwise engaged, or even asleep, then one might think the woman has reasonable alternatives to deadly self-help, such as calling the police or escaping the home.

In hearing cases involving battered women who kill their batterers, courts came to realize that it is unacceptable to insist that women wait until an attack is imminent or on-going before they can engage in self-defensive actions. Such a requirement would condemn women to death or grievous bodily harm at the hands of their attackers, since self-protection may be impossible once the violence has begun. Yet the courts also went further, thinking that they had to modify the tests for self-defense when applied to battered women, assessing the reasonableness of the defendant's beliefs against a standard of the reasonable woman or reasonable battered woman rather than the reasonable person (*State v. Kelly* 97 N.J. 178, 478 A2d. 364 [1984]; *R. v. Lavallee* 1 S.C.R. 852 [1990]).

Use of the reasonable battered woman as a standard of reasonableness in self-defense cases is deeply problematic, however, because it converts self-defense from a justification into an excuse. Although the line has become blurred in some recent work on legal defenses, the distinction between justification and excuses is important. Defenses that function as justifications have both a different rationale and a different internal structure than excuses. Justifications rest on an assumption that all persons should be subject to the same laws and held to the same standards of conduct. They focus on the action in question, and ask whether it should be recognized as a universal qualification of a legal rule the violation of which is at issue. Thus, for example, under the modern understanding of self-defense as a justification, it operates as a universal exception to the homicide laws in particular types of circumstances. This is important, because exceptions to general rules are accepted when the behavior in question is not wrong (whether actually laudable or just permissible). Both morality and law recognize that killing in self-defense is an exception to the general wrongness of killing and ought to be permitted. Anyone who kills in self-defense acts permissibly. Structurally, justifications rest on a presumption of voluntary and intentional choice. The point is not to determine whether the defendant *could* have acted otherwise than she did in acting self-defensively, but whether she *should* have acted differently. With respect to questions of justification, reasonableness is relevant in determining whether a universal qualification of the relevant legal rule would be justified, right or at least tolerable as a general rule.

Excuses function very differently. If an action is excused, it is deemed wrongful but the actor is excused because she is thought not to be responsible for it. Admitting excuses does not result in a modification of the legal rule at issue. Rather, excuses focus on the blameworthiness of particular defendants in their specific circumstances. Excuses rest on a recognition that individual characteristics of the defendant (such as mental disorder) or her circumstances (being faced with dire peril, whether caused by coercion or natural causes) make it practically impossible for her to obey the law; her behavior is in some important sense morally involuntary. The question at issue concerns what the defendant *could* or *could not* do in the circumstances, rather than on what she *should* do or have done. If what she did was determined by external forces or circumstances, rather than free choice or persistent internal character traits or dispositions, then her behavior was not voluntary and so she is not responsible[8] (Heller 1998).

The categories of justification and excuse have been distinguished in multiple ways by moral philosophers and legal scholars. Among the most common distinctions are these: (1) justified action is warranted or not wrongful, while excused action is unwarranted or wrongful; (2) justified action may be undertaken properly by others, whereas others may not similarly perform merely excused actions; (3) the justified action of one person may be assisted by others, and interference with such actions is wrongful, whereas actions that are merely excused may not be assisted by third parties and interference with them is not itself wrong; (4) justified actions are general or objective, while excused actions are individual or subjective; (5) justified actions are such that the actor has a pre-existing right to perform them, while excused actions are not grounded in a right; and (6) justified actions are those which have received prior legal authorization by the state, whereas excused actions have not been so authorized. These considerations are not, of course, mutually incompatible; indeed, they might all be thought to reflect implications of the most basic (and commonly drawn) difference between justified and excused behavior, as behavior which is right or at least permissible and that which is wrongful but excused. 'A justification speaks to the rightfulness of the act; an excuse, as to whether the actor is accountable for a concededly wrongful act' (Fletcher 1978, p. 759). Such a distinction is compatible with diverse approaches for determining whether an act is right or wrong.

To say that justifications are general and objective while excuses are personal and subjective reflects the fact that if one person is justified in violating the law in a certain set of circumstances then others similarly situated must also be justified in doing so; when a person's otherwise illegal behavior is merely excused because of personal characteristics (such a mental disorder), by contrast, it does not follow that others are permitted to perform the same action (though others with the same personal characteristics will be similarly eligible for an excuse) (Fletcher 1978, pp. 761–762; Greenawalt 1984, pp. 1915–1918).

The view that justifications are privileges legally authorized in advance has some plausibility: use of force by police officers or by parents in disciplining their children, for example, as well as self-defense, are all actions authorized by the state. Actions taken in accord with such provisions are then legally justified. This was the historically dominant view (associated most obviously with St Thomas Aquinas) prior to the modern era, and has able defenders today (Finkelstein 1996, Thorburn 2006).

George Fletcher argues that the crucial distinction between justified and excused actions actually lies in the rights of third parties. Third parties may assist but not try to prevent justified actions, while they may properly try to prevent and may not assist merely excused actions (Fletcher 1978). Likewise, potential victims may defend themselves against actions that are merely excused, but not against others acting with justification.

However we distinguish justifications from excuses, there are three dominant approaches to filling in the story of justifications: the superior interests view, the moral rights view and the contractarian view. On the superior interests view, one begins with a general recognition that the criminal law protects a specific set of interests, hierarchically ordered in some fashion or other. Specific defenses (self-defense, duress, necessity, provocation and the like) are then classified as justifications only if allowing the defined conduct protects superior interests over those which are sacrificed by the act. Self-defense may thus be justified because it protects superior interests. The interests of potential victims in defending themselves, as well as the public interest in promoting general peace, outweigh the interests of aggressors in being free from assault or even death (Eser 1976, p. 632; Fletcher 1978; Robinson 1982). Given the idea of weighing interests here, this account can easily explain the limitations or restrictions that most jurisdictions place on the justification: the duty to escape or retreat in some cases, its unavailability to those who provoke the aggression from which they then seek to defend themselves, and the proportionality requirement that the harm inflicted in self-defense not be grossly disproportionate to that threatened by the aggressor. Self-defense is justified if and when it produces more social utility than it sacrifices (when it is the lesser of two evils, as the point is often expressed), or when the person acting in self-defense reasonably believes that it will. Alternatively, one might take a natural rights perspective and say that self-defense is justified because it is the exercise of a right that is not (perhaps cannot be) surrendered to the state and cannot be limited by penal law. This is its status, as a peremptory norm, in international law (Motala and ButleRichie 1995; but for problems with the view see Kaufman 2004). Or one might say that rational agents establishing a system of criminal law for their mutual advantage would recognize this limitation on rules prohibiting violence (Kadish 1976).

It is my contention that self-defense should generally be thought of as a justification rather than an excuse, and that this is so even in standard cases of battered woman who kill their batterers in response to threats of future violence. Bringing such cases within traditional self-defense doctrine does not require abandoning any of the bases upon which we judge such actions to be justified, nor does it require introducing any special woman's self-defense claim or reasonable woman standard. To the contrary: reliance upon a special woman's or battered woman's defense, and use of a reasonable woman standard, converts the defense from a justification to an excuse, with pernicious results.[9]

At issue here is whether we consider the self-defensive actions of battered women reasonable and justified or wrong but understandable and excusable. Some scholars who rely upon battered woman's syndrome (BWS) do so in order to explain the distorted perceptions and pathological reactions the syndrome may cause. Thus they use the history of battery, with the heightened state of fear and feelings of helplessness it induces in its victims, to explain why a woman in such circumstances may have been acting in a subjectively reasonable way when she acted with deadly force against a perceived threat to her physical security. Such explanations can only excuse.

This is the position of Cathryn Jo Rosen, for example, who argues that the battered woman's defense may demonstrate that a woman who kills her abuser in circumstances that do not meet the traditional tests of self-defense may have been acting in a subjectively reasonable way, but that genuine justifications require objectively reasonable behavior, behavior that is deemed right for all people similarly situated and as such should be encouraged in society because it benefits society. She denies that the behavior of battered women who kill meets the criteria of genuine justification. Rather, she argues, their actions are wrongful, even if understandable, the product of extraordinary pressures and impaired mental functioning for which they should be excused (Rosen 1986). Claire Finkelstein likewise distinguishes standard cases of self-defense from the 'special defense for battered women' that is predicated on BWS, which treats BWS as a psychological condition that defeats responsibility on grounds of incapacity or impairment of rational functioning. Such a defense, even if it could be rendered coherent and an explanation could be given as to why it excuses violence against one's batterer but not other crimes, would at most render the resulting behavior excused but not justified (Finkelstein 1996, p. 632).[10]

Kevin Heller also thinks that employing a reasonable woman or reasonable battered woman standard converts self-defense from a justification into an excuse (Heller 1998). This reconceptualization of self-defense is very problematic, and yet it is invited by the use of BWS as pathology. As Heller argues, the particularized standard operates as an excuse, on the assumption that the particular characteristics are considered to be relevant because they are thought causally to determine how the defendant perceives and responds to the threatening situation (Heller 1998, p. 82). They must also be thought to impede the ability of those sharing the characteristic to act in objectively reasonable ways. 'For example, it only makes sense to use a "reasonable battered woman" or a "reasonable battered child" standard instead of a "reasonable person" standard if being battered prevents women and children from perceiving and acting as reasonable persons. [FN This is precisely what advocates of the 'reasonable battered woman' standard claim...]' (Heller 1998, p. 83–84). Persons who invoke any particularized factor to excuse their behavior must have been determined by that factor to perceive and act in certain ways, and those ways must be unreasonable as determined by the reasonable person standard. A similar determinist analysis is offered by Armour (1996, pp. 535–538).

Most discussants of self-defense in battered women cases treat BWS as determinative of perception and action, though they also insist (contra Heller) that the perceptions and actions are objectively reasonable. Barbara A. Venesy's treatment of the subject is typical. Relying upon the work of Lenore Walker in modeling BWS, Venesy argues that BWS 'attempts to explain the reactions of women trapped by domestic violence in terms of the cycle theory of violence and the theory of learned helplessness' (Venesy 1989, p. 94). The cyclical nature of the battery, and the feelings of helplessness it generates, not only result in battered women perceiving the situation as one of imminent threat, but make that perception reasonable. 'The unrelenting cycle of violence and feelings of helplessness place the battered woman in a constantly heightened state of terror because she believes that one day the batterer will kill her. Thus, to a battered woman, the threat of violence is continuously imminent, the abuser's earlier threats are still in force, and the imminent danger arguably justifies self-defense even in a period of apparent calm' (Venesy 1989, p. 95). Although used to argue that the woman's perception of the situation – that the threat of death or serious bodily injury was imminent and that deadly force was necessary to repel the threat – was reasonable, reasonableness itself is determined against the standard of the reasonable battered woman, a characterization focused on particularized facts about the defendant.

As used by the courts, it is clear that the reasonable battered woman falls short of the reasonable person, and that deterministic assumptions underlay its use. Consider the reasoning of a Kansas court when distinguishing between imminence and immediacy of the threat (quoted with approval by Venesy).

The abuse is so severe, for so long a time, and the threat of great bodily harm so constant, it creates a standard mental attitude in its victims. Battered women are terror-stricken people whose mental state is distorted and bears a marked resemblance to that of a hostage or prisoner of war. The horrible beatings they are subjected to brainwash them into believing there is nothing they can do. They live in constant fear of another eruption of violence (*State v. Hundley*, 236 Kan. At 467, 693 P.2d at 479, quoted in Venesy 1989, p. 99).

Venesy's analysis implicitly invokes an excuse rather than a justification model (though she had properly characterized self-defense as a justification early in her paper). She writes that the 'reasonably prudent battered woman' standard calls for the following inquiry: 'Could a reasonably prudent battered woman living in constant fear and under life-threatening conditions, have acted differently than [the defendant] acted?'[11] The defendant is described as having developed survival skills which 'narrow the battered woman's perceptions so she focuses only on survival and misperceives other important information' (Venesy 1989, p. 101). And yet, Venesy continues to insist that courts have admitted BWS evidence to explain the reasonableness of women's perception of danger and that the right to self-defense asserted by battered women is no different than that asserted by other victims of assault. The combination is incoherent.

The most significant shortcoming of introducing a particularized standard of reasonableness in self-defense cases is precisely this transformation of self-defense from a justification to an excuse. Such a move requires that we see the self-defensive actions of women as wrongful, but not blameworthy because we cannot hold battered women to the normal standards of reasonableness. Their actions must be seen as unreasonable, though excusable. This is surely wrong: a woman who protects herself, even with violent self-help, in the context of domestic battery, acts objectively reasonably, and in a way which is fully justified.[12]

George Fletcher similarly thinks that battered women who kill in non-confrontational settings cannot be justified in doing so, though they may well be excused. This is in part because he assumes that what feminists have been urging is adoption of special rules or expansion of self-defense 'to make it easier to acquit women who kill their husbands under circumstances that would not ordinarily qualify as self-defense' (Fletcher 1996, p. 555). Thus he sees feminists' efforts here as a case of special pleading, rather than an assertion of equal rights to a fair trial (as Elizabeth Schneider characterizes her own and many others' work, discussed below). This is not surprising, given the confusion we have noted just above in the use of BWS in self-defense cases.

Fletcher's reasons for thinking that battered women who kill their batterers cannot be justified in doing so are tied to his broader understanding of justifications, however, which requires not merely reasonable beliefs that the justifying conditions are realized (imminent threat, no escape and necessity of deadly force), but that those conditions in fact obtain. Thus if one falsely (even if reasonably) believes that the conditions of justification are met and one acts on them, then one has at most a putative defense, which can excuse but cannot justify. Only if the objective conditions are realized in fact can an act of self-defense be justified. Because he thinks past battery can be relevant only to the reasonableness of the belief that those conditions obtain, rather than to the fact that they obtain, and reasonableness of belief is irrelevant to justification, he concludes that evidence of a history of battery is irrelevant to the question of justification (Fletcher 1996, pp. 563–564; but see Stewart 2003).

Besides being overly demanding (Sebok 1996) and misunderstanding the position of many who argue in favor of thinking that battered women who kill in self-defense in contexts of battering relationships are justified in doing so (Schneider 1996), Fletcher's position rests on a conflation of warrant and truth. The objective conditions make the claim that one was acting in self-defense true, but justification is about warrant rather than truth. One may well be warranted in believing as one believes, and acting as one does, even though the situation is not as one reasonably believed it to be.

That we should reject Fletcher's insistence on the objective facts being realized and so the threat of imminent death being actualized is made clear, I think, in an example from Benjamin Zipursky: 'V puts a .44 Magnum to a shopkeeper's head in the middle of a hold-up, and says, when the money has been taken, "Now I'm going to blow your brains out." The shopkeeper reaches under the cash register for a gun and kills the robber. The police learn that the Magnum was unloaded' (Zipursky 1996, p. 603; see also the excellent examples in Stewart 2003). Zipursky argues, persuasively, that the shopkeeper is justified in killing the robber, even though his reasonable belief that he faced imminent death is false. The reason is because we must focus on the *threat*, rather than what will or will not result from the threat. The shopkeeper is justified and not merely excused, 'because the shopkeeper was, in fact, faced with an imminent threat of death or grievous bodily harm through [V]'s aggression. What it means to be faced with an imminent threat is to be presented with conduct that, under the circumstances, would lead a reasonable person to believe that immediate defensive force would be needed to avoid death or grievous bodily harm' (Zipursky 1996, p. 603). The circumstances determining whether conduct is objectively threatening may include particular details about the person threatening, including his or her history of inflicting abuse. If, by contrast, one person has not engaged in objectively threatening conduct, then another person can at most be excused even if she reasonably believes she is under imminent threat and acts accordingly. Threatening conduct is the key.

> On this account, one reserves the right to act aggressively where the assailant has engaged in threatening conduct. What triggers the right is not the existence of conditions rendering self-defense necessary, but the existence of threatening actions. Arguably, a person in the original position would want to reserve for herself the right to use force when the threatening conduct is engaged in, because this is something that she is better at knowing about than the future-oriented question of whether death or bodily harm *will* ensue (e.g., she can tell whether a gun is pointed at her head, but she cannot tell whether it is loaded). She would rationally decide to reserve a right that permits response to perceivable threats, rather than indeterminate outcomes (Zipursky 1996, p. 606).

Such an approach does not leave individuals at the mercy of just anyone who believes they are a threat (reasonably or not), because justified self-defense may be used only against persons engaging in behavior that they know or should know is imminently threatening. Applied to cases where the defendant lacks genuine access to alternative forms of assistance (whether in fact or putatively), Zipursky's account suggests that killing in self-defense may be justified in these cases too.

> What triggers the right to self-defense (in nonimminence situations) would be conduct that the victim knows, or should know, would lead a reasonable person to believe that, because of the absence of genuine alternatives, and because of the impending violence of the assailant, if she does not resort to defensive aggression, she will inevitably suffer death or grievous bodily harm by the assailant. Such conduct might be described as *conduct presenting a 'menace of inevitable death or grievous bodily harm'* (Zipursky 1996, p. 609).

He concludes that rational persons would reserve for themselves a right of self-defense against conduct presenting a menace of inevitable death or grievous bodily harm.[13]

This idea, that a batterer may actually engage in threatening behavior and pose a danger to his victim even in non-confrontational settings, is important in understanding another limitation of Fletcher's view. Fletcher repeatedly assumes that we are dealing with cases in which the woman's reasonable beliefs are *mistaken.* 'Reasonable mistakes in self-defense cases are about actions that are harmful to innocent people – unjustifiable, unlawful actions that can, at most, be excused on grounds of mistake' (Fletcher 1996, p. 567). This paradigm does not fit the majority of cases that feminists are concerned about, however. The batterer is not 'innocent'; he has issued credible threats of violence to kill or seriously harm the woman he batters. His behavior is immoral and unlawful. Thus the situation is importantly different than that of Mr Young, who assaulted police officers effectuating a lawful arrest in the mistaken belief that they were unlawfully assaulting the youth they were arresting (Fletcher 1996, p. 566, discussing *People v. Young* [1962] 183 N.E.2d 319). Batterers engaged in menacing behavior are engaged in unlawful assaults against which self-defense must be permissible.

Fletcher thinks, by contrast, that women's violent responses to threats of future attack are pre-emptive. Preemptive attacks are not permitted under domestic or international law as self-defense. 'They are illegal because they are not based on a visible manifestation of aggression; they are grounded in a prediction of how the feared enemy is likely to behave in the future' (Fletcher 1996, p. 557). Fletcher's conclusion from this commonplace observation, however, is puzzling. He allows that states need not wait until an attack is actually underway to take defensive action: 'the requirement of imminence does not require that guns actually fire, that bombs be in the air' (Fletcher 1996, p. 558). Yet when applied to women who kill in non-confrontational settings, he seems unwilling to 'relax' the imminence requirement (Fletcher 1996, p. 571). He insists that whether a given action is an imminent threat depends just upon what the threatener says and does at the time; past history between the parties, or disparities in power, are irrelevant to whether one is an imminent threat to the other. This entirely ignores the larger context in which non-confrontational killings happen, i.e., in response to a particular threat of serious harm at a relatively determinate time ('when I wake up', 'when the guests leave', 'when we get home'). The threat of serious violence is itself an assault and expression of hostility; from the time such a threat is made (and remains operative, not having been withdrawn), the woman is under attack. The imminence requirement is fulfilled. Thus while threats of future violence always leave open the possibility that the attack will not come (he might change his mind), so that the perceived need to take defensive action is false, it does not follow (contra Fletcher) that the danger posed by such threats is non-imminent, nor that her perception of the need for defensive action is mistaken.

Self-defense is justified, and many women who kill their batterers should be able to avail themselves of the traditional defense. This is the view of Elizabeth Schneider, whose scholarship and advocacy has been pioneering in highlighting the multiple sources of gender bias faced by women who kill, impeding their ability to a fair trial. Schneider denies that the need to introduce evidence of battery in such cases is part of an attempt to introduce a 'special defense for battered women, either as self-defense or as a special "battered woman defense"' (Schneider 1996, p. 486). Rather, evidence of a history of battery is relevant in applying the traditional framework to women who kill. Evidence of battering 'is relevant because it helps the jury to understand the woman's particular experiences with her batterer. It gives the jury insight about the development of her heightened ability to sense that she was in grave danger at the time of the killing. It provides the jury with the appropriate context in which to decide whether her apprehension of imminent danger of death or great bodily harm was reasonable' (Schneider 1996, p. 511; Armour 1996). Likewise, evidence introduced on battering relationships and BWS can help juries understand why it may be reasonable for a woman to believe that she could not safely escape a threatened attack; evidence that past attempts to leave the abuser resulted in escalating levels of violence, that past attempts to seek aid from legal authorities had failed to protect her, and the like, may help juries understand why a woman might reasonably believe she could not escape the violence threatened by her non-confrontational batterer (Armour 1996).

Although recognition of the relevance of battering to judgments of reasonableness does not entail modification of our traditional understanding of self-defense, introducing evidence of battering requires one limited change to how the law is applied. Self-defense claims were historically assessed against quite rigid temporal limitations: the fact-finder was only to asses the reasonableness of the defendant's fear of the decedent given the circumstances occurring at or immediately before the killing (Armour 1996, p. 526). Evidence of prior history between the defendant and the decedent, as well as knowledge the defendant might have about the effectiveness of legal remedies based on prior attempts to escape, were not typically admitted. But this limitation is not required under any of the traditional tests of self-defense (imminence, necessity or legal alternative). And it is wholly unjust. To see why, consider a different self-defense case. If the fact-finder is to assess the objective reasonableness of the defendant's fear and beliefs, surely the fact that she had been raped by the decedent in the past is relevant. When she is now alone and unexpectedly confronted by him, his saying 'So, here we are again' or 'I knew you'd come back for more' may be objectively good grounds for her to fear another violent attack. The reasonableness of her fear cannot be understood without the history of their prior interactions, and would certainly not be apparent from an examination confined to what he said and did just before her defensive attack. But allowing evidence concerning their prior history does not require modifying the conditions under which self-defense is permissible, nor is the rationale for doing so limited to female defendants. Their prior history is essential for understanding her fear as not just subjectively reasonable, but objectively reasonable as well.

The above discussion, it must be acknowledged, risks reinforcing commonly held stereotypes about battered woman, especially those who kill. First, it might be thought to suggest that all battered woman are alike; they are not. Second, it focuses on the problematic case of women who kill in non-confrontational settings. A 1991 study by Holly Maguigan reveals that 75–80% of appellate-reviewed cases involving battered women who killed actually did so during an ongoing attack or under imminent threat (referenced in Schneider 1996, p. 500). The focus on non-confrontational cases is not due to their statistical preponderance, therefore, but rather because they invite us to think more deeply about the traditional requirements of self-defense.

Consider one final objection to treating self-defense as justified in these kinds of cases. An argument not infrequently heard against recognizing self-defense as a justification, either in general or at least in batterer homicides, is that even the most vicious batterers would not typically be eligible for the death penalty (Fletcher 1996, Rosen 1986, Finkelstein 1996). Since most jurisdictions in the world have abolished capital punishment for any crime, this is trivially true most everywhere. The thought behind the objection is more substantial, however, namely that the woman acts as 'judge and executioner' when she kills her batterer (Fletcher 1996, p. 556). Since the state does not claim the authority to put people to death for their battering actions, it cannot authorize or permit others to put batterers to death for them either. There are a number of problems with this line of reasoning. First, even in the United States, rape and kidnapping cannot be punished by the death penalty, though most states allow deadly self-defense to prevent these offenses. Second, and more importantly, in characterizing the woman as 'judge and executioner', Fletcher suggests that the woman is killing her batterer *for his battery*. But this is untrue. If a woman killed her batterer because of his prior battery, she would be taking revenge. At most she might be excused for doing so, and usually not even that. Or perhaps she should be eligible for a provocation defense, as argued for by Brenda Baker (1998). But we are concerned with women who kill their batterers because they believe they must do so to save themselves from death or serious bodily harm. If (agents of) the state believed that deadly violence was necessary to save a woman from unlawful deadly attack, they would allow intervention; they would allow anyone to act to save the woman, i.e., to act as judge and executioner. Justified self-defense is not employed against an innocent, contra Fletcher, because the assailant must have knowingly or negligently engaged in imminently threatening conduct. Once we understand imminence as relative to threats, rather than attack, we see that the traditional defense must be available to many battered women who kill.

Much of this discussion has focused on the need to differentiate killings that are justified from those which are merely excused. Given that both lead to complete acquittal, those of a realist bent might think there is no practical point to be served by such an exercise. In a different vein, Kent Greenawalt has argued against seeking a precise schema of categorization for justifications and excuses in the law itself. But Greenawalt's arguments, like the realists', do not undermine the importance of keeping justification and excuse distinct in self-defense cases. For our evaluation of those who act in self-defense will depend upon how we classify their behavior. The symbolic value of the classifications is very different. To be excused is to be unreasonable and non-responsible, incapable of meeting the standards expected of persons; to be justified is to be reasonable and responsible, to meet the standards of conduct we demand of everyone. To be excused is a threat to one's self-respect; to be justified is to have the basis for a legitimate claim to self-respect.[14] Thus the distinction has a moral and political point in the context of our discussion, even if that point cannot be generalized to motivate a search for an exhaustive and definitive differentiation of the categories in all their legal uses.

Conclusion

The current use of reasonableness in sexual harassment cases is defective because it focuses attention on the attitudes and behavior of the victim rather than on the actions and attitudes of the alleged harasser. Justice would be better served were the demands of reasonableness to be placed directly on the actions and beliefs of alleged harasser, rather than on their victims. There is no need to introduce specific gendered standards of reasonableness in the law to produce the desired result.

The situation is different for women who claim to have killed their batterers in self-defense. Here the focus must be on the attitudes and actions of the women who kill. They must demonstrate that their actions were reasonable responses to threats of death or grievous bodily harm. This does not require, however, that we introduce a new subjective standard of reasonableness in the law. Their actions are reasonable if they faced objectively threatening behavior from which they had no escape. Expert testimony on effects of battering is useful for explaining to the triers of fact the reasonableness of women's perceptions that they are in imminent danger and their belief that no non-violent remedy is available to them. But this is fully compatible with the recognition that women who kill their abusers, honestly and reasonably believing themselves to be in mortal danger, thereby act as we think they should. Battered women may act self-defensively without waiting for an immediate attack. Such women act permissibly, tragically to be sure, but permissibly. What they do is not wrong, for precisely the same reasons that anyone who kills in self-defense is not wrong to do so.

But there is more to say about the case of battered women from the point of view of reasonableness. The very context in which they act is one of extreme unreasonableness. The actions of batterers are unreasonable and intolerable. They are the aggressors. They create the situation of desperate fear that leads to their deaths. The law recognizes the moral significance of being an aggressor. In these cases, fact-finders should be much more firmly focused on the actions of the aggressors, and the threat to life and physical security that their actions constitute. Seen against such a backdrop, the actions of those who take self-protective measures against the unreasonable aggression of others are more readily seen as what they are: both reasonable and justified.

Notes

1. The 'unwelcome' requirement is problematic, given differentials of power within the workplace and beyond. As employed by the courts, moreover, it operates as a rebuttable presumption that sexual advances are welcome. The onus is on victims to prove that they conveyed that the harasser's conduct was unwelcome.
2. For a review of some cases decided under the 'reasonable person' standard, and the shocking results produced by those courts, see Brenneman (1992).
3. Judge Keith of the Court of Appeals for the Sixth Circuit argued in favor of adopting a reasonable woman standard, for many of these reasons, in his dissenting opinion in *Rabidue v. Osceola*; his reasoning is reflected in the cases referred to in note 4.
4. Cf. *Yates v. Avco Corp.*, 819 F.2d 630 (6th Cir. 1987); *Lipsett v. University of Puerto Rico*, 864 F.2D 881 (1st Cir., 1988); *Andrews v. City of Philadelphia*, 895 F.2d 1469 (3rd Cir., 1990); *Robinson v. Jacksonville Shipyards, Inc.*, 760 F. Supp. 1486 (M.D. Fla. 1991); *State v. Town of Milton*, No. S1149-87 CnC (Vt. Super. Ct. Chittenden County filed 4 Nov. 1987); *Ellison v. Brady*, 924 F.2d 872 (9th Cir. 1991).
5. Shoenfelt, Maue and Nelson (2002) claim that it seems not to matter to findings of hostile-environment harassment whether a gender-specific or gender-neutral standard is used by fact-finders.
6. These behaviors and many more are documented in the various articles and cases referenced above.
7. Jeremy Horder (1998), following Suzanne Uniake (1994), argues against the requirement of 'unlawful assault' in favor of an 'unjust threat' condition for justified self-defense. I cannot address this suggestion here.
8. This is meant to leave open adoption of either the 'choice' or the 'character' theory of criminal liability and its corresponding theory of defenses. See Hart (1968); Moore (1990); Robinson (1984); Bayles (1982); Fletcher (1978); Lacey (1988); Huigens (1995).
9. This is not to deny that self-defense, like duress and necessity, may sometimes function as an excuse and sometimes as a justification. It is simply to point out that the standard cases in which women kill their abusers can and should be brought within the justification category, but doing so requires that we retain the objective reasonable person test for self-defense.

10. Both Rosen and Finkelstein share the unusual view that no case of killing in self-defense is justified, however, insisting that it is at most excused. Nonetheless their discussions of the distinct defense for battered women are representative of the kind of view in which I am interested.
11. The defendant killed her batterer while he slept.
12. Golding (2002) disagrees, arguing that we should see such non-confrontational killings as only excused, rather than justified, precisely because we should not send the message that such killings are right, appropriate or proper. The idea that justified actions must be not merely permissible but right is shared by most scholars who favor treating self-defense as merely excused, including those discussed in this paper. See Stewart (2003) for an excellent discussion.
13. There are significant evidentiary advantages to this approach as well: it doesn't require a judge or jury to conclude that going to the police or seeking escape would have failed, but only to assess whether a reasonable person would have found the conduct menacing and whether the assailant knew or should have known that it was menacing. It also provides a nice explanation of the permission of deadly self-defense in kidnapping cases, even though death is not imminent. See Zipursky (1996, pp. 610–612). David Gauthier speculates that the imminence requirement is necessary on a social contract view of self-defense to avoid licensing anticipatory (Hobbes) or retaliatory (Locke) violence (Gauthier 1996). Neither is licensed on Zipursky's model, however, given its requirement of objectively menacing conduct.
14. This discussion parallels in many respects that drawn by John Gardner between the defenses of provocation or diminished capacity in English law and their importance in batterer homicides (Gardner 1998).

References

Abrams, K., 1989. Gender discrimination and the transformation of workplace norms. *Vanderbuilt law review*, 42, 1183.

Abrams, K., 1992. Social construction, roving biologism, and reasonable women: a response to Professor Epstein. *DePaul law review*, 41, 1021–1040.

Alder, R.S. and Peirce, E.R., 1993. The legal, ethical, and social implications of the 'reasonable woman' standard in sexual harassment cases. *Fordham law review*, 61, 773–827.

Alexander, L., 1993. Self-defense, justification and excuse. *Philosophy and public affairs*, 22, 53–66.

Armour, J., 1996. Just deserts: narrative, perspective, choice, and blame. *University of Pittsburgh law review*, 57, 525–552.

Baker, B.M., 1998. Provocation as a defence for abused women who kill. *Canadian journal of law and jurisprudence*. 11, 193–211.

Bayles, M., 1982. Character, purpose and criminal responsibility. *Law and philosophy*, 1, 5–20.

Blackwood, E.M., 1992. The reasonable woman in sexual harassment law and the case for subjectivity. *Vermont law review*, 16, 1005.

Brenneman, D.S., 1992. From a woman's point of view: the use of the reasonable woman standard in sexual harassment cases. *Cincinnati law review*, 60, 1281.

Cahn, N.R., 1992. The looseness of legal language: the reasonable woman standard in theory and practice. *Cornell law review*, 77, 1398–1446.

Chamallas, M., 1992. Feminist constructions of objectivity: multiple perspectives in sexual and racial harassment litigation. *Texas journal of women and law*, 1, 95.

Childers, J., 1993. Is there a place for a reasonable woman in the law? A discussion of recent developments in hostile environment sexual harassment. *Duke law journal*, 42, 854.

Crenshaw, E.K., 1989. Demarginalizing the intersection of race and sex: a black feminist critique of antidiscrimination doctrine, feminist theory, and antiracist politics. *University of Chicago legal forum*, 139.

Christopher, R., 1998. Self-defense and defense of others. *Philosophy and public affairs*, 27, 123–141.

Dennisen, L., 1993. An argument for the reasonable woman standard in hostile environment claims. *Ohio law journal*, 54, 473–496.

Dolkart, L.J., 1994. Hostile environment harassment: equality, objectivity, and the shaping of legal standards. *Emory law journal*, 43, 151–244.

Duff, R.A., 2002. Virtue, vice, and criminal liability: do we want an Aristotelian criminal law? *Buffalo criminal law review*, 6, 147–184.

Eser, A., 1976. Justification and excuse. *The American journal of comparative law*, 24, 621–637.

Finkelstein, C.O., 1996. Self-defense as a rational excuse. *University of Pittsburgh law review*, 57, 621–649.

Finkelstein, C.O., 2002. Excuses and dispositions in criminal law. *Buffalo criminal law review*, 6, 317–359.

Fletcher, G.P., 1978. *Rethinking criminal law*. NY: Little Brown.

Fletcher, G.P., 1988. *A crime of self-defense: Bernard Goetz and the law on trial*. NY: Free Press.

Fletcher, G.P., 1996. Domination in the theory of justification and excuse. *University of Pittsburgh law review*, 57, 553–578.

Gardner, J., 1998. The gist of excuses. *Buffalo criminal law review*, 1, 575–598.

Gauthier, D., 1996. Self-defense and the requirement of imminence: comments on George Fletcher's 'Dominance in the theory of justification and excuse'. *University of Pittsburgh law review*, 57, 615–620.

Golding, M.P., 2002. The cultural defense. *Ratio juris*, 15, 146–158.

Greenawalt, K., 1984. The perplexing borders of justification and excuse. *Columbia law review*, 84, 1897–1927.

Gutek, B., 1985. *Sex and the workplace*. San Francisco, CA: Jossey-Bass.

Haag, S.L., 1993. The reasonable woman standard: perpetuating sex discrimination in the workplace. *University of Florida journal of law and public policy*, 5, 329–341.

Hall, J., 1976. Comment on justification and excuse. *The American journal of comparative law*, 24, 638–645.

Harris, A.P., 1990. Race and essentialism in feminist legal theory. *Stanford law review*, 42, 581.

Hart, H.L.A., 1968. *Punishment and responsibility*. Oxford: Clarendon Press.

Heller, K.J., 1998. Beyond the reasonable man? A sympathetic but critical assessment of the use of subjective standards of reasonableness in self-defense and provocation cases. *American journal of criminal law*, 26, 1–120.

Hochschild, A. and Machung, A., 1989. *The second shift: working parents and the revolution at home*. NY: Viking Press.

Horder, J., 1993. Criminal culpability: the possibility of a general theory. *Law and philosophy*, 12, 193–215.

Horder, J., 1998. Self-defense, necessity and duress: understanding the relationship. *Canadian journal of law and jurisprudence*, 11, 143–165.

Huigens, K., 1995. Virtue and inculpation. *Harvard law review*, 108, 1423–1480.

Kadish, S.H., 1976. Respect for life and regard for rights in the criminal law. *California law review*, 64.

Kaufman, W., 2004. Is there a 'right' to self-defense? *Criminal justice ethics*, 23, 20–33.

Lacey, N., 1988. *State punishment*. London: Routledge.

Lustberg, L.S. and Jacobi, J.V., 1992. The battered woman as a reasonable person: a critique of the Appellate Division decision in *State v. Kelly*. *Seaton Hall law review*, 22, 365.

MacKinnon, C., 1989. *Toward a feminist theory of the state*. Cambridge, MA: Harvard University Press.

Minow, M., 1987. The Supreme Court, 1986 Term Forward: justice engendered. *Harvard law review*, 101, 10.

Minow, M., 1990. Feminist reason: getting it and losing it. *Legal education*, 38, 47.

Moore, M., 1990. Choice, character, and excuse. *Social philosophy and policy*, 7, 29–58.

Motala, Z. & ButleRichie, D.T., 1995. Self-defense in international law, the United Nations, and the Bosnian conflict. *University of Pittsburgh law review*, 57, 1–33.

Otsuka, M., 1994. Killing the innocent in self-defense. *Philosophy and public affairs*, 23, 74–94.

Robinson, P.H., 1984. Criminal law defenses: a systematic analysis. *Columbia law review*, 82, 199–291.

Rosen, C.J., 1986. The battered woman's defense. *The American university law review*, 36, 35–56.

Sebok, A.J., 1996. Does an objective theory of self-defense demand too much? *University of Pittsburgh law review*, 57, 725–756.

Scalet, S.P., 2003. Fitting the people they are meant to serve: reasonable persons in the American legal system. *Law and philosophy*, 22, 75–110.

Scheppele, K.L., 1991. The reasonable woman. *The responsive community, rights, and responsibilities*, 1, 36–47.

Schneider, E.M., 1996. Resistance to equality. *University of Pittsburgh law review*, 57, 477–524.

Schulhofer, S.J., 1990. The gender question in criminal law. *Social philosophy and policy*, 7, 105–137.

Shoenfelt, E.L., Maue, A.E. and Nelson, J., 2002. Reasonable person versus reasonable woman: does it matter? *Journal of gender, social policy and the law*, 10, 633–672.

Spelman, E.V., 1998. *Inessential women: problems of exclusion in feminist thought.* Boston, MA: Beacon Press.

Stewart, H., 2003. The role of reasonableness in self-defence. *Canadian journal of law and jurisprudence*, 16, 317–336.

Tadros, V., 2005. *Criminal Responsibility*. Oxford: Oxford University Press.

Thorburn, M., 2006. Justification and state actions. Unpublished manuscript.

Triades, M.O., 2002. Finding a hostile work environment: the search for a reasonable reasonableness standard. *Washington and Lee race and ethnic law journal*, 8, 35–73.

Uniacke, S., 1994. *Permissible killing: the self-defense justification of homicide.* Cambridge: Cambridge University Press.

Venesy, B.A., 1989. State v. Stewart: self-defense and battered women: reasonable perception of danger or license to kill. *Arkon law review*, 23, 89–104.

Zipursky, B.C., 1996. Self-defense, domination, and the social contract. *University of Pittsburgh law review*, 57, 579–614.

Environmentalism, fairness, and public reasons

Mathew Humphrey

Introduction

Green political theory has recently taken what might be described as a 'deliberative turn'. There has been a tendency for green theorists to endorse deliberative democracy (in one variety or another) as the form of democratic governance that is most likely, through its levelling of the discursive playing field, to offer environmental reasons the greatest scope to influence the outcomes of the political decision-making process. This claim is not the naïve one that deliberative democracy will deliver green outcomes, but a more realistic belief that deliberative democracy will give green reasons their best opportunity to wield influence, by comparison with forms of democracy that, for example, rely upon mere preference aggregation.[1]

A serious commitment to deliberative democracy entails, of course, a commitment to its moral and dispositional demands. One of these demands is that those engaged in certain forms of political activity, across specific parts of the political realm, adhere to the dictates of public reason in their political justifications.[2] Public reason features in two of the three essential elements of deliberative democracy delineated by John Rawls (1999, p. 580). It is there in its own right, and along with a framework of constitutional democratic institutions, it features in the desire on the part of citizens to follow and realise public reason in their political conduct. Rawls is not, of course, alone: a commitment to giving public reasons in political argument infuses the literature on democratic deliberation.[3] As public reason is considered such a central element of democratic deliberation, it is worth reflecting upon its relationship to the ideals and political demands of the environmental movement, given the interest of environmental political theorists in deliberative democracy.

In particular, I want to assess the possibility that the demands of public reason are *unfair* to political doctrines that seek to transform political morality, and I take environmentalism, at least in its more radical forms, to be one such doctrine. I will undertake this task by revisiting a debate from the mid-1990s between Jeremy Waldron and Lawrence Solum on the fairness of public reason with respect to novel reasons. I will suggest that Waldron's original charge that public reason is unfair to novel reasons holds in an attenuated form after we allow for Solum's counter-argument. Even in this attenuated form the potential unfairness remains considerable. For this reason green theorists should be far more circumspect than they have been so far in their embrace of deliberative democracy. They may otherwise find themselves undermining the legitimacy of the substantive positions they support.

I should note at the outset that using the arguments of environmentalists as a 'test' of public reason might seem bizarre, as Rawls himself suggests that environmental questions are ones to which the dictates of public reason do not apply. Public reason most clearly applies to 'constitutional essentials and matters of basic justice' i.e., 'fundamental matters', but 'Many if not most political questions do not concern those fundamental matters, for example ... statutes protecting the environment and controlling pollution; establishing national parks and preserving wilderness areas and animal and plant species' (Rawls 1996, p. 214). There are three points to note in respect to this. Firstly, Rawls himself hedges on this distinction. His claim is that public reason applies most clearly to fundamental matters – if we cannot establish the need for it there, we cannot establish it anywhere. However, after this, other issues such as the environment will 'sometimes' involve fundamental matters, and a 'full account' of public reason would explain how they differ from constitutional essentials and why the dictates of public reason do not apply, or at least not as strictly (Rawls 1996, p. 215). Secondly, as Jonathan Quong notes, even on supposedly non-fundamental issues such as the environment, we are still dealing with coercive authority, and the need for justification for the use of coercive power remains. As long as 'there are reasons available to us that are suitably public in nature ... what possible reason can we give that would justify ignoring them?' (2004, p. 246).[4] Thirdly, for many of the more radical green arguments, the question of what constitutes 'basic justice' is precisely what is at stake, the argument being that principles of distributive justice need to be extended in order to take into account the interests of (at least some) non-human animals, or even all of non-human life.[5] For all of these reasons, a turn by environmentalists to deliberative democracy leads to a need for us to enquire into the relationship between public reason and environmental politics.

The unfairness objection, green reasons and public reason

The argument that the limitations of public reason constitute unfair constraints with respect to novel reasons can be put in the following form:[6]

(1) On the 'inclusive' Rawlsian view, public reasons must be offered as the *decisive* justification for the legitimate use of coercive power in political life with respect to 'fundamental matters'. This may be the coercive power of the state, but would also include the coercive power of, for example, social movements engaging in forms of political direct action.
(2) Public reasons have to meet a criterion of reasonableness.
(3) Public reasons have to meet a criterion of being 'widely shared'.
(4) (2) and (3) set demands that, without sufficient reason, actively militate against political justifications that seek to transform public political morality (such as ecocentric or animal rights-based reasons).
(5) Therefore, the public reason restriction on political justification is unfair to groups and individuals seeking to offer such justifications.

The key objections here are to conditions (2) and (3) which are both taken to impose restrictions on justification for public policy or certain forms of political protest that impose unfair constraints on novel political moralities.

To take one relevant example, an ecocentric state (should such a thing ever exist) could be expected to construct a policy framework that would in the name of its own comprehensive doctrine frustrate many people in the pursuit of their conception of the good. Restrictions on economic development, forms of travel, trade, and the treatment of non-human nature could all be expected. Even if ecocentrism itself is taken to be a reasonable comprehensive doctrine,[7] imposing such restrictions on human activity in the name of a single comprehensive moral doctrine would not be agent-reasonable in that their imposition stands in denial of the liberal ideal of reciprocity and the burdens of judgement. That is, such imposition would not recognise that 'many of our most important judgements are made under conditions where it is not to be expected that conscientious persons with full powers of reason ... will all arrive at the same conclusion. ... These burdens of judgment are of the first significance for a democratic idea of toleration' (Rawls 1996, p. 58).

This raises a question regarding the 'fit' between 'reasonableness' on the one hand, and public reason on the other. In what sense (if any) does Rawls expect public reasons to themselves *be* reasonable? As the above paragraph suggests, it may be that public reasons must be belief-reasonable, or that they must be held in a manner that is agent-reasonable, or that both of those are necessary conditions for a reason to be public. For Rawls, the two forms of reasonableness are connected. Reasonable citizens affirm the criterion of reciprocity and want to co-operate on terms that all can accept. Furthermore they recognise the burdens of judgement and the impossibility of reaching agreement around a single, comprehensive conception of the good under conditions of reasonable pluralism. Agents who are reasonable in this way would not affirm an unreasonable comprehensive doctrine, when a condition of doctrine-reasonableness is that it 'does not reject the essentials of a democratic regime' (1996, p. xviii). Doctrines that are unreasonable in this sense must be contained, so that they do not 'undermine the unity and justice of society' (1996, p. xix). Agent-reasonableness and doctrine-reasonableness combine to affirm public reason on matters of basic justice and constitutional essentials, as reasonable persons 'see that the burdens of judgment set limits on what can reasonably be justified to others, and so they endorse some forms of liberty of conscience and freedom of thought. It is unreasonable for us to use political power ... to repress comprehensive views that are not unreasonable' (Rawls 1996, p. 61). Thus, reasonable people would not endorse a comprehensive doctrine that was unreasonable, and would affirm the doctrine of public reason.

By contrast, the principles of ecocentrism are not principles that people in a plural society can be expected to endorse voluntarily from a variety of comprehensive moral doctrines, and so are not 'political' values in that sense. Appeals on the part of radical environmentalists to ecocentric principles, deep ecology, or primitivism cannot constitute a reasonable justification for coercive activity.

Nor are such principles already 'widely shared' in the public culture, unlike certain notions of 'common sense' and 'non-controversial' scientific findings and methods. If the principles of ecocentrism are not widely shared, and their imposition would contravene norms of reasonableness, should we have any cause to regret their exclusion, as forms of justification, from the domain of fundamental questions? The unfairness objection suggests that we should. As Jeremy Waldron puts it, 'what this conception seems to rule out is the novel or disconcerting move in political argumentation ... Rawls' conception seems to assume an inherent limit in the human capacity for imagination and creativity in politics, implying as it does that something only counts as a legitimate move in public reasoning only to the extent that it latches on to existing premises that everyone already shares' (1993, p. 838).

If this is a fair account of the strictures of public reason, as demanded of deliberative democrats by Rawls, it is also worth reflecting upon the relationship between deliberative democracy and the political philosophy with which Rawls' name is most readily associated, liberalism. Are these restrictions on what counts as legitimate political argument consistent with liberalism's commitment to free speech and toleration? For Rawls, the ideal of public reason, and citizens' commitment to realising that ideal, realizes the principle of reciprocity that is foundational to his account of political liberalism. Rawls discusses the 'role of the criterion of reciprocity as expressed in public reason' and holds that

'The criterion of reciprocity is normally violated when basic liberties are denied' (1999, p. 579). The idea of public reason 'specifies at the deepest level' the basic values of political liberalism and demands reasons on constitutional essentials and matters of basic justice that 'might be shared by all citizens as free and equal'. By contrast, any 'insistence on the whole truth' in politics is 'incompatible with democratic citizenship and the idea of legitimate law' (1999, p. 579).

Of course it is precisely the purpose of ecocentric thinkers (and animal rights activists) to present 'novel or disconcerting' arguments, related to their conception of 'the whole truth' into the public sphere. Any transformative political discourse will by definition not partake of commonly shared political beliefs already existent in a society. In the same way as it once would have challenged deeply entrenched and widely shared beliefs (amongst white males, at least) to advocate the end of slavery, or to promote racial or sexual equality, it now challenges widely shared beliefs to propose that animals have rights grounded in justice, or that biodiversity protection should take moral priority over economic growth. Nothing hangs here on whether these propositions are right, Waldron's point is merely that such doctrines, if allowed to enter political debate over constitutional essentials and basic justice, might themselves become widely shared. Many (not all) of the arguments put forward by Martin Luther King were cast in terms of a comprehensive Christian doctrine.[8] Liberals (now) tend to tolerate that fact, as the outcome was greater justice in society – 'the abolitionists and King would not have been unreasonable ... if the political forces they led were among the necessary historical conditions to establish political justice, as does indeed seem plausible in their situation' (Rawls 1996, pp. 250–251).

The point here is that, from the perspective of a future society in which the meat trade and animal experimentation are abolished, and in which animals are taken to have rights grounded in justice, it may well appear to be the case that earlier activists, making their case in terms of comprehensive moral doctrines, also intended to bring about 'a well-ordered and just society in which the ideal of public reason could eventually be honored' and whose political force was also 'among the necessary historical conditions to establish political justice'. If, however, their arguments rooted in comprehensive moral doctrines are disbarred from the public political realm on *a priori* grounds, this situation may never be achieved. Thus 'we have reason to be cautious about Rawls' insistence that the idea of public reason "excludes comprehensive religious and philosophical doctrines" in favour of "the plain truths *now* common and available to citizens *generally*"' (Waldron 1993, pp. 839–840, emphasis in original). The point is that what now look like non-political reasons rooted in a comprehensive doctrine, adhered to by a minority of citizens, may come to be public reasons in the Rawlsian sense if they are allowed the space to compete for allegiance in the political field. They may come to be widely shared, and be in accordance with common sense and the non-controversial elements of science (ecocentric theories frequently appeal to 'new' scientific beliefs, grounded, for example, in quantum physics or ecology (see, for example, Mathews 1991, Goldsmith 1996).

Unfairness reconsidered

If unfairness to novel political doctrines is to be avoided, then for Waldron the public reason restriction in its Rawlsian form has to be weakened, if not removed completely. We should take a Millian rather than Rawlsian view of public discourse. Greens should be free to engage their comprehensive doctrines in all aspects of political debate, including those concerning constitutional essentials and basic justice, and, indeed, use those comprehensive doctrines in order to *change* what 'we' think of as constitutional essentials and matters of basic justice. The Rawlsian response, as put forward by Lawrence B. Solum in answer to Waldron's critique, is to deny that this liberal version of public reason is unfair to novel political arguments. The Rawlsian response can be stated as follows:[9]

(1) The unfairness objection fails to distinguish between the acceptability and availability of reasons.
(2) The unfairness objection confuses universal agreement with wide agreement.
(3) The unfairness objection fails to explain why novel reasons cannot be sufficient.
(4) The unfairness objection incorrectly assumes the exclusive view of public reason.

On (1) the riposte is that the unfairness objection focuses on the idea of *accepted* reasons and ignores what Rawls has to say about the *availability* of reasons. As Solum puts it, 'Waldron assumes that for a reason to be public in Rawls's sense, it must be accepted by the public at large. Recall, however, that what Rawls said was a bit different; Rawls referred to reasons "now widely accepted, or available, to citizens in general"' (Solum 1996, pp. 1476–1477). Solum presses on the distinction between 'accepted' and 'available', on the grounds that reasons can quite plausibly be available to citizens even if they are not widely accepted. The question that arises in response to this argument is what it means, exactly, for a reason to be 'available' to people, and can *novel* reasons be available to citizens (by comparison with widely accepted reasons) in a manner that would overcome the unfairness objection? If it is to have any purchase, 'availability' has to mean more than that a reason has been put forward by someone, somewhere in the public realm. Availability might be understood as a social or communicative criterion (a reason is 'available' if it is easily accessible to citizens – perhaps offered in the mainstream media) or, as Solum interprets it, it might refer to a reason having an ideational or psychological affinity with people's existing beliefs or modes of thought. Thus reasons would be available if they 'fit with the citizen's other beliefs', or follow 'from the citizen's other beliefs', or if a reason is 'intuitively plausible and does not contradict any of the citizen's other firmly held beliefs'. Even reasons that 'contradict current beliefs might be available if minor adjustments would render the whole system of belief more attractive with the addition of the novel reason' (Solum 1996, p. 1477). This list is not intended to be exhaustive but demonstrates a certain understanding of what it means for a reason to be 'available' to a citizen.

Is the 'availability' response sufficient to remove most of the force of the unfairness objection, as Solum suggests it is? The response is not as decisive against the unfairness objection as Solum believes it to be, for at least three reasons. The first is simply a textual response: there are many more passages where Rawls cites the 'acceptance' or 'acceptability' rather than the 'availability' of ideas as the necessary criterion for them to have the status of public reasons.[10] The claim that we should appeal 'only to *presently accepted* general beliefs and forms of reasoning' (1996, p. 224) is, presumably, intended to mean what it says. Solum argues that although Rawls may 'occasionally' state the ideal of public reason in terms of 'pre-existing agreement', there 'is nothing in his underlying arguments that requires this restriction' (1996, p. 1477). This is not obviously true. The 'underlying arguments' are presumably those that deal with how a society marked by 'reasonable pluralism' can obtain a moral agreement on constitutional essentials and basic justice, and part of this is that they must each be able to endorse a constitutional settlement because it is justified according to principles that they can accept as reasonable and rational. The underlying argument suggests that reasons that cannot be accepted as reasonable and rational will not form the basis of a stable and justified constitutional agreement. It is not clear that 'availability' can do the same work here as 'acceptability', but this will partly depend, as we will see below, upon how availability is interpreted.

The notion of an idea being 'available' might be interpreted in any one of a number of ways. Solum, as we have seen, relates it to the ways in which new ideas might be integrated with citizens' pre-existing beliefs – they may be 'intuitively plausible', they may 'fit with' or 'follow from' other beliefs that we have, and even ideas that contravene existing beliefs might be available if they could render an entire system of beliefs 'more attractive'. We should focus on the latter of these examples; clearly the concern that motivates the unfairness objection is not that ideas that might easily conform with our existing beliefs might be precluded but rather that ideas that represent a fundamental challenge to pre-existing norms are excluded because they *cannot* conform to the demands of public reason. This leads us to the second problem with Solum's understanding of availability, which lies in the way it is decontested in order to give it substantive meaning within the theory of public reason, in that it appears to collapse the distinction between acceptability and availability. If a reason is recognised, now, as making our overall thought system 'more attractive' when it is included in that thought system, then it is acceptable. Accepting it is precisely what we are doing when we integrate it into our system of thought. It may be true that citizens would endorse ecocentrism or animal rights, were they to accept them as extensions of their existing moral beliefs, or as elements that make their overall package of moral beliefs more attractive, but accepting them is what they would be doing. To say they are 'available' if they can be so integrated into people's belief systems is to say no more than that they are 'acceptable' – whether or not they are actually accepted.

If 'availability' is to be held distinct from 'acceptability', then Solum's understanding does not suffice, as it collapses availability back into a version of acceptability. An alternative reading of availability would simply be to assert that an idea is 'out there' in the public culture at large. An idea is available to the citizen in the sense that it is open to him or her to make use of. This sense of availability would have nothing to say about how such an idea might 'fit' with a citizen's pre-existing beliefs, or how 'attractive' it might make the citizen's overall package of beliefs. This gives us conceptual separation between acceptability and availability, but it raises the third problem in that it comes at an obvious price in terms of maintaining the grounds of public reason. If all that was necessary for an idea to count as a public reason was its availability in this sense, then this particular distinction between public and non-public reasons collapses, or at least the class of non-public reasons becomes vanishingly small. On this view the Roman Catholic arguments cited by Waldron (1993, passim) would be public reasons even though they make a direct appeal to a comprehensive religious doctrine, because they are well-known, widely understood and available to anyone who is sufficiently interested.

It does not appear, then, that Solum's reliance upon the acceptability/availability distinction can suffice to defeat the unfairness objection, because that distinction is unstable. Availability either collapses back into acceptability or if held distinct from it, serves instead to collapse the distinction between public and non-public reasons. Rawls (usually) employs the criterion of acceptability for good reason, and against this the unfairness objection remains undefeated.

The second defence of public reason holds that the unfairness complaint confuses universal agreement with wide agreement. Solum is correct in his complaint against Waldron that the latter is guilty of this confusion. It could not be a reasonable requirement of public reason that, within a pluralistic society, there be literal unanimity about the acceptance of a reason before it can count as public. The interesting question is whether any plausible version of the unfairness complaint would have to be guilty of this same confusion (so the question is whether the demand that a belief be widely shared is itself an unfair restriction). The point that Waldron makes in this regard is that an idea that is not widely shared at the current time may come to be widely shared if enough people are exposed to its argumentative force, but that this is not going to happen if any such idea is excluded *a priori* from the realm of political debate on the grounds that it is not already widely shared now. Solum's response – that a reason does not have to be widely shared *now*, but rather be something that *could* be widely shared (that is, be 'widely available') falls to the problems of maintaining a meaningful distinction between acceptable and available discussed above.

The third response holds that the unfairness objection cannot show why it is the case that novel public reasons cannot be sufficient. Solum's response to Waldron's version of the unfairness objection is to distinguish between different varieties of novel reasons. Waldron proposes a 'premise that no one has thought of before', and of course novel reasons may take this form. Solum reminds us that there are, however, 'other models of political argument', and a novel reason could emerge as the outcome of a Rawlsian process of reflective equilibrium, but itself be based upon widely shared principles and premises. Thus the unfairness objection 'only applies to a subset of novel political arguments, those that cannot themselves be supported by considerations of public reason', and this subset may be insufficiently large to 'underwrite' the unfairness objection (Solum 1996, p. 1480–1481). This argument may indeed demonstrate that only some novel reasons are treated unfairly if they are *a priori* excluded on the grounds of public reason, as others can be supported by acceptably public reasons in a process of reflective equilibrium. Nonetheless this is a strange response unless the residual category of novel reasons is null or vanishingly small. For any novel reasons that cannot be supported by public reasons in the appropriate way are still, on this view, being treated unfairly; it is merely that there are not as many in this category as we might have thought there were before encountering this response. But how large does a category of reasons have to be before it is large enough to 'underwrite' the unfairness objection?[11]

The fourth response suggests that the unfairness objection incorrectly assumes an exclusive view of public reason, whereas Rawls recommends an inclusive or 'wide' notion of public reason. It is certainly true that Rawls' conception of public reason became 'wider' (more accommodating to non-public reasons) in his later works, culminating in the 'wide view of public political culture' outlined in 'The idea of public reason revisited'. This view 'allows us to introduce into political discussion at any time our comprehensive doctrine, religious or nonreligious, provided that, in due course, we give properly public reasons to support the principles and policies our comprehensive doctrine is said to support' (1999, p. 584). This is what Rawls terms the *proviso*, which specifies public political culture as opposed to the 'background culture'. Standards of public reason are here not violated when non-public reasons are employed in political discussion, provided that properly public reasons are also provided in due course for the principles or policies that the non-public reasons were held to support. As Solum comments, 'One can imagine that novel political argument would be introduced in cases in which the proviso was satisfied, that over time these novel arguments would become part of the public political culture, and thus, that eventually, the novel arguments would become public reasons' (Solum 1996, p. 1482). This is a potentially powerful response to the unfairness objection. Ecocentric or animal rights arguments, even when rooted in comprehensive doctrines, can still be employed as arguments in the public political arena without violating the dictates of public reason as long as the proviso is satisfied and public reasons are provided in due course and a principle is not adopted for *merely* non-public reasons. How could this be unfair to novel reasons when they are explicitly *not* being excluded from public political debate?

The response would have to distinguish between *allowing* the expression of non-public reasons in political discourse and *allowing non-public reasons to be decisive* in political justification. The wide view of public reason allows the former but not the latter. This is a credible distinction which allows the unfairness objection to retain some force although not as much as Waldron holds it to have, but the problem for Waldron is that he only considers public reason in its 'exclusive' version. Does it matter that non-public reasons cannot be decisive? Isn't this something that liberals (rightly) applaud, that non-public grounds such as religious doctrine cannot stand as decisive reasons for adopting public policy – at least not in the area of constitutional essentials and basic justice? This is what allows liberals to enforce, for example, women's rights against those comprehensive religious doctrines that would seek to curtail such rights for non-public reasons.

Whilst this is true, not allowing non-public reasons to be decisive has wider ramifications, in particular we have to consider the justifications available for politically and discursively disadvantaged groups seeking to protest against existing laws, policies and attitudes in society. As novel reasons are very unlikely to be public reasons on the grounds that, at the very least, they will not be widely shared, then it is at least possible, if not likely, that such groups will not have public reasons available to them in order to justify political action against the prevailing laws, institutions, or norms. The arguments of radical environmentalists are rooted in a comprehensive moral ideal regarding the relationship between human and non-human nature and the ontological status of the latter. These views are not 'widely accepted' (Rawls) and are not widely available in any of Solum's senses. Ecocentrism and its biocentric cousin are believed to fundamentally challenge a whole range of intuitions that people have about the nature of reality, the relative moral standings of different species, and the ways in which we judge the relationship between capacities and rights (Taylor 1986, pp. 14–24). If justifications for ecocentric ideas are judged against these background assumptions, most people would hardly expect their overarching moral framework to 'become more attractive' if it is thrown into turmoil through an attachment to something like Naess' 'biospherical egalitarianism' (Naess 1989). Such a belief may be consistent with principled egalitarianism, for example, but it is not necessarily implied by it. In short, those who seek to transform the moral beliefs of existing society through novel reasons are unlikely, by virtue of that very transformative potential and novelty, to have public reasons available to them. Does this make it acceptable that society should deny them any justification for taking protest actions against existing laws, policies and norms on the grounds that they lack such reasons?

The problem is that the argument against non-public justification looks arbitrarily biased. A major premise that justifiably decisive reasons will be public, combined with a (possibly unintended) minor premise that novel reasons cannot be public reasons, results in a conclusion that political acts based on novel arguments cannot be justified. This problem is especially acute when novel doctrines seek to extend the very notion of the 'public'. 'Public reason' in its liberal version has to satisfy the principle of reciprocity between humans. There is a sense in which ecocentric theory seeks to extend the notion of the affected public to non-human nature as well, such that we would have to ask of the exercise of political power whether non-human entities could be expected to endorse it as well. Whatever the metaphysical problems raised by trying to think about non-human entities 'endorsing' anything, there is clearly dispute here as to the nature of the 'public' to whom the notion of public reason is applied, and this dispute cannot be settled through an appeal to public reason that takes the scope of the public to be pre-determined. On the view defended here, then, the disbarring of non-public reasons from decisiveness in political justification is indeed unfair on those seeking to argue on the basis of novel reasons.

Conclusion

If we believe that we should not disbar non-public reasons from decisiveness, on the grounds that to do so is unfair to novel reasons, what follows, politically? We may after all accept the truth of the claim but suggest that it leaves us normatively untroubled. The protection offered by the demands of public reason against sectarian use of state power is so important that its marginal unfairness to some groups trying to make new political arguments is of relatively little importance. To think otherwise is to risk something like a return to the wars of religion, and all of the old bloody mess from which liberalism has managed to extricate us. This is an important argument, but one needs to step back a little and consider the wider context of political action. Theorists of deliberative democracy oppose what they see as coercion in political life, except when it is justified by reasons that all should be able, reasonably, to accept. This opposition to unjustified coercion applies across all areas of political life, to non-deliberative forms of protest[12] as well as the use of state power. But this view of political life has to be disaggregated, and we require an account of political justification that is more nuanced than that so far offered by theorists of deliberative democracy. Looking back on the twentieth century we know just how dangerous an entity the state is, and even those of us who believe that the state is an essential component for delivering social justice can accept what is empirically obvious: states have access to awe-inspiring means of literally destroying their enemies. Thus states have to be hedged around with constitutional laws and institutional arrangements that seek to limit their use of this power and ensure that state activity accords with society's political morality. Groups of protestors seeking to challenge existing political morality do not have the political means available to them that states do. The catalogue of damage done by environmental direct activists, for example, includes many instances of damage to property, trespass, and obstruction, but nothing that even begins to approach the violence that has been done to people in the name of the state. We can accept along with deliberative democrats that these *are* forms of political coercion that seek to change the behaviour of agents by imposing costs upon them, but does it follow from this that all forms of political coercion require the same level of justification? Or the same form of justification, i.e., reasons that are pubic in the appropriate way?

It may be rather that we require a more contextual understanding of political justification, that we should differentiate various levels and forms of coercion in political life and apply different standards of justification between them. We should take seriously Rawls' comment that standards of public reason may vary across different political fields.[13] Being the dangerous entities they are, states should have to satisfy high standards of public reason in order to justify laws and policies with regard to fundamentals and any other area in which public reason is available. For non-state actors we may want to impose a weaker standard of political justification. This does not entail that the state should not prosecute activists for acts of destruction against property, for example, but rather that such action should be seen as 'conscientious' (but not civil) disobedience and dealt with accordingly.

Thus if a court can accept that the protagonists had a genuine belief in the justification of their action for political reasons, then there is *potentially* a reason for relative leniency of the same sort that is applied to acts of civil disobedience (it is the reason, note, which is of the same sort, the level of leniency may well be different). If we do not accept that non-public reasons *can* justify political disobedience, we could not accept that Martin Luther King's contention that God created all men equal (King 1963) could justify conscientious disobedience in the name of civil rights, as it is rooted in the comprehensive religious doctrine of a Baptist minister, and in a society that included a significant number of atheists, this could not be a public reason. If belief in God was not widely accepted, and if there were no other reasons than these available, then the civil rights movement would lack justification on the public reason view. But this would be a strange conclusion, as King was trying to *change* public opinion, and in particular, of course, to get the white south to accept blacks as equals. To the extent that he succeeded, and belief in racial equality now seems 'obvious', we should accept that the possibility of today's established wisdom being yesterday's contentious new idea should warn us against delegitimising novel arguments on the grounds of public reason.[14] Public reason can serve as a useful check on state activity, but risks placing a stifling burden of justification upon those seeking to challenge entrenched, but possibly misguided, beliefs.

This argument may seem to lead to a paradoxical or at least inconsistent conclusion, as a result of the consequences of restrictions on state activity not applying to the activities of other groups in society. Thus a 'green' state would not be justified in taking actions for 'green reasons' when these reasons are non-public. Thus it would not be justified in designating large areas of land as 'wilderness' in the way that Laura Westra wants to,[15] on the basis of a controversial ecophilosophy that was not 'widely accepted' in society. Nonetheless a green protest group in society could be justified in taking direct action for the same ecophilosophical non-public reasons on the grounds that they are (a) seeking to challenge conventional morality, and (b) they are a discursively marginalised group.

There are at least three points to make in response to such an observation. Firstly, the concern about the power of the state by comparison with the power of protest groups justifies this distinction. States are the kinds of entities that require strong moral constraints to hedge in their field of legitimate activity. However, even if we adopt Quong's view, which I believe is consistent with the demands of public reason, and apply the canons of public reason where they can be applied, rather than arbitrarily delimiting their field of operation, this will still leave many areas, including many areas of environmental policy, where public reason either does not apply or applies inconclusively. In these cases we may think that the appropriate path of justification for a political act comes through non-public reason, even for a state.[16] Secondly, if a 'green state' really was to come into existence via the democratic process, we might usually expect that this indicates that at least some green arguments that were once non-public have now become sufficiently widely accepted that they 'count' as public reasons. Finally, the argument that direct action forms of protest may be morally justified by non-public reasons does not entail either that (a) there are not independent constraints on legitimate protest activity, or (b) that such activity should necessarily go unpunished by the state. On (a) 'direct action' can take a variety of forms, from classical civil disobedience to out-and-out terrorism. Most forms of environmental action are clearly between these two extremes. On the one hand, they may be clandestine and often seek maximal rather than minimal damage to property. On the other hand, they normally target inanimate objects, and such groups often have strong moral strictures against harming living creatures of any sort. We require a normative category of 'conscientious direct action' or similar[17] to capture this kind of activity. This does not entail that direct attacks on people, for example, can be justified however marginalised a protest group is, as there are independent reasons for rejecting this activity (which I assume to be stronger than injunctions against attacking inanimate objects – on this I would endorse Keane's [2004] view). With respect to (b), even where the conscientiousness of the protestors is recognised, it does not entail that, when caught, they should not be punished in accordance with the law. What it *does* entail is the recognition that motivations matter, and that rather than treat political protestors more harshly than other law-breakers (as campaigners against so-called 'ecoterrorism' are seeking to do), there should be a *prima facie* assumption towards leniency, on the grounds of conscience, as each case is judged on it merits.

In light of the above discussion, those who seek to promote environmental values in our society should be cautious about hitching a ride on the wagon of deliberative democracy. The latter's commitment to making moral and dispositional demands upon those who engage in democratic debate and it insistence upon norms of public reason for the justification of political action places additional burdens upon already marginalised positions.[18] Both radical environ-mentalists and animal-rights activists engage in non-deliberative forms of poli-tics with good reason. They are starting out from a discursively disadvantaged position with little access to 'mainstream' channels of communication. Their direct-action forms of politics should not be considered unjustifiable *merely* because they do not comply with *a priori* restrictions on what constitutes an 'acceptable' justificatory reason (there may of course be other reasons why such forms of politics are unacceptable in certain cases). We require a far more open and conflictual conception of democracy if we are to offer transformative political doctrines the political space they require to get citizens to reconsider those things they currently take for granted.

Notes

1. See, for example, Gunderson (1995), Goodin (2003), Dryzek (2000), Smith (2003), Maldonado (n.d.). It should be noted that a number of these works seek to go 'beyond' conventional accounts of deliberative democracy, and a more adequate treatment of the issues raised here would engage with these developments. For the purposes of this paper, however, the focus is on public reason.
2. The use of public reason as a standard of justification has been criticised on a number of grounds, including its inability to reflect the depth of pluralism in contemporary society and its intimate connection with 'sectarian' liberal doctrine; see for examples Frohock (1997), Bohman (1995), Westmoreland (1999). The focus of this essay, however, will be the 'unfairness to novel reasons' objection.
3. See, for example, Gutmann and Thompson (2004), although it is worth noting that Rawls believes that Gutmann and Thompson seem 'to work from a comprehensive doctrine' (1999, p. 578).
4. Rawls clearly thinks that there *are* public reasons that can apply in this field (Rawls 1996, p. 245). See also Bell (2002).
5. On the former see Regan (2001); on the latter Taylor (1986).
6. Adapted from Waldron (1993).
7. That is, in the sense specified by Rawls (1996, p. 59). Even if a comprehensive doctrine satisfied these three criteria of reasonableness, it may still be unreasonable to coercively impose said doctrine on the citizenry, or to appeal to it in justification of certain types of political action.
8. See King (1963); also Medearis (2004, p. 62–65). Cf. Rawls (1999, p. 593).
9. These are taken from Solum (1996), upon whom this section draws extensively. What I call the 'unfairness' objection he calls the 'novelty' objection. I do not consider Solum's final response here.
10. For example: 'our exercise of political power is proper ... only when it is exercised in accordance with a constitution the essentials of which all citizens may reasonably be expected to endorse in the light of principles and ideals *acceptable* to them as reasonable and rational' (Rawls 1996, p. 217). '[I]n making these justifications we are to appeal only to *presently accepted* general beliefs and forms of reasoning' (1996, p. 224).
11. Ecocentrism and animal rights arguments, for example, for all that they may draw on a logic of egalitarianism, also rely upon novel (or at least non-public) understandings of the relationship between human beings and non-human nature.
12. See, for example, Rawls' moral constraints governing civil disobedience (1999, pp. 176–189).

13. See, for example, Rawls (1999), p. 575–576.
14. This is not to deny that King and the other civil rights campaigners also made use of recognisably public reasons. What if, contra that facts of the matter, they had *only* their Christian beliefs to fall back on – would we want to argue that their campaign of direct action would under those circumstances be unjustified?
15. See Westra (1998).
16. On this see Reidy (2000); for a critical counter-argument, see Williams (2000).
17. See Martin's attempt to develop a concept of 'conscientious wrongdoing' in this regard (1990).
18. On this see Medearis (2004, p. 60).

References

Bell, D., 2002. How can liberals be environmentalists? *Political studies,* 50, 703–724.
Bohman, J., 1995. Public reason and cultural pluralism: political liberalism and the problem of moral conflict. *Political theory,* 23(2), 253–279.
Dryzek, J., 2000. *Deliberative democracy and beyond.* Oxford: Oxford University Press.
Frohock, F., 1997. The boundaries of public reason. *American political science review,* 91(4), 833–844.
Goldsmith, J., 1996. *The way: an ecological worldview,* revised ed. Totnes: Themis Books.
Goodin, R., 2003. *Reflective democracy.* Oxford: Oxford University Press.
Gunderson, A., 1995. *The environmental promise of democratic deliberation.* Madison: University of Wisconsin Press.
Gutmann, A. and Thompson, D., 2004. *Why deliberative democracy?* Princeton, NJ: Princeton University Press.
Keane, J., 2004. *Violence and democracy.* Cambridge: Cambridge University Press.
King, Jr., Martin Luther, 1963. *Letter from a Birmingham Jail.* Available from: http://www.africa.upenn.edu/Articles_Gen/Letter_Birmingham.html.
Maldonado, M., n.d. *Green politics and deliberative democracy.* Berkeley Workshop on Environmental Politics Working Papers WP04-13.
Martin, M., 1990. Ecosabotage and civil disobedience. *Environmental ethics,* 12, 291–310.
Mathews, F., 1991. *The ecological self.* London: Routledge.
Medearis, J., 2004. Social movements and deliberative democratic theory. *British journal of political science,* 35, 53–75.
Naess, A., 1989. *Ecology, community, and lifestyle.* Cambridge: Cambridge University Press.
Quong, J., 2004. The scope of public reason. *Political studies,* 52, 233–250.
Rawls, J., 1996. *Political liberalism.* New York: Columbia University Press.
Rawls, J., 1999. *Collected papers,* ed. S. Freeman. Cambridge, MA: Harvard University Press.
Regan, T., 2001. *Defending animal rights.* Urbana, IL: University of Illinois Press.
Reidy, D., 2000. Rawls's wide view of public reason: not wide enough. *Res Publica,* 6, 49–72.
Smith, G., 2003. *Deliberative democracy and the environment.* London: Routledge.
Solum, L., 1996. Novel public reasons. *Loyola of Los Angeles law review,* 29(4), 1459–1486.
Taylor, P., 1986. *Respect for nature: a theory of environmental ethics.* Princeton, NJ: Princeton University Press.
Waldron, J., 1993. Religious contributions in public deliberation. *San Diego law review,* 30, 817–848.
Westmoreland, R., 1999. The truth about public reason. *Law and philosophy,* 18, 271–296.
Westra, L., 1998. *Living in integrity: a global ethic to restore a fragmented earth.* Lanham, MD: Rowman & Littlefield.
Williams, A., 2000. The alleged incompleteness of public reason. *Res Publica,* 6, 199–211.

Democratic reasonableness

Thomas A. Spragens, Jr

The topic of this essay is the legitimacy, power, and limits of reasonableness in democratic self-governance. Addressing this topic will require, in turn, attending to a number of specific questions, including: What does it mean to be reasonable? Is it appropriate to expect reasonableness of democratic citizens? What difference does democracy make to norms of reasonableness? What benefits can we expect from having reasonable citizens and reasonable procedures? What desirable political outcomes are beyond the capacity of reasonableness to deliver? The central thesis of the essay will be that it is proper and important to encourage the habits and capacities of reasonableness among a democratic citizenry, that devotion to norms and practices of reasonableness is highly advantageous to social comity and good policy in a democratic society, but that expecting or demanding too much of reasonableness can be counterproductive.

Reason, politics, and democracy

It is entirely possible for political societies to be managed without significant admixtures of rationality or reasonableness. In fact, that may be more the rule than the exception. The strongest group or class within the populace may simply impose its rule upon the rest. Marx, for one, regarded this pattern as pretty much a universal phenomenon, simply the way the world worked unless and until an advanced form of human society could abolish classes altogether. Or societies can be run more or less by a kind of social inertia in which convention, custom, and tradition provide habitual norms and pathways of political conduct. The politics of force and inertia have their hazards and serious limitations, however. So, many social analysts and idealists have long insisted that the systematic deployment of what seem to be distinctively human powers of reasoning can have significant and benign effects on the organization of human relations. These powers have been conceived in different ways. It might be the powers of noetic reason, deemed able to intuit the patterns of moral and political order. It might be the capacities of phronesis or practical reasoning, depicted as capable of ascertaining the human good and the way thereto. It could be gnosis, or sophia, or scientia – all of which in various ways were believed to have the power of vouchsafing to their practitioners crucial ends and means of successful human social action and organization.

The concrete political scenarios and normative sociologies generated by these accounts of reason in politics were in inception almost uniformly elitist and hier-archical. It was assumed that only the possession of special capacities, specialized training, or both, enabled people to be 'reasonable' in the relevant senses. The triumph of what we could call 'public reason' in the generic sense, therefore, generally involved placing these special knowers into positions of authority from which they could 'rationalize' their societies. They might be philosophers who instructed potential rulers in the academy or priests who instructed their sheep in the structures of the logos or the phronimoi who practiced aristocratic rule or Comtean savants who would give the law to industriels who would in turn put it into practice. The common folk, in contrast, were assumed to be incompetent or ignorant or preoccupied in ways that made them in effect only what we might call, in parallel with Hegel's notion of 'objects of history', 'objects of reason'. Like the doomed cavalry in Tennyson's *Charge of the Light Brigade*, it was not theirs to reason why but only to do and die – that is, to be obedient to the reason-ing class and accept whatever role or fate reason dictated for them. Even in the early stages of the Enlightenment, we should recall, the philosophes ventured from their salons when they sought political relevance not to somehow make the general populace more reasonable but to scurry to the courts of kings and queens they wished to enlighten. That strategy may have been quite understandable, as even Thomas Jefferson confessed himself daunted by the intellectual deficits of the Parisian mobs; but it clearly left the politics of reason as a 'trickle-down' theory at best.

Ready or not, the striking and inexorable process of democratization that stirred in the seventeenth century and gathered speed in the eighteenth and nineteenth centuries in Europe and America – a process Tocqueville called a Prov-idential fact and one which induced in him a kind of religious awe – altered the whole landscape of political reason quite dramatically. The arrival of modern democratic governance meant that the context and locus of political reason would have to be different from what it was in its aristocratic origins. In the first place, in a democracy the people are sovereign. They rule themselves – or at least some preponderant or majority part of the whole populace will rule themselves and the rest of citizenry. This devolution of power and authority ups the ante for political reason and makes the prospects for its successful deployment more challenging and problematic. With democratization it can no longer suffice to enlighten the few: it is the many who now must somehow be reasonable in their attitudes, their conduct, and their judgment. This was a prospect that profoundly dismayed Hobbes, leading him to fasten his hopes for democratic stability upon the dissemination of his 'theorems of moral doctrine' among the whole populace via the mandate of his mortal god, the democratically authorized sovereign. Two centuries later, defenders of the devolution of power and the extension of the franchise such as John Stuart Mill and Walt Whitman confessed themselves similarly daunted by the challenge of wedding reasonableness with democracy, but they hoped that the development and education of the people would permit this to happen. In any case, the challenge was logically quite clear: in order for democracy to be effective, reasonableness has to be achieved wholesale and not just retail.

The other fundamental alteration in the landscape of political reason occasioned by democratization was not a technical challenge – how can such a larger and more extensive attainment of reasonableness be accomplished? – but a change in the substance of reasonableness itself. This change was a function of the triumph of the democratic moral postulate of human equality. In a generic and abstract sense, it need not be sensible or mandatory – hence 'reasonable' – to presume that all human beings or all citizens must be considered as equally important. In fact, that insistence is on its face counter-intuitive. Clearly, some members of any society are more talented than others and do more for humankind than others and are more crucial to their society's flourishing. It would seem, then, perfectly reasonable to count the welfare of those more important and accomplished people for more than one would count the welfare of lesser folk. But the moral axioms of the democratic faith insist to the contrary that every citizen must ultimately be considered as worthy of equal concern in any political calculus. Democratic reasonableness is not reasonableness simpliciter. It is not open to any propositions inconsistent with the postulate of the ultimate moral equality of persons. There is in this sense a fundamental component of moral dogmatism within the norms of democratic reasonableness that provides it with some of its content.

The meaning of reasonableness

It would be useful at this point to take a step backward to reflect upon the core meaning of the term 'reasonableness' itself. For certainly this is a notion that is both multivalent and ambiguous. It is also ubiquitous. The result is a lot of room for misunderstanding, circularity, and stipulation when the term is invoked. Consider in this context the constant invocation of reasonableness in the later political philosophy of John Rawls, together with his apparent reluctance to provide any clear definition of the notion itself. Samuel Freeman, who edited Rawls's collected papers, acknowledges this pattern and the apparent problem therein, but goes on to offer a defense of it:

> The idea of reasonableness plays a major role in … the idea of public reason. What does it mean? Throughout his career Rawls used the idea of reasonable – or 'the Reasonable' – in a number of ways. At some point or another he refers to 'reasonable acceptance', 'reasonable political conceptions', 'reasonable conditions on agreement', and 'politically reasonable'. [Indeed, I once counted twenty-seven uses of the term 'reasonable' or some variant thereof within two pages of one of Rawls's journal articles – AU.]. In all instances he refused to offer a definition of 'reasonable' in terms of necessary and sufficient conditions. Many express frustration at this, and say the idea of reasonableness only masks appeals to inchoate intuition. But any attempt to provide a definition of 'reasonable' would be incapable of capturing all that is involved in the many uses of this rich concept (Freeman 2004, p. 2035).

Although I share at times both the frustration of Rawls's critics and also the suspicion that Rawls sometimes uses the term to appeal to his own inadequately specified or defended moral intuitions, there is something to be said for Freeman's apologia for Rawls in this passage. If the meaning of a term is, as Wittgenstein insists, its use, then it seems apparent that 'reasonableness' is at best what Wittgenstein calls a 'family term' – a term deployed to refer to similarities, not necessarily a single similarity across the board, among a number of things or activities. The breadth and import of its use closely resembles that of the term 'good,' whose multivalence, generality, and performative features have puzzled analytic philosophers and led some of them to characterize its use as an expression of emotion or approval rather than a cognitive claim. As a result, it seems that Rawls is to the concept of the reasonable as Justice Potter Stewart was to the concept of obscenity: neither of them felt capable of providing a definition of the term in question but both of them thought they knew it when they saw it.

If there is a general definition of the obscene, it would have to be something along the lines of 'tending to degrade human beings or to defile human dignity'. But the problem comes when we try to identify images or representations that in fact do this. For example, First Amendment jurisprudence regarding the obscenity exception to free speech rights often revolves around competing views of whether erotica are obscene per se or if not what kinds or forms of depictions of sexuality are degrading in the relevant sense. Definition doesn't get us very far at all. Hermeneutics and casuistry are 90% of the story. The same is true of 'reasonableness'. Its general definition would be very general and unspecific indeed, something on the order of 'fitting and proper in light of all the relevant features of the situation and the issue at hand'. Only an adjectival characterization of that breadth and nonspecificity could cover all the many ways in which we invoke the notion of reasonableness. A commodity up for sale is 'reasonably priced' when the amount demanded for it seems fittingly proportioned to all the factors properly relevant to monetary evaluations. Doctrines are 'reasonable' when they comport properly to the understandings of the relevant empirical realities and the moral criteria that seem appropriate. Persons are 'reasonable' when they behave and respond in ways that seem suitable to the situation at hand and to the powers, rights, and responsibilities which they bear. And so on.

Whenever we characterize an act or belief as being reasonable, therefore, we are in effect commending features of these actions and beliefs that make them seem fitting and proper. In a sense, attending to the sum and substance of someone's uses of the term provides us with the clues upon which we can rely and with particulars from which we can attend in order to comprehend both the user's core moral intuitions and his or her fundamental conception of how the world works. To that extent, the critics' characterization of Rawls's use of the idea of the reasonable is entirely accurate, but it does not designate something unique to Rawls and in itself it does not constitute a valid criticism. Rawls might be faulted, however, for not specifying as clearly as he could what might be called the intermediate or middle-range defining features of his conception of the reasonable. And he might also be faulted for using the term to confer moral privilege upon certain substantive beliefs for which he offers inadequate justification.

In point of fact, Rawls actually identifies rather clearly for us what the intermediate defining features are that shape his use/definition of what is morally and politically reasonable. It is just that he scatters these features throughout the exposition of his theory and doesn't refer to them under the heading of determining features of reasonableness. He establishes the first axis of his core moral intuitions at the outset of *A theory of justice* where he tells us that justice is 'the first virtue of social institutions' and refers to 'our intuitive conviction of the primacy of justice' (Rawls 1971, p. 4). He identifies a second axis of the moral intuitions that drive his conception of political reasonableness in his response to Michael Sandel's argument that his theory of justice presupposes a particular metaphysic of selfhood. No, Rawls responds. My conception does not depend upon any single metaphysic of selfhood. Instead, it takes its bearings from a normative and political conception of the person: namely, the free and equal democratic citizen. Finally, he establishes a third axis of the intuitions beneath his conception of reasonableness when he tells us what the 'veil of ignorance' will cover and specifies the parameters of the 'morally arbitrary'.

If we want to know, then, how Rawls would 'define' political reasonableness, we can pretty much answer that question by saying: for Rawls, political actions, doctrines, and principles should be deemed reasonable when they are what someone would do, believe, or accept were he or she to presume that human beings are properly treated as free and equal, that the right takes priority over the good, and that social inequalities are almost wholly the result of contingencies for which people cannot properly be held accountable. The content of 'reasonableness' thus is indeed reflective of and driven by the moral intuitions of those who use the term. In Rawls's case, these intuitions can hardly be said to be 'inchoate', even if Rawls does not do the work of specifying the pattern of his intuitions for us in the context of defining his conception of the reasonable. If we wish to understand how the notion of reasonableness does meaningful work in rendering moral and political judgments, therefore, we need to recognize and affirm from the get-go that the operative notion cannot be merely the generic notion of the fitting and proper. Instead, to have any real bite to it, a conception of political reasonableness must take its leave from some substantive and hence contestable moral intuitions or presuppositions which those who deploy that notion should, in the name of self-understanding and intellectual probity, do their best to specify.

Rawls's moral intuition that the right is prior to the good and his intuitions about the scope of the morally arbitrary play an important role in justifying Rawls's contention that his difference principle represents the 'most reasonable' conception of fair terms of social cooperation. These intuitions are, I think, not as generally shared among all the citizens of contemporary liberal democracies as Rawls seems to suppose. Rawls's explicit affirmation that one of the fundamental moral reference points for his account of justice and public reason is a conception of the person which incorporates the moral status and capacities of the democratic citizen, however, identifies a less contestable moral intuition. It is not that no reasonable person could ever contest this attribution to all people (who are not afflicted by some deep cognitive incapacity or developmental failure) of the moral properties of democratic citizens. Alasdair MacIntyre tells us in a different context that we must choose between Nietzsche and Aristotle, for example. And neither of these philosophers would accept this moral intuition. But all who are committed to the core principles of democratic legitimacy would seem bound to affirm this normative conception of personhood. Specifically, all of them (us) would seem as a corollary of their (our) most fundamental democratic values to be required to share and endorse the claim that all democratic citizens should be deemed free and equal persons who possess what Rawls calls the two basic moral powers of a sense of justice and a conception of the good. Here, indeed, is a specific, particular, and contestable set of moral intuitions which are nonetheless logically obligatory upon all who affirm the most central assumptions of democratic self-governance.

Such, then, are the requisite intermediate principles which can make 'reasonableness' something more potent and determinate for us than a very general admonition to do and believe what is fitting and proper. (These principles are not as specific and exclusionary, however, as an insistence upon deontology or upon more specific beliefs about the scope of human agency.) Let us call this normative conception, then, 'democratic reasonableness'. Exactly how potent and determinate this normative conception of political reasonableness can and should be is the topic of the rest of this essay. The imperatives of democratic reasonableness, I shall argue, generate some very important moral attitudes and constraints incumbent upon those who would be good democratic citizens. And the norms of democratic reasonableness also provide some extremely significant guidelines for proper democratic practices and procedures. There are, however, limits to the purchase of democratic reasonableness that need to be recognized and respected, for transgressing them can create delusive expectations and damage social comity.

Democratic moral reasonableness

Political reasonableness has several layers or dimensions: moral, procedural, and substantive. People can be said to be morally reasonable when they have an appropriate conception of themselves and their standing in relation to their fellows and when they understand and accept the obligations and constraints upon their aspirations and behavior which derive from that conception. People act in accord with norms of procedural reasonableness when they understand and comply with the requirements of the practices and institutionalized relationships logically appropriate to the norms of moral reasonableness and the purposes of their political association. Social policies and allocations of the benefits and burdens of a political association are substantively reasonable when they embody sound judgments of practical reason within the constraints of moral reasonableness. The content of each of these dimensions of political reasonableness will in any political association be governed first and foremost by the constitutive moral axioms and purposes of the association. We can speak meaningfully of democratic reasonableness within each of these three dimensions, therefore. In each case, reasonableness means consonance with the democratic understanding of a legitimate polity as an association of free and equal moral persons joined together in pursuit of 'liberty and justice for all' and the 'general welfare'. The sum of these several dimensions of reasonableness is democratic reasonableness *tout court*.

What, then, does it mean, first, to be morally reasonable within the context of the constitutive axioms of democratic legitimacy? The central criterion of democratic moral reasonableness is that each member of a democratic society should regard himself or herself and his/her fellow citizens as morally equal participants in an association in which, as Hegel wrote, not merely the one or the few but all are to be free (Hegel 1953, p. 24). Significant further implications for the standards of moral reasonableness also follow upon that postulate.

It follows, first, that democratic moral reasonableness requires the recognition of something like human rights. It implies that all human beings qua human beings possess moral dignity and that within the framework of a democratic polity every fellow citizen must be treated with respect. Respect here does not connote honor. Nor does it mandate anything so particular and demanding as the 'recognition and affirmation' of everyone's specific moral identity or conception of the good. It simply requires affirmation that one's fellow citizens have the capacity to be autonomous moral agents. As such, they are entitled to be regarded as ends-in-themselves and not as beings who may legitimately be subordinated to anyone else as mere means to their ends. Obviously, this moral terrain has a very Kantian cast to it. And this is neither inappropriate nor fortuitous, since Kant's transcendental deduction of 'pure practical reason' is precisely an excavation of the prescriptive implications consequent upon the recognition of people as being free, equal, and rational. His model of the 'kingdom of ends' accordingly provides us with the most apt abstract logical rendering available to us of the moral structure of a democratic society.

A second implication for moral reasonableness derivative from the fundamental democratic axiom that all citizens are free and equal is the stipulation that all valid moral judgments and precepts must be capable of assuming the form of generality. Because each and all are free equals, a valid moral precept cannot be predicated upon interests or suppositions specific to a particular one or few. Hume argued that this was a requisite of moral language and moral judgment as such – that all moral language qua moral language intrinsically had to be based upon a general perspective. Moral judgments, he wrote, cannot be predicated upon particular interest but 'must be moulded on some more general views, and must affix the epithets of praise and blame, in conformity to sentiments, which arise from the general interests of the community'.[1] I am not so sure that this claim about the logic of moral language and judgment represents a universally valid empirical generalization, since one could clearly object that many purportedly moral languages are in fact predicated upon the superior value of particular groups – that, empirically speaking, a lot of moral languages have their 'lessers' and their 'others'. But Hume's proposition does seem normatively appropriate to any society based upon democratic assumptions of citizens as free and equal. In democratic reasonableness, all legitimate moral judgments and associated imperatives must indeed take a general point of view and be predicated upon general interests, for there are in the moral universe of democracy no legitimate grounds for invidiously discriminating among human beings, each of whom stands as morally equal to the rest.

A third corollary of this core conception of democratic moral reasonableness is the requirement of reciprocity in the relationships and exchanges among democratic citizens. Rawls properly depicts reciprocity as a central norm both for fair terms of social cooperation and for the legitimacy of government authority itself. Reciprocity is accordingly modeled in the 'device of representation' of his original position and for that matter in all contractarian arguments in which the participants are represented as free, equal, and rational. And the requirement of reciprocity is also central to what Rawls designates as the 'liberal principle of legitimacy' – to wit, that morally appropriate exercises of government power and legal compulsion must be defensible on the basis of justificatory grounds which are, at least theoretically, generally accessible and potentially plausible to all citizens who themselves comport with the norms of moral reasonableness (Rawls 1996, p. xliv ff. and lectures I and II, passim).

The reciprocity demanded by democratic reasonableness, moreover, is a strong form rather than a weak form of reciprocity. It demands not simply some element of *quid pro quo* in social relations and exchanges, for that exists in almost all kinds of political relationships other than outright subjugation – including very hierarchical, inequitable, and not fully consensual relationships. The lord of the manor and his villeins or serfs, for example, were bound by mutual obligations which worked to their mutual advantage. But the background conditions and power relations which set the terms of these exchanges did not satisfy the 'free and equal' criteria of democratic moral reasonableness and hence would not have satisfied the strong sense of reciprocity embodied there. The reciprocity required by democratic moral reasonableness is the kind that characterizes exchanges and relations among persons who enter the relationships and agree to the exchanges on the terms and within conditions of freedom and equality. That strong demand is why feminists, for example, are entitled to depict the marital relations established on the basis of patriarchal legal institutions as departures from genuine reciprocity, hence as violations of democratic moral reasonableness, and therefore as presumptively illegitimate.

The defining criteria of democratic moral reasonableness also provide the logical reference point for the identification and characterization of the standard democratic vices. Consider in this context: the central civic republican vice of corruption, which consists in a disposition to privilege private interests over the general welfare; the specifically democratic form of pleonexia, which is the disposition to demand and seek to obtain more than one's proper share of scarce goods; what Milton Friedman calls 'special pleading' and attempts to be a free rider on the labor or sacrifices of other citizens; and intolerance of different races or religious persuasions. In their respective ways, each and every one of these democratic vices or violation of norms of good citizenship represents a failure to abide by the norms of respect, generality, and reciprocity that define reasonableness in the relations among people who are conceived as free and equal to one another.

Democratic procedural reasonableness

Procedural reasonableness refers to norms governing the way reasonable people conduct their business. The business of politics is to manage conflict and to coordinate collective activity on behalf of the general welfare. Democratic procedural reasonableness therefore refers to the practices and institutional procedures appropriate for the accomplishment of these political purposes by a free and equal citizenry. It comprises the institutional implications of democratic moral reasonableness and adds to these the institutional imperatives of democratic rational will formation.

The procedural norms implicit in the standards of democratic moral reasonableness turn out to be potent, extensive, and quite familiar to us. Some have been accorded constitutional status in the United States and elsewhere, while others are part of the public morality or ethos governing the ways democratic citizens are supposed to comport themselves when dealing with each other in the performance of political tasks. These procedural norms are sufficiently familiar and so widely accepted as self-evident standards for law and policy that we tend not to reflect upon the principled assumptions from which they are derived; but clearly our tacit understandings and commitments regarding what it means for free and equal people to behave 'reasonably' are powerfully at work here.

Consider first in this context the important notion of the rule of law. The superficial accounts of what that phrase means normatively are that 'we are a government of laws, not of men' and that legitimate legal mandates in a democracy represent the declared will of the majority of the people. But clearly these formulations are not adequate to explain the principled normativity of this familiar procedural ideal. People, after all, make the laws; so the alleged distinction between rule of law and rule of human beings *per se* is neither meaningful nor useful. And as almost all serious democratic theorists fully recognize, the will of a majority may be morally opprobrious even when duly enacted and encoded in 'promulgated standing laws'. Express publicity and formality alone cannot justify the moral normativity we like to attribute to the rule of law.

The crucial additional element in the normativity of rule of law is the generality principle in democratic moral reasonableness. Rule by law is superior to rule by people only because and to the extent that the legal mandates take a general object. Only then do they possess the moral universality that makes them more than gussied-up exertions of the will or interest of some at the expense of others. Rousseau understood the nature and significance of this constraint, making the generality requirement an essential defining feature of law. A rule counts as a law, he says, only if 'the matter about which the decree is made is ... general'. He continues:

> When I say that the object of laws is always general, I mean that law considers subjects *en masse* and actions in the abstract, and never a particular person or action. Thus the law may indeed decree that there shall be privileges, but cannot confer them on anybody by name. It may set up several classes of citizens, and even lay down the qualifications for membership of these classes, but it cannot nominate such and such persons as belonging to them ... In a word, no function which has a particular object belongs to the legislative power.[2]

The force of this principle of procedural reasonableness is made amply evident when democratic legislatives violate it. Hypocrisy, as has been well said, is the tribute vice pays to virtue. So it is notable that when the US Congress, say, wants to abridge the generality principle of rule of law and disburse favors to particular clients, it usually pays tribute to the principle it is violating by constructing a pseudo-general category or criterion as camouflage for its act of favoritism. To take one real-world example, a tax break once log-rolled on behalf of one particular oil company was written into law in language to the effect that 'this provision shall not apply to companies engaged in exploration for oil incorporated in the state of Oklahoma in the period between the years x and y'. There was in fact only one such entity, but the creation of a pseudo-generality helped to mask the transgression of democratic procedural reasonableness taking place.

The constraints of democratic procedural reasonableness also place significant limits upon the legitimacy of laws that 'set up several classes of citizens' (to recall Rousseau's words) at all, even where these classes are defined abstractly rather than by designating particular people. Constitutionally, in the American system, these limitations are enforced by the courts' insistence that any such categories or classifications among citizens have to be rationally related to a legitimate public purpose. Applying that standard, of course, is not always easy or automatic. But the deep principle involved here is the reciprocity requirement of democratic reasonableness. The pertinent constitutional norm is the 'equal protection of the law'. Locke articulated this principled constraint of democratic reasonableness early on in the ascendance of liberal legitimacy when he wrote that the 'bounds' incumbent on 'the legislative power' included the stipulation that its laws were 'not to be varied in particular cases, but to have one rule for rich and poor, for the favorite at Court and the countryman at plough'.[3]

A third element of democratic moral reasonableness, respect for the dignity and integrity of each citizen, actually is omnipresent in norms of democratic procedures and institutions. Liberal democratic regimes are very rights-oriented in their laws and values, and respect for persons (as rational beings and ends-in-themselves) provides the core rationale for the whole notion of individual rights. The provisions of the Bill of Rights are suffused by the implicit normativity of respect for persons, from the guarantees of free speech and exercise of religion to the prohibition against unwarranted search and seizure to the procedural protections accorded the accused to protections against the invasion of privacy.

Norms governing the procedures for formulating public policies also derive from the logic of democratic reasonableness: they represent the logically fitting and proper mode of communal decision making by a political association of free, equal, and rational moral persons. Call these the norms of democratic rational will formation. The two fundamental mechanisms here are democratic deliberation and voting with universal suffrage for competent adults. They work in tandem in the way captured by the central provision of the 'constitution' of the Moravian settlement in Winston-Salem, North Carolina. Visitors to the restored site of this settlement can see this provision prominently displayed in the meeting room where decisions were made there: all decisions, it reads, shall be made by casting of the lot, provided that no vote shall be taken prior to providing the opportunity for a full and free discussion of the issue at hand.

In recent years, Habermas and Rawls *inter alia* have emphasized and thematized the core procedural norms of practical dialogue among equal and reasonable citizens. Among the most important of these procedures and institutions are the creation, protection, and sustenance of a vital public sphere and the understanding of, the dedication to, and the ability to practice the art of public justification.

The notion of the public sphere applies to all those venues, channels, and mechanisms of communication through which citizens can share their ideas about public affairs and public policy. It is important that most of these venues and mechanisms be informal, in the sense of not under the control of governmental bodies. In a healthy democratic society, these exchanges of ideas begin at the very informal grassroots level – on street corners, in pubs, in barbershops, and in neighborhood gatherings. In a more organized fashion, the discussions can be conducted in meetings of civic associations and public forums arranged by groups like the League of Women Voters. The availability of journals of opinions, op-ed pages in the newspaper press, and various kinds of talk shows such as 'Meet the Press' and 'Firing Line' on television and radio are an important part of the public sphere. And in the fast-evolving information age, new information sources and discussion venues such as weblogs and chatrooms may play an increasingly significant role in helping citizens make informed and reasonable judgments. The venues for public comment provided by governing bodies such as administrative agencies and local school boards can also serve as a means of more reasonable and less arbitrary public decision-making, although in the former setting they may at times be little more than another forum for so-called 'cozy triangles' and in the latter setting they may be little more than occasions for aggrieved parties to hurl verbal abuse at public officials.[4]

At the level of formal governmental decision-making, a very important expression of the norms of democratic procedural reasonableness is the expectation that the parties involved systematically offer public justification for their positions and decisions. 'Justification' here means the provision of relevant reasons to warrant the judgments being rendered. 'Public' refers both to the public expression and availability of these rationales and also to their conformity to the demands of democratic moral reasonableness.

A paradigmatic institutionalization of public justification constrained by norms of democratic moral reasonableness is the expectation that justices voting on matters of public law will write or join in endorsing written and public explanations of their decisions (e.g., Rawls 1996, pp. 231–240, Macedo 1990, chap. 4). The justices would not be seen as acting properly were they simply to say, 'appellant wins'. They are expected to defend their decisions by careful explication of the logic and relevant considerations that led them to endorse one interpretation and application of the law over other possible readings urged upon them by the unsuccessful litigants in the case. Legislators are subject to similar but somewhat different expectations of public justification when they make their proposals and render their decisions. Legislators' decisions and hence their public justifications are less tightly constrained than in the case of their judicial counterparts: they are making law, perhaps from whole cloth, and are not bound by *stare decisis*. But when they address legislative proposals on the floor, legislators are expected to provide the rationale for their support or opposition to them. At their best, these discussions may lend credence to boasts about being 'the greatest deliberative body in the world'. Less remarked, but equally important, are the written committee reports that accompany legislative proposals to the floor in the US Congress.

When democratic citizens or their representatives are engaged in making judgments on law and policy, operating in conformity with the constraints of democratic procedural reasonableness helps to generate and in turn is sustained by a kind of ethos or public morality. This ethos was absolutely central to Dewey's claims that democracy was not a set of institutions but a way of life. It relies upon the capabilities Habermas thematized under the heading of 'communicative competence.' It includes what John Stuart Mill alluded to as 'the real morality of public discussion'. And it also incorporates much of what Rawls praises as the 'political virtues' of 'civility and tolerance, reasonableness, and the sense of fairness' (Habermas 1970a; Mill 1958, p. 67; Rawls 1996, p. 194). Being a good democratic citizen and conducting one's public life in accord with the norms of democratic reasonableness thus turn out to be very closely related. In order to participate legitimately and effectively in the public life and decision-making of a democratic society, citizens have to be reasonable people. They have to have the capacities and dispositions appropriate to Aristotelian phronimoi (people capable of sound practical judgment) who are engaged in communal endeavor with other free and equal reasonable citizens. Both good democratic citizens and reasonable persons have to recognize and live in accord with formal principles of right. They must be deliberatively competent. They must be willing to provide relevant 'general' reasons to their fellow citizens on behalf of laws and policies they espouse, and they must be wiling in turn to listen to the reasonable arguments of these others. Finally, because they recognize and accept the epistemic limits and frailties of even the best and best-intentioned practical reasoning (of which, see below), both reasonable people and democratic citizens have obligations to be civil and tolerant to all those who adhere to the norms of reasonableness but who nonetheless have views and reach conclusions different from their own.

Substantive democratic reasonableness

The final layer or dimension of democratic reasonableness is substantive. The question here is whether there is such a thing as substantive democratic reasonableness. That is, can the norms and constraints of democratic reasonableness produce determinate substantive conclusions about matters of law and policy? If all democratic citizens were to behave in a morally and procedurally reasonable and proper fashion, could we anticipate that the result would be substantive rules and policies all reasonable people should accept?

Here things become dicier – much more complicated and contestable. Our intuitive assumptions on this score seem in some respects hard to reconcile. Consider in this context two familiar phrases sufficiently common to have achieved the status of platitudes: 'come let us reason together' and 'reasonable people may differ'. The first of these nostrums seems to presuppose what we could call the dynamics of rational convergence. Presumably, the implicit expectation informing the admonition to reason together is not that people should simply serially ventilate their divergent views, which then just lie there in a kind of suspended antagonism. Instead, the clear hope and supposition is that the reasoning process will have the power dialectically to winnow out unconvincing claims and produce some form of substantive agreement among the parties. On the other hand, the cautionary warning that reasonable people may differ suggests that even when reasonable people reason together they may not be able to reach agreement. So, the question here becomes: is there such a thing as democratic substantive reasonableness? If democratic citizens are morally reasonable in our sense and if they abide by all the canons of democratic reasonable procedure, to what extent can we expect the result to be a determinate substantive answer to the 'what ought to be done' question – an answer which can deservedly be designated as the only or most reasonable principle or policy?

In their different ways, both Habermas and Rawls have seemed to endorse the hopeful anticipation that democratically reasonable people following the right deliberative procedures can arrive at some form of 'rational consensus'. Habermas has written, for example, that 'public discourse is supposed to eliminate all force other than that of the better argument' and that majority decisions are 'only a substitute for the uncompelled consensus that would finally result if discussion did not always have to be broken off owing the need for a decision' (Habermas 1970b, p. 7). And elsewhere he tells us that 'practical discourse must guarantee that the participants ... must be in a position to develop that language system which permits them to say what they want ... and to say – on the basis of a universal consensus – what they ought to want' (Habermas 1973, p. 252).

In conformity with his affirmation that there are multiple reasonable comprehensive conceptions of the good, Rawls does not contemplate the possibility of achieving a consensus among all reasonable persons about 'what ought to be done' in an omnibus sense. However, it is central to his account of the stability of a well-ordered democratic society that reasonable citizens can be expected to reach 'an overlapping consensus on a political conception of justice' (Rawls 1996, p. 145). That does not mean, Rawls wrote in a later introduction to *Political liberalism*, that there is only one single reasonable political conception of justice. There is, however, only a specific subset of extant or possible political conceptions of justice entitled to be considered as reasonable. As he puts it, there is 'a family of reasonable liberal political conceptions of justice', and membership within that family is conditional upon certain conditions including not only a specification of democratic liberties and opportunities but also an insistence upon 'adequate all-purpose means to make intelligent and effective use' of these liberties and opportunities. Rawls also claims that his theory of justice as fairness 'should have a special place' in this family and can be presented as 'the most reasonable' conception (Rawls 1996, pp. xlviii, lx, lxii).

I want to argue here that both of the apparently contradictory nostrums about the capability of reasonable democratic citizens to achieve a substantively reasonable and determinate consensus contain an important truth. The canons of democratic reasonableness do possess, for those who embrace and adhere to them, the power to force some degree of convergence upon substantive conclusions about principles and policies. A failure to understand and exploit this practical power of 'acting reasonably', moreover, makes democratic societies less likely to be stable and less likely to make collectively prudent policy decisions. The importance Habermas and Rawls attribute to the idea or goal of rational consensus among democratic citizens therefore has genuine meaning and validity. There are at the same time, however, very real and insurmountable limits upon the likely reach and specificity of such a consensus of the reasonable. Failure to appreciate and to respect these limits has its own potentially adverse consequences, including the heightening of social conflict and the fostering of the kind of political cynicism produced by disillusionment. Recognizing these limits requires us to understand the ideal of reasonable democratic consensus on substantive matters of justice and policy in a specific and constrained way.

When citizens who are morally reasonable by democratic standards reach their decisions through procedures which themselves embody the constraints of reasonableness, a large number of possible substantive outcomes are exposed as illegitimate. To be sure, these illegitimate-because-democratically-unreasonable outcomes may still be pursued by partisans and special interests; but exposed as special pleadings unjustified by good reasons, these proposed policies lose the credibility and the democratic *bona fides* important to their chances of acceptance. They and their supporters tend to lose out because they fail to survive what might be called the discipline of reason. In a well-ordered democratic society, policy options are tested by the demands of public justification through democratic dialogue. This dialogic justificatory process must in turn conform to the constitutive norms of reasonable practical discourse. And these norms exert a constraining and hence selective power over contending substantive policy proposals in several important ways. One way to put this dynamic is to say that the normativity of democratic procedural reasonableness demands the giving of good reasons by advocates of public policy, and the normativity of democratic moral reasonableness places significant demands and limitations upon what can qualify as a good reason.

Argumentative warrants in practical discourse have to meet both moral and empirical tests. On the moral side, principles invoked as regulatory standards, and social purposes invoked as animating goals, are forced by the logic of moral discourse to conform to what Kurt Baier has aptly termed 'the moral point of view' (Baier 1958). Good moral reasons are forced toward the moral 'objectivity' of adopting a general viewpoint and serving general purposes. To maintain *prima facie* plausibility as a democratically legitimate outcome, any substantive policy proposal must be able to demonstrate *prima facie* conformability to principles of justice predicated on the moral equality of all citizens. And it must also be able credibly to present itself as oriented to achieving the general welfare rather than to privileging particular interests. We are, as democratic citizens, familiar with and habituated to these demands of reasonableness in our public utterances and advocacy. We know that we can present no acceptable reason for a policy we support that is discriminatory among the various sectors of our pluralistic society; and we know that if we want to be seen as providing a credible warrant for a tax proposal that would benefit our particular economic interests, we must be able to say how and why it is also in the best interest of the economy as a whole.

Making this last kind of claim also subjects its expositors to the requirements of empirical reasonableness. Social policies always are predicated upon certain assumptions about how the world works, and these empirical assumptions also have to survive critical examination. The discipline exerted by the norms of reasonableness force upon participants in the policy process not only acceptance of moral objectivity but also conformity to the reality principle. If you are going to justify going to war on the grounds that this must be done to prevent the dissemination of weapons of mass destruction, they had better be there. And if you want to justify cutting taxes on capital gains, you need to have a reasonable case not only for the fairness of the change but also a credible case for how we can reasonably anticipate the advantageous consequences you predict.

In societies which have a dominant ethos of democratic reasonableness, then, and when they have decision-making practices and institutions embodying the norms of democratic procedural reasonableness, the result is a powerful and benign narrowing of the substantive policy outcomes likely to attain credibility and to emerge successfully from the policy process. Where norms of democratic reasonableness are operative, serious policy options have to come with plausible *prima facie* cases on behalf of their conformability to standards of democratic equity, their orientation to the general welfare, and their compatibility with relevant social realities and causal forces. In a healthy public sphere, numerous critics will emerge to hold policy advocates to these tests. In this sense, the court of public opinion can function in a way approximating Condorcet's hopes that it can constitute 'a tribunal, independent of all human coercion, which favors reason and justice, a tribunal whose scrutiny it is difficult to elude, and whose verdict it is impossible to evade' (Condorcet 1955, p. 100). Operative norms of democratic reasonableness can in fact serve to give force to the better argument, as Habermas contends, and to push a democratic citizenry toward a rough consensus about political justice, as Rawls argues. Hence it can be said that there is at least such a thing as a domain or range of the democratic substantively reasonable. Cynics who portray invocations of reasonableness in democratic deliberation as nothing more than an empty facade masking rhetorical discourses of power are therefore mistaken. And heeding their counsel would deprive democratic societies of a crucial moral mechanism regulating their political conduct and policy choices.

While insisting upon the moral force and political power of the adherence by democratic citizens to canons of reasonableness, however, it is equally important to have a clear sense of the inescapable limits upon this power. In substantive terms, canons of reasonableness can rarely if ever produce a single determinate outcome. These limitations upon the substantive determinacy of reasonableness result from what Rawls terms 'the burdens of judgment'. By that phrase he is referring to 'the sources, or causes, of disagreement between reasonable persons' (Rawls 1996, pp. 54–55) and it might therefore more aptly have been designated as signifying the impediments to achieving consensus among reasonable people in their practical judgments.

Three of these burdens or impediments deserve specific mention. Rawls recognizes the first two of these but not (or not sufficiently) the third. First, the complexity of the social world makes it impossible for even the most informed, most morally reasonable, and most judicious among us to say with certainty what all the social facts and all the causal relationships relevant to choice among possible social policies may be and how they are likely to play out. These are weaknesses of our theoretical or scientific reasoning capabilities rather than a limitation on the powers of our moral reasoning, but their weaknesses undermine the certainty and precision of practical judgments based upon them. Consider in this context the contentious but nonetheless reasonable disagreements over the causes of crime or the consequences of trickle-down economic policies. However confident we all might be that our judgments are better than those of our adversaries on such policy-relevant theoretical questions, we have to admit that these judgments are to some degree speculative and that reasonable and knowledgeable people might reach conclusions different from our own.

The second principal epistemic frailty leading to reasonable disagreement on matters of social principles and policy is one brought home to us by Sir Isaiah Berlin. As Berlin insisted, human life is characterized by a plurality of genuine goods. These plural goods, moreover, may not be entirely reconcilable or simultaneously attainable. Indeed, in some instances, achieving one of these goods may be possible only at the cost of sacrificing some or all of another good. The result is a kind of tragedy in the moral economy of human goods. Moreover, we have no definitively reasonable algorithm to commensurate or adjudicate the tragic conflicts and choices thus engendered and thereby to produce determinate solutions to them (Berlin 1990). Consider, for example, the tensions between the virtues of traditional ways of life and the technological advances necessary for economic development. Or consider the tensions between equity and efficiency in economic policy or trade-offs between individual liberties and communal security. The fact is that fully reasonable people in our sense of the term may reach different conclusions about the proper balances or compromises in these cases where there is, as the current mantra goes, 'nothing without loss'.

The third important impediment to the capacity of reasonableness to deliver determinate substantive outcomes on social principle and policy stems from what I have elsewhere characterized as 'the antinomies of social justice' (Spragens 1993). The problem here is the presence *vis à vis* the right and just of moral conflicts and tragedies paralleling those which Berlin observed *vis à vis* the good. These conflicts and tragedies result from the difficulty of knowing the right way to deal with certain kinds of gratuitous inequalities. Gratuitous inequalities are *prima facie* unjust by the democratic moral axiom of the equal worth of persons. But when gratuitous inequalities are ineluctably connected with other important moral norms or moral goods, there is no single morally reasonable way to handle the resulting moral tensions. How, for example, can we eliminate the unfairness consequent upon the natural inequalities among human beings without infringing to some extent upon the integrity and moral inviolability of persons? How can we honor and give full play to the many human goods produced by familial bonds without perpetuating inequalities simultaneously generated by them? What is the right way to deal with suffering that can be assuaged only by imposing great costs upon people who bear no responsibility for inflicting it and who would themselves suffer in turn?[5]

Although he generally appreciates the significance of the 'burdens of judgment' when it comes to empirical theoretical knowledge and when it comes to adjudicating genuine goods not mutually attainable, Rawls seems not to appreciate the burdens or impediments that place real limitations upon our ability to settle upon specific principles of distributive justice entitled to be seen as uniquely reasonable or most reasonable. Because he implicitly incorporates into the criteria for reasonableness not merely the norms of what we have called democratic moral and procedural reasonableness but also a belief in certain reasonably contestable moral and speculative beliefs, he winds up depicting libertarians, utilitarians, and anyone who thinks that differential work warrants differential rewards as morally unreasonable.

This argumentative strategy has the virtue, if it be that, of bracing polemical chutzpah. It parallels the cheeky bravado and, in a way, the underlying logic of Rorty's counsel that democratic partisans should not bother to engage in fruitless discussion with anti-democrats like Nietzsche but instead should just dismiss them as 'mad'. But such an attempt to ramp up the substantive content of reasonableness in this way and to claim on its behalf the power so to discriminate among competing conceptions of justice in such a definitive way is both inappropriate and costly. Rawls's construction of the content and specificity of reasonableness strains credulity by demanding that we construe philosophers such as Hume, Mill, Kant, and Hayek – not to mention most of his fellow citizens – as unreasonable people. Making such extravagant claims on behalf of and in the name of reasonableness not only raises understandable ire among thoughtful people so dismissed as unreasonable, it tends also to discredit and undermine the normativity of democratic reasonableness by raising the kind of suspicion mentioned earlier by Samuel Freeman that invoking it is nothing more than a rhetorical gloss over one's partisan views or personal moral intuitions. In effect, by attempting to squeeze more political and moral specificity out of reasonableness than it can deliver, Rawls plays inadvertently into the hands of the Stanley Fishes of the world who are only too happy to seize upon such overreaching as confirmation of their insistence that liberal appeals to reasonableness are purely rhetorical and/ or delusional (see, *inter alia*, Fish 1994).

Conclusions and implications

Condensed to its essentials, my argument has incorporated four main claims. The first of those has been that it is both meaningful and valid to invoke the normativity of reasonableness in political and moral practice and policy. The second main thesis has been that reasonableness *per se* – bare bones or generic reasonableness, if you will – can only refer to beliefs or behavior that seem fitting and proper in the context of the best understanding of our social world we can obtain through the conscientious use of our cognitive faculties. Democratic reasonableness brings into play in addition to the constraints of generic reasonableness more specific constraints generated from an insistence upon the bedrock axioms of democratic morality – specifically, that all citizens are to be treated as free, rational, and equal in moral worth. Because these moral axioms are constitutive of democratic principles, these additional constraints and the more specific criteria of reasonableness they engender (reciprocity and universal admission to democratic deliberation, for example) also have a strong claim to normativity in democratic societies. Third, the norms and constraints of democratic reasonableness so understood can exert a significant and felicitous impact upon political practices, institutions, policies, and public justification when they are widely understood and accepted. Fourth, there are irremovable impediments to the power of democratic reasonableness to produce determinate substantive convergence – a rational consensus – on social policy or principles of justice even where all citizens are able and willing to subject their self-interested inclinations to the discipline of democratic reasonableness. These impediments result from the 'burdens of judgment', which is to say from limitations upon our ability to do two things: first, to ascertain with any certainty the realities and causal consequences pertinent to policy choice; and second, to adjudicate in any definitive way the conflicts among multiple but mutually unattainable goods and among competing principled ways of dealing with the antinomies of justice created by moral tragedies endemic to the human condition.

Taken all together, these several theses lead to the additional conclusion that the idea of a rational political consensus about the best thing to do or an overlapping consensus about political justice, even within a setting of universally accepted democratic axioms, should be understood as what might be called a normatively valid impossible possibility. Each term in this formula should be respected. The hope of reaching such a consensus among all (democratically) reasonable people is impossible to fulfill because of burdens of judgment we can neither escape nor transcend. It is nonetheless a normatively valid goal, in an abstract theoretical sense, because it is logically derivative of our status as rational animals and as democratic citizens. And it is a possibility of sorts: first in the practical sense that we can in fact eliminate many potential alternatives for political institutions, practices, and policies by subjecting them to the constraints of democratic reasonableness; and second, in the abstract sense that were we somehow capable of transcending the epistemic frailties and moral tragedies beneath the burdens of judgment, we could in principle achieve such a consensus or a close approximation thereof.

These claims carry, in turn, several significant implications I have space only to state rather than develop here. The first of these implications is a theoretical one regarding the cultural conditions of functional democratic regimes. Tracing the lineaments of democratic moral and procedural reasonableness and recognizing the importance of the constraining influence upon political behavior they exert when operative should lead us to appreciate the depth and intimacy of the structural and causal nexus between a culture of democratic reasonableness and successful democratic institutions.

John Stuart Mill's insistence that democratic institutions are not appropriate for all societies is often seen today as a piece of insufferable ethnocentric prejudice. Mill contributes to this reading – and in today's multicultural ethos to the dismissal – of his argument by using Enlightenment tropes of backwardness to characterize those societies he sees as not ready or able to sustain what he calls 'representative government' (Mill 1861, esp. chap. 4). My argument here suggests that we should bracket any such concerns, however legitimate, to recognize an important truth that underlies Mill's concern with what he sees as the cultural requisites for successful democratic governance. For if we set aside any adjectival labeling of different kinds of cultures and look at the specific capacities and dispositions Mill itemizes as essential to democratic functioning, we can see that many of these are capacities and dispositions necessary for and pursuant to a culture of democratic reasonableness. Charitably understood in the context of our argument here, Mill's central concern is to point out that democracies require for their survival and certainly for their flourishing the sustenance and support of reasonable citizens – citizens who are able and willing, *inter alia*, to take a moral point of view, to seek the general good, to reason together, to treat others as moral equals, and to accept norms of moral reciprocity.

This theoretical recognition of the close structural and causal nexus between making democracy work and a culture of democratic reasonableness has practical correlates. It should suggest to us the enormous importance of all those institutions of civil society that serve to socialize people into the ethos of democratic reasonableness. It also suggests a sobering recognition of the serious difficulties in attempting to transplant democratic institutions and practices into places where norms of democratic reasonableness and their moral and intellectual sources are weak or not available. This recognition does not imply that democratic governance can take root only in scientifically and technologically advanced societies. Nor does it suggest the necessity of any particular religious or philosophical heritage. What is does suggest is the necessity for any likely venue of successful democratization to possess strong sources of cultural support for norms of universal respect, moral reciprocity, reasonable dialogue, the rule of law, and so on. There are many possible ways of sustaining these norms of democratic reasonableness, but if none of these are widely influential the prospects for stable and effective democratic institutions have to be seen as disconcertingly slim.

Finally, due respect for the limited capacity of democratic reasonableness to produce a concrete rational consensus carries important implications, as well. It suggests that we need to appreciate the impropriety and the costs of claiming greater determinacy for reasonable argumentation than it can in fact produce.

Claiming too much capability for operative norms of reasonableness, forgetting the 'impossibility' part of the aspirations for rational consensus, leads to stigmatizing perfectly reasonable political opponents as being beyond the pale of democratic legitimacy. That in turn sharpens social conflict and ironically tends to weaken the normativity and the practice of democratic deliberation. Given the limits upon the power of democratic reasonableness to produce consensus upon substantive policies, there will always be an unavoidable and legitimate role for standard practices of compromise and voting. We can only hope that these staple political practices will function within the constraints of democratic reasonableness and not in their stead.

Notes

1. David Hume, *An enquiry concerning the principles of morals*, Section 5, Part 2.
2. Jean-Jacques Rousseau, *The social contract*, Book Two, Chapter 6.
3. John Locke, *Second treatise of civil government*, Chapter 11, Section 142.
4. For an interesting recent consideration of the opportunities and issues surrounding public comment broadly construed within the rule-making procedures of administrative agencies, see Richardson (2002).
5. Three very different kinds of texts whose core problematics arise from these kinds of circumstances are Vonnegut (1968), Fishkin (1983), and Balkin (1986).

References

Baier, K., 1958. *The moral point of view*. Ithaca, NY: Cornell University Press.

Balkin, J.M., 1986. The crystalline structure of legal thought. *Rutgers law review*, 39(1), 1–110.

Berlin, I., 1991. The pursuit of the ideal. *In*: I. Berlin, *The crooked timber of humanity*, ed. H. Hardy. New York: Knopf, 1991, 1–19.

Condorcet. 1955. *Sketch for a historical picture of the progress of the human mind*, trans. J. Barraclough. London: Weidenfeld and Nicolson.

Fish, S., 1994. *There's no such thing as free speech*. New York: Oxford University Press.

Fishkin, J., 1983. *Justice, equal opportunity, and the family*. New Haven, CT: Yale University Press.

Freeman, S., 2004. Public reason and political justifications. *Fordham law review*, 72(5), 2021–2072.

Habermas, J., 1970a. Towards a theory of communicative competence. *Inquiry*, 13(4), 360–375.

Habermas, J., 1970b. *Toward a rational society*, trans. J. Shapiro. Boston, MA: Beacon Press.

Habermas, J., 1973. Wahrheitstheorien. *In*: H. Fahrenbach, ed. *Wirklichkeit und Reflexion*. Neske: Pfullingen, 211–265.

Hegel, G.W.F., 1953 [1837]. *Reason in history*, trans. R. Hartman. Indianapolis, IN: Bobbs-Merrill.

Hume, D., 1751. *An enquiry concerning the principles of morals*. *In*: Aiken, H.D., ed., *Hume: Moral and Political Philosophy*. New York: Hafner Press, 1948.

Locke, J., 1690. *Second treatise of civil government*. London: J.M. Dent and Sons, 1955.

Macedo, S., 1990. *Liberal virtues*. Oxford: Clarendon Press.

Mill, J.S., 1861. *Considerations on representative government*. London: Parker, Son, and Bourn.

Mill, J.S., 1958. *On liberty*. Indianapolis, IN: Bobbs-Merrill.

Rawls, J., 1971. *A theory of justice*. Cambridge: Harvard University Press.

Rawls, J., 1996. *Political liberalism.* New York: Columbia University Press.

Richardson, H., 2002. *Democratic autonomy: public reasoning about the ends of policy.* Oxford: Oxford University Press.

Rousseau, J-J., 1762. *The social contract.* Translated by Cole, G.D.H. New York: E.P. Dutton, 1950.

Spragens, T.A., 1993. The antinomies of social justice. *Review of politics,* 55(2), 193–216.

Vonnegut, K., 1968. Harrison Bergeron. *In: Welcome to the monkey house.* London: Panther, 7–14.

Reasonable utility functions and playing the cooperative way

Gerald F. Gaus

The rational, the reasonable and utility maximization

In *Political liberalism* Rawls draws the important distinction between the rational and the reasonable. The rational

> applies to a single, unified agent (either an individual or corporate person) with the powers of judgment and deliberation in seeking ends and interests peculiarly its own. The rational applies to how these ends and interests are adopted and affirmed, as well as to how they are given priority. It also applies to the choice of means, in which case it is guided by such familiar principles as: to adopt the most effective means to ends, or to select the more probable alternative, other things equal ...

> What rational agents lack is the particular form of moral sensibility that underlies *the desire to engage in fair cooperation as such*, and to do so on terms that others as equals might reasonably be expected to endorse. I do not assume the reasonable is the whole of moral sensibility; but it includes the part that connects with the idea of fair social cooperation (Rawls 1996, pp. 50–51, emphasis added).

Because the rational and the reasonable are distinct in these ways, says Rawls, it is a mistake to try to derive the moral (qua the reasonable) from the rational; thus he appears to criticize David Gauthier's project of basing morality on the theory of rational choice qua utility maximization (even though it was Rawls's earlier work that inspired Gauthier; Rawls 1996, p. 53; Gauthier 1986, p. 4). Others have followed up this idea, and have argued that, given decision theory's focus on instrumental rationality qua the maximization of utility, decision theory cannot adequately capture the ideas of the moral or the reasonable insofar as they manifest 'the desire to engage in fair cooperation as such'. In this vein, Paul Clements and Emily Hauptmann (2002) argue that, while decision theory's modeling of the rational leads to problems such as the Prisoner's Dilemma (PD), drawing on the reasonable allows us to make sense of playing a PD in a cooperative way.

In this essay I dispute this conception of the utility and decision theory, which ties it to means-end, instrumental, reasoning. I show that the decision theoretic framework has no deep problems accommodating the 'reasonable' qua a desire to engage in fair cooperation as such. I focus on the claim that, while rational choice-driven agents are caught in the Pareto-inferior outcome, reasonable agents could 'solve' the PD and cooperate. Not so, I shall argue. All evaluative criteria relevant to choice can be built into a von Neumann-Morgenstern utility function; given this, if reasonable people find themselves in PD situations – that is, if their utility functions ordered the outcomes in a way that defines the PD – they too would follow the dominant 'defect' strategy. The difference between simply rational agents and those who are also reasonable is not that they would behave differently in Prisoner's Dilemmas, but that reasonable people are more successful in avoiding the Prisoner's Dilemma and tend to play more cooperative games.

The prisoner's dilemma and utility

The all-too-familiar story behind the prisoner's dilemma goes like this. Two suspects, Alf and Betty, have been arrested by the police. The police have enough evidence to convict both on a relatively minor charge. If convicted of this charge – and the police can obtain a conviction – each will get two years in prison. The police, however, suspect that Alf and Betty acted together to pull off a bigger crime but the police have inadequate evidence to convict them of that crime. They make the following offer to Alf (the same offer is made to Betty). 'Alf, turn state's evidence against Betty, and we'll let you go free; we'll demand the maximum penalty for Betty, so she will get 12 years. Of course if Betty confesses too, we're not going to let you both go free: you'll each get 10 years. However, if you keep quiet and she confesses, we'll let her go free, and you will be the one to get 12 years. But if neither of you confess to the bank job, we won't have enough evidence to prosecute. We will then proceed with the lesser charge, and you'll get two years each.' Figure 1 displays their problem in terms of years in jail; Alf's 'payoffs' (time in jail) are depicted in the lower left of each cell, Betty's in the upper right.

Alf reasons: 'If Betty confesses, and I keep quiet, I'll get 12 years; if Betty confesses and I confess too, I'll get 10 years; so I know one thing: if Betty confesses, I better confess too.' What if Betty keeps quiet? Alf reasons: 'If Betty keeps quiet

Betty

Keep Quiet   *Confess*

	Keep Quiet	Confess
Keep Quiet	2	0
Alf	2	12
Confess	12	10
	0	10

Figure 1.   PD in terms of years in jail.

and I keep quiet too, I get 2 years; if Betty keeps quiet and I confess, I go free. So if Betty keeps quiet, I do best by confessing.' But now Alf has shown that confessing is a *dominant strategy*: no matter what Betty does, he does best if he confesses. And Betty will reason in a parallel way; she will conclude that no matter what Alf does, she does best by confessing. So they will both confess, and get 10 years. Hence the (sole) equilibrium outcome is strongly Pareto-inferior to the non-equilibrium outcome {keep quiet/keep quiet}.

This, however, is simply a story in terms of jail time. We have simply assumed that the players want to stay out of jail, and that their utility functions are monotonic with minimizing jail time. In order to really get the result that the rational thing for them to do is to confess, we need to say something about their *preferences* over outcomes. We can generate an ordinal utility function for any person in terms of his preference rankings for the different outcomes if his rankings satisfy the standard conditions of completeness, asymmetry of strict preference, symmetry of indifference, reflexivity and transitivity.[1] Ordinal utility functions map rankings of outcomes on to numbers. Let us assume that most preferred outcome is mapped on to the highest number, the next preferred to a smaller number, the next to a yet smaller number and so on. The sizes of the differences, or ratios between the numbers, provide no additional information.

Assuming that in both of their preference orderings less years in jail are preferred to more years (and, remember, our ordinal scale is one in which *larger* numbers designate *more* preferred outcomes), we get Figure 2.

Figure 2 is the general ordinal form of the prisoner's dilemma. Each ends up with his/her third ranked outcome (utility 2), yet {keep quiet/keep quiet} would

Betty

Keep Quiet   *Confess*

	Keep Quiet	Confess
Keep Quiet	3	4
Alf	3	1
Confess	1	2
	4	3

Figure 2.   General PD form in ordinal utility.

Betty

		Keep Quiet	Confess
Alf	Keep Quiet	x / x	1 / 0
	Confess	0 / 1	y / y

where $1>x>y>0$

Figure 3.   The general cardinal form of a PD.

give each his/her second choice (utility 3). Thus even though there is a strongly Pareto-superior outcome (i.e., one that is preferred by each) they cannot achieve it. Ordinal utility only allows us to distinguish more and less preferred outcomes; rather than {4, 3, 2, 1} we could have used {1000, 999, 4, 1}, which would give precisely the same information. If we wish to (roughly speaking now) get some idea of the relative preference distances between the outcomes (again, roughly how much more one thing is preferred to another),[2] we then can generate cardinal utilities, using some version (there are several) of the standard von Neumann-Morgenstern axioms. On one accessible view, four further axioms are required.[3] The key to this approach is to assume certain preferences over lotteries (risky outcomes), and then confront agents with lotteries involving their ordinal preferences. Their ordinal preferences *over the lotteries* allow us to infer a cardinal scale (or, rather a set of such scales, since the results are unique only up to linear transformations). This is an incredibly powerful idea, for it generates a cardinal utility measure from series of ordinal preferences. We can define a cardinal utility PD as in Figure 3:

Figure 4 gives one example of how such cardinal utilities might come out.

So Alf and Betty reason themselves into an outcome that, on each of their cardinal scales, each ranks as giving him/her .1 out of 1, whereas the {keep quiet/ keep quiet} outcome would give each .85 out of 1.

Betty

		Keep Quiet	Confess
Alf	Keep Quiet	.85 / .85	1 / 0
	Confess	0 / 1	.1 / .1

Figure 4.   A PD in cardinal utility.

Can the utility of being a reasonable person be included in the game?

The idea, then, is that purely rational, means-end oriented, agents will sometimes find themselves in PDs. If, though, they reasoned in another, more cooperative, way they could avoid the Pareto-inferior outcome. Recall that Rawls describes a reasonable person as one who has a 'desire to engage in fair cooperation as such'. Thus we might say that while purely rational people will only be cooperative when doing so is the path to largest payoff, rational and reasonable players will gain intrinsic utility from taking the cooperative move (they have a desire to be cooperative 'as such'). Of course, Rawls also adds that a reasonable person is one who is concerned with conditions of *fair* cooperation. So we might say that a reasonable person intrinsically values taking the fair cooperative move. This means that she will choose the cooperative move when others do so as well, since it is not fair to demand that anyone be an unconditional cooperator; proposing that others cooperate on those terms – 'You cooperate no matter what I do' – is not reasonable. Assume, then, that the players are reasonable insofar as they have a preference to be conditional cooperators: people who cooperate when others do. Apart from the payoffs to which such a cooperative stance might lead, each has a preference to be a conditional cooperator rather than a person who seeks to gain by unilateral defection. So, someone might be tempted to say, rational and reasonable people might cooperate in a PD.

Now the obvious response by a traditional game theorist is to insist that all the utility that is relevant to the game must be built into the game. Suppose, then, that each player values being seen as a cooperative person, but not as a sucker (that is, each puts intrinsic value on cooperating when the other cooperates, but not on cooperating when the other takes advantage of one). Adding .2 extra units of utility for performing the cooperative act, we get the game in Figure 5:

In this game {keep quiet/keep quiet} is in equilibrium (if one player keeps quiet, the other cannot improve his/her total utility of 1.05 by confessing). Unfortunately, like so many attempts to 'solve' the Prisoner's Dilemma, we have done so by converting it into another game, in this case the 'Assurance Game': the utility of the outcomes no longer conforms to Figure 3, the general form of the

Betty

		Keep Quiet	Confess
Alf	Keep Quiet	.85 (+.2) .85 (+.2)	1 0
	Confess	0 .1	.1 .1

Figure 5. The transformation of a PD into an assurance game by adding the utility of cooperative action.

Prisoner's Dilemma. In the Assurance Game there are two equilibria: {keep quiet/ keep quiet} and {confess/confess}.

Important decision theorists, however, insist that this is not the proper analysis. It looks now as if in Figure 5 we stipulate that *cooperating is the path to the most utility*, but this seems to miss the idea that in some sense our reasonable and rational cooperators could gain by defecting. Thus Amartya Sen argues that those in a Prisoner's Dilemma who constrain their pursuit of the best payoffs act 'as if' they are in an assurance game, but they are not apparently really playing one (Sen 2004, p. 218). Robert Nozick agrees. He insists that some utility cannot be integrated (as I have done in Figure 5) into the payoffs in the game. Sometimes, Nozick argues, an act's utility 'is not determined solely by that act. The act's meaning can depend upon what other acts are available with what payoffs and what acts are also available to the other party or parties' (1993, p. 55). Thus an act's utility 'may depend on the whole decision or game matrix. It is not appropriately represented by some addition or subtraction from utilities of consequences *within* the matrix' (1993, p. 55, emphasis in original). So the idea seems to be that a certain utility may depend not just on the value of a consequentially resulting state of affairs, but on the entire game, including what other options are available to both players. Nozick insists that this cannot be captured within, as we might say, any single cell but depends on the relation between the cells (the 'whole game matrix').

Sen, then, thinks that reasonable cooperators are playing 'as if' they were in assurance game; Nozick believes that we need to distinguish payoffs which are simply the *results* of an action from payoffs that depend on players having confronted certain options in the course of the game. Is there any way to analyze the game in Figure 5 that makes sense of these intuitions? Nozick focuses on the 'matrix' – the strategic representation of the game. However, as soon as we become concerned about the information available at different points in a game (which player had what options), the strategic form is inappropriate, and we should consider the extensive form of the game. Figure 6 provides the extensive form of our game in Figure 5 – 'Transformation of the PD into an assurance game by adding the utility of cooperative action game' (hereafter the 'Reasonable Cooperators Game').

Squares indicate decision nodes, filled dots are terminal nodes that indicate the end of the game, or the payoffs of the game (the utilities are given in cardinal numbers, first Alf's, then Betty's, at each terminal node). The advantage of the extensive form is that at each node we can identify the information sets available to the players. We can specify that in games of 'perfect recall' information sets include knowledge of the prior moves of both oneself and the other player made at each node. The extensive form builds into games the order of the moves; in Figure 6 Alf makes the first move. However, in prisoner's dilemma-like games, the moves are simultaneous. This feature is accommodated in Figure 6 by the dotted line connecting Betty's decision nodes; she must make her first move without knowing which node she is at (her information set at this node is thus not a singleton, as she does not know which of the two nodes she occupies). Consequently, the same game could be displayed with Betty having the first move, and

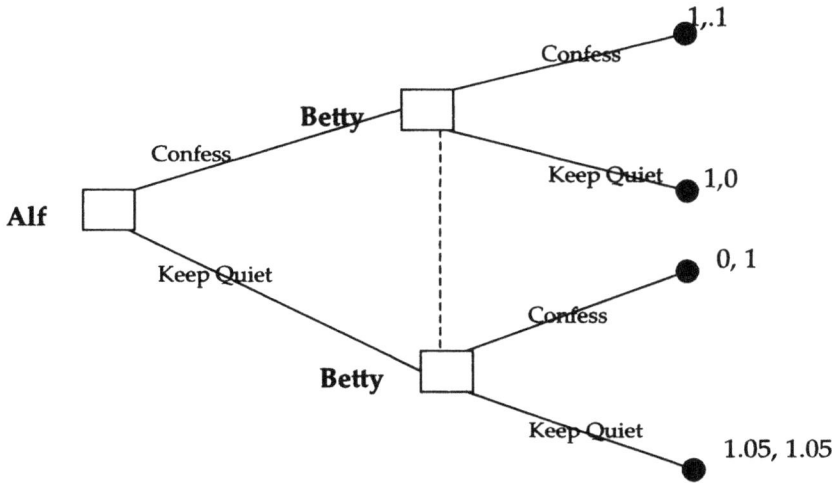

Figure 6. The reasonable cooperators game in extensive form.

Alf making the second move with his information set incomplete in a similar way. Now when we think outside the box (strategic form) of the game in this way, we see how the utilities at the terminal nodes can be affected by information about what nodes the players have passed through. Alf's utility of 1.05 (the same holds for Betty) is produced (partly) by his knowledge that at choice points (nodes) where he might have ratted on Betty and she might have ratted on him, they *both* chose not to, and instead took a more cooperative path.

Is it legitimate to interpret a game in this way – where the utility of the terminal nodes is dependent on the players' knowledge of what decisions have been made at earlier nodes, and what this tells them about each other? Consider the game of chicken in Figure 7:

Figure 7 is a familiar textbook game. Its standard name comes from the teenage game in the 1950s, in which two teenage boys (or, as Bertrand Russell put it, 'youthful degenerates') drove toward each other with the pedal to the metal, and the first one who swerved was 'chicken'. So the winner gets 1 out of 1 if he keeps driving straight and the other swerves (say the swerver gets .5 out of 1); if both swerve their reputations take a bit of a hit (say their payoff is .8 out of 1). If, on the other hand, neither swerve they both take a much bigger hit and crash (0 out of 1).

What is seldom appreciated in the textbook rendition is how much of the intuitive description depends on the knowledge by each player at the end of the game what turns at each node he has or has not taken and what turns at each node the other has or has not taken. Like the Reasonable Cooperators Game, the intuitive account of the game is crucially about what sort of person one is and this is determined by the choices one made at each node. So far from this utility – derived from knowledge from each other's choice set – being 'outside the game',

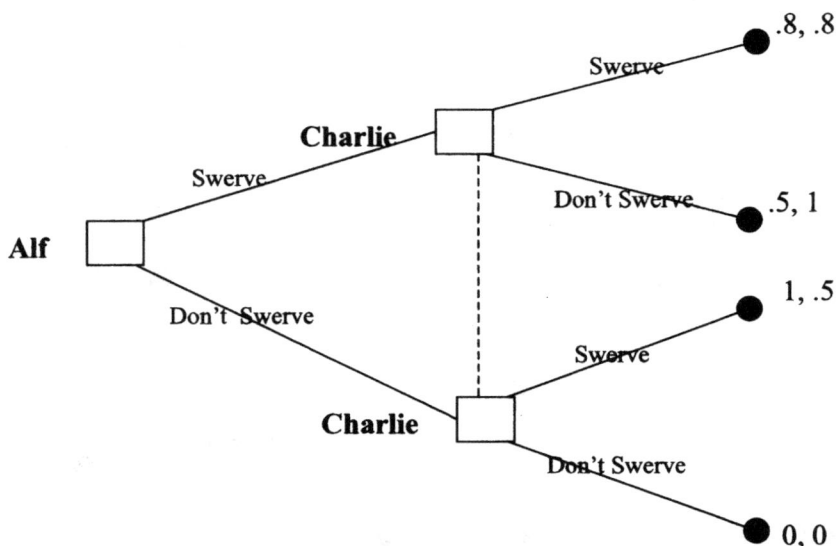

Figure 7.   Chicken.

it is most of the game (along with the disutility of surviving or being killed). To better see this, suppose that it was discovered that one of the cars was made in Sweden and had a safety auto-swerve device such that, when another car was approaching, at a distance of 30 feet the car automatically turned away. Although in *some sense* (see p. 227) the consequences would be 'the same' as if one player chickened (we get to a 'swerve, didn't swerve' terminal node), the payoffs would change, since the swerving was not the result of the other player making a chicken choice at one of the nodes.

Often all games with the payoffs ordered as in Figure 7 are considered the game of Chicken. I believe this is wrong. Consider a different game of 'Chicken' drawn from Dennis Mueller (2003, p. 16). Suppose Alf's goat wanders into Betty's garden and eats her veggies while Betty's dog wanders on to Alf's property, scaring his goat so that it does not give milk. A fence would be a public good between the two of them. Assume that each would benefit by unilaterally building the fence (each would be better off building the fence alone than not having one) but, of course, each would prefer that the other build the fence. So each has the following ordering: (1) the other builds, (2) we split the cost (3) I build; (4) neither builds. We get the following game in ordinal utility (4=best).

This game has the same ordinal strategic representation as the game of Chicken of Figure 7, but it is crucially different. Here the payoffs in no way depend on having traveled through certain choice nodes: Alf's and Betty's payoffs are determined exclusively by the resulting state of the world (whether a fence is built or not, and who pays) and they get no payoff at all from knowing that the other party 'chickened' out.

Betty

	Builds	Doesn't Build
Builds	3 / 3	4 / 2
Doesn't Build	2 / 4	1 / 1

Figure 8. 'Chicken' in providing a public good.

Figures 7 and 8 represent different games *even though the orderings of the payoffs are identical*: the decision trees for the two games have different properties. To see the importance of this, compare the following two choice situations confronting Alf:

(1) *Betty's reward*: Betty says to Alf, 'I don't want you to go the football game this afternoon or go drinking with your friends tonight. Forgo both and you will get a kiss from me this evening.'

(2) *Alf's trek to Betty*: Alf wants to see Betty this evening and get a kiss (if he turns up at her door, he *will* get a kiss), but on the way will confront choices between seeing a football game or continuing on, and then he will confront the choice between going into the bar or continuing on to see Betty. If he goes to the football game he will be too late to drink beer or see Betty; if he goes drinking he will also be too late to see Betty.

Figures 9 gives Alf's decision tree for Betty's reward and Figure 10 gives it for Alf's trek.

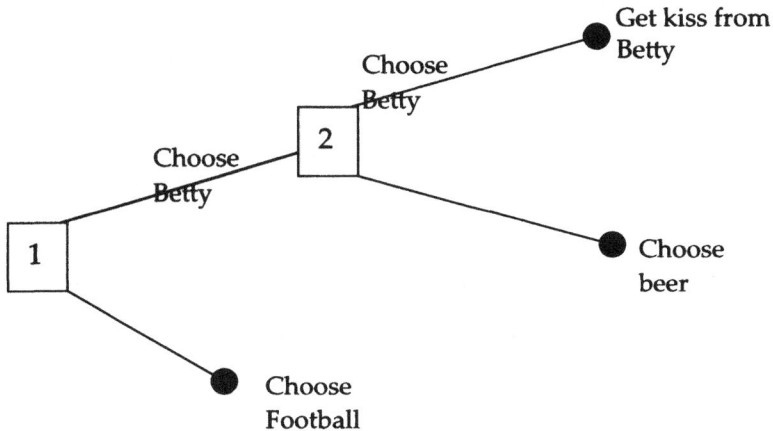

Figure 9. Alf's decision tree for Betty's reward.

116   *G.F. Gaus*

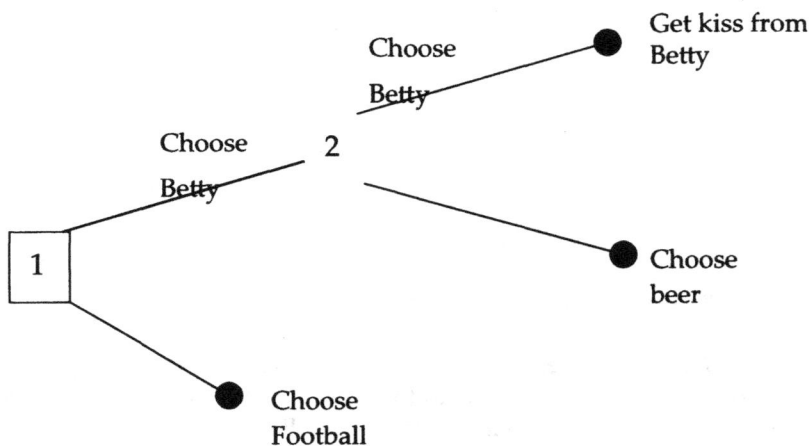

Figure 10.   Alf's decision tree for Alf's trek.

These trees look identical; however, they differ in a crucial respect. The tree in Figure 10 is *separable*, in the sense that if we truncate the tree, starting at node 2 rather than 1, this separated part of the tree is the same as it was when it was part of the larger tree (McClennen 1990, p. 120ff). In Figure 10 Alf has the exact same choice open to him at node 2, whether we begin the tree at node 1 or node 2: Betty's kiss or beer. But not so in Figure 9: the payoffs there depend on passing through both nodes, so it makes no sense to truncate the tree.[4] Alf cannot start at node 2. Clearly in *some* decision trees the payoffs are necessarily conditional on confronting a series of choices and so, in such cases, a separable game cannot be started at a node that does not include one of the choices. Trees are not always simply 'access routes to prospects' (cf. McClennen 1990, p. 120). Because in a genuine game of 'Chicken' as well as the 'Reasonable Cooperators Game,' the payoffs depend on proceeding through certain nodes, the players' decision trees will have similar difficulties with separability, since the structure of the decision tree is part of the payoffs (Hammond 1988, p. 26).

Nozick and Sen are (of course) right. Just because two games have the same payoffs – the games are the same in their strategic form – they may nevertheless be different games in their extensive form. The decision trees for the players may have different properties even though they lead to the exact same utilities. But this by no means justifies the idea that somehow the utilities gained by the players from their knowledge about what moves have been made cannot be integrated into the payoffs of the terminal nodes (or cannot be included 'in the matrix'). All the utilities at stake in a game are part of its payoffs. The difference between a standard Assurance Game and the Reasonable Cooperators Game is not that there are some extra payoffs lurking somewhere outside the matrix in the latter. The difference is not in the payoffs at all, but in the characteristics of the game, which make the payoffs depend on passing through certain nodes.

Nevertheless, reasonable agents thus described find themselves in strategic interactions that are versions of the Assurance Game; and so understanding such games looks crucial to grasping how reasonable and rational others will interact (Skyrms 2004). It is not discovering how to 'cooperate in PDs,' but finding the cooperative equilibrium in these types of Assurance Games, that explains the emergence of cooperation of rational and reasonable individuals.

Self-sacrifice arguments against integrating all utility into the payoffs

My claim, then, is that in a game everything of normative relevance for choice – 'even the structure of the decision tree itself' – is part of the consequence domain (Hammond 1988, p. 26). The utility at the terminal nodes sums up all the normatively relevant considerations. In some ways, Sen agrees that the moral person is a maximizer, but in other ways, Sen argues, she isn't. After all, she derives utility from taking a *less* attractive option. Thus, says Sen:

> A person's preferences over *comprehensive* outcomes (including the choice process) have to be distinguished from the conditional preferences over *culmination* outcomes *given* the act of choice. The responsibility associated with choice can sway our ranking of our narrowly defined outcomes (such as commodity vectors), and choice functions and preference relations may be parametrically influenced by specific features of the *act* of choice (including the *identity* of the chooser, the *menu* over which the choice is made, and the relation of the particular *act* to behavioral social norms that constrain particular actions) (2002c, p. 159).

Sen distinguishes the 'comprehensive' outcome (which can include the utility of the choice process) from the distinct state of affairs that is produced by a choice, the 'cumulative' outcome. Insofar as part of the outcome derives from what it shows about one or the options confronting one, this is part of the comprehensive, but not the cumulative, outcome.

Sen has in mind cases in which the utility of the states of affairs depends on the fact that one passed up what looked to be a more attractive option.

> You arrive at a garden party, and can readily identify the most comfortable chair. You would be delighted if an imperious host were to assign you to that chair. However, if the matter is left to your own choice, you may refuse to risk it. You select a 'less preferred' chair. Are you still a maximizer? Quite possibly you are, since your preference ranking for choice behavior may well be defined over 'comprehensive outcomes', including choice processes (in particular, who does the choosing) as well as outcomes at culmination (the distribution of chairs).

> To take another example, you may prefer mangoes to apples, but refuse to pick the last mango from the fruit basket, and yet be very pleased if someone else were to 'force' that last mango on you (2002c, p. 161, footnote omitted).

Now, on the face of it, this sort of chooser seems to act irrationally. Suppose one is confronted with the option {mango, apple}; given one's preference not to take the last mango, one will choose an apple. But now suppose that one is confronted with the set {mango, mango, apple}. Now one will pick a mango. But our last mango refuser will violate what many take to be basic axioms of consistent rational choice – the contraction and weak expansion properties. According the *contraction* property, if *x* is chosen from the entire set *S*, it must be chosen from all subsets of *S* in which *x* is included. Our polite mango refuser violates this by selecting a mango from the set {mango, mango, apple} but an apple from the subset {mango, apple} (Anand 1993, pp. 56–58). Our chooser will also violate the *weak expansion* principle: if an option is chosen from each of two subsets, it must still be chosen when the sets are combined.[5] Suppose our person is confronted with two sets {apple, apple, mango} and {apple, mango}. Because she will not take the last mango, she will chose {apple} from the first set and {apple} from the second. But if we combine the two sets to get {apple, apple, apple, mango, mango} she will choose a mango, thus violating the weak expansion principle.

Suppose, as I think is clearly the case, that having such preferences is rational, and so we want to allow for them in an account of consistent choice; it may look as if we must follow Sen in developing new axioms of rational choice, distinguishing choices from menu-independent sets (where the contraction and weak expansion principles may hold without modification) from axioms of choice involving options, like the choice of our mangoes, that are chooser or menu-dependent.[6] Thus when Sen argues that conditional cooperators act 'as if' they are in an assurance game, the idea is that the best modeling of their utility function is that they maximize their goals subject to a self-imposed restriction to a certain menu. That is, rather than (as I have argued) building into the cooperative person's utility function their preference for cooperative acts, Sen argues that we can better capture their deliberations as constraining their maximization behavior to a certain subset of the options.[7] So on Sen's view we model the person as first restricting her action options by identifying a 'permissible' subset of her options 'reflecting *self-imposed* constraints, and then seeking the maximal elements' within that remaining set (2002c, p. 189ff).

This proposal fits well with some understandings of the reasonable, *viz.*, in which deontological principles function as side constraints. However, the idea of a self-imposed menu constraint does not obviously capture deontological *requirements*, which do not function primarily as constraints on maximization. Principles that require positive action are not easily interpreted as menu constraints. If the principle requires performance of *x* out of the set {*x,y,z*}, it doesn't look as if the principle is one of constrained maximization: it dictates a choice. To be sure, it might be said that in this case the principle constrains the option set to one item and then that is maximized, but it is not clear what it means to appeal to maximization to determine what option to select from the restricted menu when the option to be acted upon has already been selected. Perhaps we could still make sense of this. After all, there is typically more than one way to fulfill a principle, and perhaps we can maximize when selecting from the various ways. Yet this too seems normatively charged; some theories may well instruct us not to appeal to our own goals when deciding among alternative instantiations of the principle, but instruct us to consult the spirit or *telos* of the principle.

I am not convinced that we should accept Sen's complication of decision theory to model this type of 'sacrificing' choice. The polite last-mango refuser only violates the principles of consistent choice (contraction and weak expansion) if each choice is viewed as ranging over enjoyable food items. If Betty has stable preferences, and is simply picking the more tasty fruit, and if Betty chooses a mango when presented with the choice between a mango, an apple and another apple, it is perplexing indeed if she then chooses an apple when confronted with the choice between a mango and an apple. It looks quite irrelevant that the first time her set included an extra apple. But, of course, the problem arises just because the relevant description changes: at one point Betty is choosing simply on the grounds of 'which fruit would I like the best?' and at the other time the relevant description is 'Should I choose the one I like the best or be polite, knowing that Alf loves mangoes?' If Betty has reasons according to which, in cases like this, being polite is more important than an enjoyable fruit fest, then she is simply acting on her total set of preferences and there is no inconsistency.

This raises the difficult issue of 'framing' and whether Betty's choices violate what Kenneth Arrow calls 'extensionality':

> The cognitive psychologists refer to the 'framing' of questions, the effect of the way they are formulated on the answers. A fundamental element of rationality, so elementary that we hardly notice it, is, in logicians' language, its *extensionality*. The chosen element depends on the opportunity set from which the choice is to be made, independently of how it is described (1982, p. 6).

Now if, when the *same option* is described in different ways a person's utility changes, extensionality (or invariance) is violated (Tversky and Kahneman 2000, p. 211.) Is Betty just framing the same choice differently? That is, can we say that she *really* has a choice between eating a mango and an apple, but she responds to different descriptions and so changes her preferences? This gets us into complex issues in the philosophy of social science, regarding the intentionality of actions. What I think is clear, though, is that there is no such thing as a set of brute action options that is independent of the descriptions (intentional states) of the choosers. Are Betty's true options: a mango or an apple to eat, a soft object or a hard one, a dull-surfaced object or a shiny-surfaced one, the superior piece of fruit to throw at a disliked political speaker, the superior fruit to put on the teacher's desk, or between being rude or being polite? One of the hopes of revealed preference theory, with its behavioral underpinnings, was that we could describe an unambiguous 'choice behavior' that had no reference to the chooser's intentional states, and so her descriptions of what she is up to. But this behaviorist project failed: action is inherently intentional. So 'framing' cannot simply be understood in terms of different descriptions of the 'same' option, for what is the 'same' option depends on the relevant description. Sen, I think, agrees: framing explains inconsistent choices, but as he sees it, Betty's fruit choices do not really seem inconsistent (2002c, p. 168n). A full account of framing, and its relation to a plausible version of Arrow's condition of 'extensionality', must involve a notion of *irrelevant* differences in description or a criterion of choice inconsistency.[8]

Decision theory: *pro tanto* or all-things-considered considerations?

So how do we model in decision theory and game theory a person's choosing as in some sense 'the best' an action that is nevertheless a self-sacrificing choice, so she (in a sense) loses utility? My suggestion is that we do not explicitly do so. Of course our intuitive description of a game can include these: we can say that in the Reasonable Cooperators Game each person has adopted a moral principle not to cheat if the other cooperates, and this can be seen as a sort of sacrifice, but it is not modeled in the game itself.

To better see the view I am espousing, contrast three conceptions of decision theory. The first I have mentioned and will put aside. Decision theory was, as I said, originally presented as a theory of consistent *choice behavior*, where it was hoped that this might entirely avoid relying on mental states. I have indicated why this aspiration was misconceived.

This leads to the second conception. Decision theory is crucially concerned with how a person's preferences over states of affairs translate into her preferences over action-options. We need to suppose, most basically, that a person can rank the possible relevant states of the world in terms of her normative criteria, whatever they are. Let us call the *consequence domain* the ordering of possible outcomes: the ordering sums up everything relevant in the person's set of normative criteria to ranking the states of the world that might obtain. Now suppose a chooser confronts a set of *action options*; she will rank the action-option highest that is associated with the highest ranked outcome in the consequence domain. This is what we mean by saying that she has more reason to choose that act: given her entire set of normative criteria, doing that act is preferred to all the other alternatives. Thus, her preferences over outcomes (the consequence domain) determine her preferences over action-options. We can think, then, in terms of mapping the ordering of outcomes on to the action-options set, producing an ordering of action-options (Morrow 1994, p. 17).

The power of decision theory is that modest principles of consistency and transitivity of preference allow us to construct a mathematical representation of a person who consistently acts on her best reasons – i.e., chooses higher- over lower-ranked options and has a complete ordering of outcomes; for cardinal representations additional and somewhat more contentious principles are required, but they too are pretty intuitive. This mathematical representation allows us to depict consistent choices for higher- over lower-ranked options as maximizing a utility function. Decision theory then formalizes a person's *all-things-considered considerations* in favor of action options based on her ranking of outcomes. It is crucial to stress that decision theory simply does not maintain that anyone *seeks* to maximize utility – that idea is a remnant of utility *qua* hedonism. Acting in a way that maximizes utility models choices that are consistent with one's ordering of action options based on one's ordering of outcomes; maximization of utility is not itself a goal.

It is absolutely fundamental to realize that there is no reason whatsoever to suppose that a person's background set of evaluative criteria must produce an ordering of outcomes that ranks states of affairs simply in regard to how well a person's *goals* or *welfare* are achieved (Cf. Morrow 1994, p. 17). Although decision theory distinguishes acts from outcomes (or consequences), and holds that the ranking of acts is determined by the ranking of outcomes, we should not confuse this sort of decision-theoretic consequentialism with the moral theory of consequentialism or the theory of instrumental action (Anand 1993, p. 84n). Among an agent's background evaluative criteria may be to conform his actions to the moral principle to 'tell the truth when under oath.' Suppose, given one's evaluative criteria, one ranks at the top the outcome 'I tell the truth under oath at the trial today.' Given this, the action of telling the truth under oath has 'high utility' – that is, the action one has most reason to perform. S.I. Benn has shown that deontological requirements can be modeled in this way (1988, ch. 3).

It is a mistake, albeit a common one, to see decision theory as a theory of instrumental action.[9] Decision theory allows us to model choice based on one's notion of the overall ordering of outcomes based on one's evaluative criteria or, we might say, one's best reasons – whatever they are. To be sure, if one also claims that all reasons are reasons to achieve one's goals, *then* decision theory does indeed model instrumental reasoning, but only because one's practical reasons have been limited to goal-seeking ones. If one's practical reasons include being a fair cooperator and these reasons lead to ranking outcomes in ways that meet the basic utility axioms, then a person acting on her best reasons can be modeled as maximizing a mathematical cardinal function. Gary E. Bolton (1991) has done this, building into players' utility function (along with the goal of getting money) a concern for fairness *to themselves* (i.e., that the player is himself treated fairly); moreover, Bolton provides experimental evidence that this model predicts choices in bargaining games.

Sen dissents from this way of modeling the action: he advises us to distinguish actions that follow from 'adhering to a deontological principle' from those that are "actually 'preferred'" (20002c, p. 191). The idea is that an obligation that requires one to act in a way that sets back one's goals or welfare (perhaps my best friend will be convicted if I tell the truth under oath) is not an action I 'prefer' to perform. Here Sen is pushing the idea of 'preference' closer to its ordinary meaning of 'liking,' where one can rationally do what one does not prefer ('I had reason to do it, but I sure did not prefer it.') (Benn and Mortimore 1976, pp. 160–161). R. Duncan Luce and Howard Raiffa hint at a similar interpretation of preferences when they refer to them as 'tastes': if preferences are tastes, then it is surely wrong to describe a Kantian as one who has a 'taste' for justice.[10] Given this, we can see that Sen, Nozick and those who resist integrating the reasonable into normal utility functions seek a third conception of decision theory: one that does not simply model the relation of *all-things-considered* orderings of outcomes to choice and action, but endeavors to model our *pro tanto* reasons and how we structure them to arrive at all-things-considered rankings and choice. Thus, as we have seen, Sen models deontic constraints differently from goal maximization. Sen (and Nozick) seek a decision theory that *models rational deliberation and its relation to choice and action.* If we have different types of reasons, then the decision theoretic model should distinguish these to stay truer to the phenomenon of rational deliberation, choice and action.

There is nothing erroneous about transforming decision theory from an account of all-things-considered rational choice to model *pro tanto* considerations as they enter into all-things-considered choice. In some ways microeconomics does this: it models preferences over consumption of goods (where the preferences are subject to further conditions, such as decreasing rates of marginal substitution) subject to budget constraints. And we have long been familiar with metapreference analysis, which supposes that a rational agent has first-level preferences and also preferences about these preferences (and so on up levels). Sen, consistent with his general approach, calls such 'metarankings ... an analytically tractable concept' that has been 'practically important' (2002a, p. 12).

Nevertheless, there are reasons to think this development of decision theory into a theory of choice based on structured *pro tanto* reasons, while in many ways interesting, is ill-advised. Not only does decision theory become increasingly complex, but more importantly, it becomes tied to different accounts of types of reasons. Sen, we have seen, develops a way of modeling deontic reasons as side constraints, but it is not clear that he adequately models deontic requirements. Nozick argues that the game theory cannot integrate the utility associated with 'symbolic' cooperative reasons, but there is good reason to doubt whether they are reasons at all (Nozick 1993, pp. 54–55; Pincione and Tesón 2001; Gaus 2002). Just what reasons we have, and how they are to be distinguished, is philosophically highly contentious. Now we might develop models for each of these: a virtue decision theory, purely instrumentalist decision theory, a side-constraint decision theory, a deontic requirement decision theory, and egoistic decision theory, and so on. But as we do so, decision theory loses its appeal as an ecumenical theory that can relate a person's (overall) rankings of outcomes to choosing actions, and so understanding how people with differently ordered outcomes may rationally interact. Furthermore, if we follow Nozick's (and Sen's) lead, and see games such as the Prisoner's Dilemma as only about how the players' goal-related reasons would instruct them to act, the games become difficult to interpret, and, crucially, *the overall rational course of action turns on reasons not identified in the game's payoffs.* Thus we have 'solutions' such as Nozick's to the Prisoner's Dilemma which really turn on the claim that the game is under-described since the reasons that tilt the balance to cooperation (that lead the players to order {keep quiet/keep quiet} above {I confess, the other keeps quiet}) are not 'in the matrix.' Essentially, games are described in terms of partial utility – *pro tanto* reasons – and the claim is that, *if* these are one's only reasons, then we will behave as the game predicts.

Conclusion: morality and utility theory

I do not want to claim that every normative criterion can be accommodated by cardinal utility theory without complications.[11] Cardinal utility theory is full of complications. Take the straightforward problem of the deontologist who places absolute weight on adhering to a moral principle. So x, the world in which he abides by the principle, is best. Suppose that the next best outcomes (worlds) are y and z. One of the axioms of cardinal decision theory, continuity, says that there must be a lottery L in which he is indifferent between y and a lottery that gives him p probability of x and 1-p of z.[12] But our absolutist prefers x for any probability over zero. As Luce and Raiffa (1957, p. 27) acknowledged, some choices may not be continuous. To use their example: even if we all agree that $\$1 > 1\textcent >$ death, not too many people are indifferent between $1\textcent$ and a lottery with chance p of $\$1$ and a 1-p chance of death. It might be thought that the whole idea of a lottery over prizes makes no sense for a deontic theorist who always has total control over his action, and so his 'prizes'. The absolutist is acting under certainty, not risk, so the lottery axioms are inappropriate.

But note that these problems concern cardinal utility measures. An absolutist still can have a complete, reflexive and transitive preference ordering (at least, as long as he has only one absolute). As Rawls notes, a strict lexicographic preference-ordering prevents formulating a cardinal utility function (1996, p. 332fn). And if we see deontologists (qua deontologists) as always acting under certainty (which I think is erroneous), then indeed we will not employ expected utility accounts, which model choices under risk. The important point, though, *is that these sorts of worries cannot show that decision theory is about instrumental reasoning (or is consequentialist in any interesting sense)*: they are objections to the lottery axioms and the development of cardinal utility. I have given games in both ordinal and cardinal utility: the difference between them is the amount of information conveyed by the utility numbers about the relation between the ranked outcomes. The difference is not that cardinal utility commits us to instrumentalism but ordinal utility does not. If so, these problems with modeling some sorts of deontic choices may be barriers to developing a cardinal utility scale modeling such choices, but this by no means shows that deontic choices cannot be modeled in decision theory because it is 'consequentialist'.

However, placing infinite weight on a moral consideration is an extreme position indeed. A person who chooses on the basis of pluralistic reasons to act, acknowledging both goal-oriented, means-end reasoning, and moral reasons that place intrinsic value on doing certain sorts of acts, and who never gives infinite weight to any reason, can be modeled according to a cardinal utility function (Benn and Mortimore 1976, pp. 185–186). Although those who insist that the moral or the reasonable cannot be integrated into utility theory are apt to see themselves as followers of Rawls, this was not, in fact, his view. 'From a purely formal point of view, there is nothing to prevent an agent who is a pluralistic intuitionist from having a utility function' (1996, p. 332fn).

Acknowledgements

Earlier versions of this paper were presented to the 2005 Fagothey Philosophy Conference, Santa Clara University and the Universidad Torcuato Di Tella, Buenos Aires. My thanks to all participants for their comments, questions, and objections.

Notes

1. *Completeness:* For every option (x,y) it must be the case that either x is preferred to y, y is preferred to x, or y and x are indifferent. Let us use '$x>y$' for 'x is preferred to y'; '$x{\sim}y$' for 'x is indifferent to y' and '$x?y$' for 'x is either preferred to y or x is indifferent to y.' So for all (x,y): $x?y?y?x$; *Asymmetry:* not $(x>y \; \& \; y>x)$; indifference is *symmetric:* if $x{\sim}y$ then $y{\sim}x$; *Reflexivity:* $x?x$; *Transitivity:* $x?y \; \& \; y?z \rightarrow x?z$.
2. If we wish to be extremely careful, we will restrict ourselves to saying that all these 'von Neumann-Morgenstern' utilities tell us are a person's preferences between lotteries or gambles, and so what he will do in situations that involve risk – where the agent does not know for certain what outcome-consequences are associated with his action-options, but can assign a specific probability p that a certain action option α will produce a certain consequence. See Morrow (1994, p. 34).
3. *Continuity:* For all (x,y,z) where $x?y \; \& \; y?z$ there must exist some probability p such one is indifferent between y and a lottery L that gives one p chance of x and 1-p chance of z; *Better prizes:* if (i) we are confronted with lotteries L_1 over (w,x) and L_2 over (y,z); (ii) L_1 and L_2 have the same probability of prizes; (iii) the lotteries each have an equal prize in one position; (iv) they have unequal prizes in the other position; then (v) if L_1 is the lottery with the better prize, then $L_1>L_2$; if neither lottery has a better prize, then $L_1{\sim}L_2$; *Better chances:* if (i) confronted with a choice between L_1 and L_2, and they have the same prizes; (ii) if L_1 has a better chance of the better prize, then $L_1>L_2$; *Reduction of compound lotteries:* If the prize of a lottery is another lottery this can always be reduced to a simple lottery between prizes. I follow Dreier (2004), but see also Hampton (1998), ch. 7; Luce and Raffia (1957, pp. 23–31).
4. As Peter Hammond (1988, n. 4) notes, 'a decision tree can hardly include, as a partial consequence, regret at missing an opportunity to have consequence y, unless there was an opportunity in the past to have had y'. Hammond argues, however, that his continuity principle over choices may still apply. In any event, note that denying separability does lead one at any node to choose what, from that node onwards in the tree, would be a suboptimal outcome. Thus the core of modular rationality is retained.
5. Weak expansion is crucial to the idea of path-independent choice. I call it the 'weak expansion' principle as it is less demanding than Sen's $\beta+$ property. See Riker (1988, p. 132ff), Mueller (2003, pp. 152–153), Craven (1992, p. 63ff).
6. Sen's argument is complex. He argues for a notion of maximization that is distinct from optimization, which itself has to drop consistency conditions. I cannot go in to these matters here. See Sen (2002c, p. 184fn).
7. For a similar approach see McMahon (2001). I examine McMahon's proposal in Gaus (2003).
8. Arrow himself refers (1982, p. 7) to people being moved by 'irrelevant' events. On justifying distinctions between preferences, see Broome (1991).

9. For an extremely insightful if contentious analysis, see Hampton (1988, ch. 7). David Gauthier (1986, ch. 2), makes the error of conceiving of decision theory as instrumental. Morrow presents a typical though erroneous interpretation: 'Put simply, rational behavior means choosing the best means to gain a predetermined set of ends' (1994, p. 17).
10. They did acknowledge (1957, p. 21) that this is a very rough interpretation. Cf. Hampton (1988, p. 239–240fn) So strong is the mistaken link between decision theory and instrumental rationality that the erroneous idea that preferences are 'tastes' (so rational agents have the goal of maximizing the satisfaction of their tastes) remains prominent even in sophisticated theorists, some of whom go so far as to talk about 'tastes for fairness.' Kaplow and Shavell (2002, p. 431) claim that 'if individuals in fact have tastes for notions of fairness – that is if *they feel better* off when laws or events that they observe are in accord with what they consider to be fair – then analysis under welfare economics will take such tastes into account' (emphasis added). Apparently if satisfying one's preference for a fair outcome does not result in one's feeling better, welfare economics cannot take it into account.
11. One interesting problem concerns whether the Better Chances axiom is inconsistent with some sorts of process-dependent moral criteria that require fair lotteries to distribute goods. See Diamond (1976), Broome (1991), Drier (2004), Gaus (2007). I think the proper analysis of this type of problem is essentially the same as my analysis of the last-mango refuser.
12. See note 3.

References

Anand, Paul, 1993. *Foundations of rational choice under risk.* Oxford: Oxford University Press.

Arrow, Kenneth J., 1982. Risk perception in psychology and economics. *Economic inquiry,* 20, 1–9.

Benn, Stanley I., 1988. *A theory of freedom.* Cambridge: Cambridge University Press.

Benn, S.I. and Mortimore, G.W., 1976. Technical models of rational choice. *In*: S.I. Benn and G.W. Mortimore, eds. *Rationality and the social sciences.* London: Routledge and Kegan Paul, 157–196.

Bolton, Gary E., 1991. A comparative model of bargaining: theory and evidence. *The American economic review,* 81, 1096–1136.

Broome, John, 1991. Rationality and the sure-thing principle. *In*: Guy Meeks, ed. *Thoughtful economic man.* Cambridge: Cambridge University Press, 74–102.

McMahon, Christopher, 2001. *Collective rationality and collective reasoning.* Cambridge University Press.

Clements, Paul and Hauptmann, Emily, 2002. The reasonable and the rational capacities in political analysis. *Politics & society,* 30(March), 85–111.

Craven, John, 1992. *Social choice.* Cambridge: Cambridge University Press.

Diamond, Peter A., 1967. Cardinal welfare, individualistic ethics, and interpersonal comparisons of utility: comment. *Journal of political economy,* 75, 765–66.

Dreier, James, 2004. Decision theory and morality. *In*: Alfred R. Mele and Piers Rawling, eds. *The Oxford handbook of rationality.* Oxford: Oxford University Press, 156–181.

Gaus, Gerald F., 2002. Principles, goals and symbols: Nozick on practical rationality. *In:* David Schmidtz, ed. *Robert Nozick.* Cambridge: Cambridge University Press, 105–130.

Gaus, Gerald F., 2003. Once more unto the breach, my dear friends, once more: McMahon's attempt to solve the paradox of the prisoner's dilemma. *Philosophical studies,* 116, 159–170.

Gaus, Gerald F., 2007. *On philosophy, politics, and economics.* Belmont, CA: Wadsworth.

Gauthier, David, 1986. *Morals by agreement.* Oxford: Oxford University Press, 1986.

Hammond, Peter, 1988. Consequentialist foundations for expected utility. *Theory and decision,* 25 (1988), 25–78.

Hampton, Jean E., 1998. *The authority of reason.* Cambridge: Cambridge University Press.

Kaplow, Louis and Shavell, Steven, 2002. *Fairness versus welfare.* Cambridge, MA: Harvard University Press.

Luce, R. Duncan and Raffia, Howard, 1957. *Games and decisions.* New York: John Wiley & Sons, 1957.

McClennen, Edward, 1990. *Rationality and dynamic choice.* Cambridge: Cambridge University Press.

Morrow, James D., 1994. *Game theory for political scientists.* Princeton, NJ: Princeton University Press.

Mueller, Dennis, 2003. *Public choice III.* Cambridge: Cambridge University Press.

Nozick, Robert, 1993. *The nature of rationality.* Princeton, NJ: Princeton University Press.

Pincione, Guido and Tesón, Frenando, 2001. Self-defeating symbolism in politics. *The journal of philosophy,* 98(December), 636–652.

Rawls, John, 1996. *Political liberalism.* New York: Columbia University Press.

Riker, William, 1988. *Liberalism against populism.* Prospects Heights, IL: Waveland.

Sen, Amartya, 1970. *Collective choice and social welfare.* San Francisco: Holden-Day.

Sen, Amartya, 2002a. Introduction. *In:* Amartya Sen, *Rationality and freedom.* Cambridge, MA: Harvard University Press, 3–64.

Sen, Amartya, 2002b. Goals, commitment and identity. *In:* Amartya Sen, *Rationality and freedom.* Cambridge, MA: Harvard University Press, 207–224.

Sen, Amartya, 2002c. Maximization and the act of choice. *In:* Amartya Sen, *Rationality and freedom.* Cambridge, MA: Harvard University Press, 159–205.

Skyrms, Brian, 2004. *The stag hunt and the evolution of social structure.* Cambridge: Cambridge University Press.

Tversky, Amos and Daniel Kahneman, 2000. Rational choice and the framing of decisions. *In:* Daniel Kahneman and Amos Tversky, eds. *Choices, values and frames.* Cambridge: Cambridge University Press, 209–223.

Are the judgments of conscience unreasonable?

Edward Andrew and Peter Lindsay

Introduction

The first article of the Universal Declaration of Human Rights declares: 'All human beings are born free and equal in dignity and human rights. They are endowed with reason and conscience and should act together towards one another in a spirit of brotherhood.' The Declaration does not define the relationship between reason and conscience, but we can surmise that, in the wake of the Holocaust, the age-old definition of man as the rational animal was deemed insufficient. Rationality could serve human animality; technique could serve bestial purposes. Instrumental reason cannot be definitive of humanity.

Reason, of course, can be understood in different ways; we might, say, think of it as prudential calculation, or as the capacity to provide reasons for one's conduct (reasons that are morally acceptable to others, as distinct from rationalizations, or reasons that seem to others as unsuccessful justifications of self-interest). Aristotle understood prudence to be more than rational calculation of one's interest. For Aristotle, prudence encompasses deliberation about the ends of human life, not just the means appropriate to achieve the end desired. However, since the time of Hobbes, prudence has typically been understood as rational calculation of means to the achievement of goals set by the passions. As Hume was to assert, reason is, and ought to be, only the slave of the passions. Deliberation on the means to obtain one's strongest desire or avert one's deepest fear provides the individual with her long-term self-interest. A prudent person looks to her long-term interests rather than her short-term passions. But rationality as prudence is quite different from conscience.

Reason, however, can be understood as reasonableness, not just prudent rationality. In his discussion (1994, ch. 15) of the fool who neither believes in God nor justice, Hobbes did not deny that one can get away with injustice or breach of contract. What Hobbes called 'successful wickedness' is all too common; with Machiavellian *virtù*, usurpers can seize power without right. What Hobbes wrote was that prudence was not justice, or rationality was not reasonableness. The successful usurper cannot give reasons to justify his actions because they would justify others usurping his power, and would undermine his own objective. 'He therefore that breaketh his Covenant, and consequently declareth that he thinks he may with reason do so, cannot be received into any Society, that unite themselves for Peace and Defence.' Hobbes was a defender of reasonableness, and an enemy to conscience, as the private judgment of good and evil. Conscience, for Hobbes, is the antithesis of law, which he defined as 'the public conscience' (1994, ch. 29), and the antithesis of reason as science. Conscience is opinion, not science or knowledge: 'men, vehemently in love with their own new opinions, (though never so absurd,)... gave those opinions also that reverenced name of Conscience, as if they would have it seem unlawful, to change or speak against them; and to pretend to know they are true, when they know at most, but that they think so' (1994, ch. 7). Reason as reasonableness, as well as reason as prudential calculation, can be at odds with conscience.

Moreover, Plato and Aristotle, who defined humans in terms of their rationality, saw that on that score, they were inherently unequal. Christianity – and other religions – emphasized that the moral choices we humans make are more crucial to our immortal destiny than our ability to reason. Our decision to obey the divine order and avoid the sinful propensity to pursue selfish rational interests, rather than respect the dignity of others, is what matters most to the salvation of one's soul. Might we, then, see the Universal Declaration as an effort to combine rationalism with the egalitarianism characteristic of the world religions? Does it point to the perils with which we, in the name of reason's light, leave conscience in the shadows?

As such questions make clear, there is between reasonableness and conscience a sharing of political labour. Both enter political thinking at the intersection of law and justice. They are, in effect, the mediators between the individual and the society at large, weighing the political obligations that bind citizens and, in so doing, guide their actions. We admire the *daimonion* of Socrates in forbidding him to obey unjust decrees and also the reasonableness of his arguments in favour of upholding Athenian law. We admire both the integrity of Sophocles' Antigone in her strict observance of the sacred law, flouting the authority of Creon, and the reasonableness of Creon (in Jean Anouihl's *Antigone*) in presenting arguments for restoring order in the face of her unreasonable intransigence. We cite Christian conscience as a motive both to obey law and worldly authority (Romans, 13, 1–7) and, since the Protestant Reformation, as a motive to disobey law. Clearly, as these and myriad other examples illustrate, reasonableness and conscience are essential to political theory, for without them the individual and the society become one. If individuals were so socially conditioned that they never felt at odds with their government and laws, politics would be stripped of all interest. That it is not reflects the tensions between individual judgments and social mores; tensions from which arise our quest for moral norms, and which give to political theory an endless array of problems to surmount, riddles to solve, or, at a minimum, debates to clarify.

One such debate is how, precisely, we might divide this labour between reasonableness and conscience. Is there a complementarity between the two, or, as much contemporary political thought has suggested, can reasonableness alone mediate the conflicts that exist between the individual and society? We suggest here that the former perspective has more plausibility than contemporary thinkers have been willing to consider. In order to defend that position, we shall, after a brief overview of reasonableness, focus primarily on conscience as it has developed through a number of modern intellectual traditions.[1] As we shall make clear in the final section, the historic reliance on conscience throws into question our contemporary reluctance to recognize the vitality of its political role.

Reasonableness

Reasonableness enters liberal thinking in response to the latter's basic presumption of multiple and often antagonistic ends. The political thought of the nineteenth and twentieth centuries tended to see the antagonism of ends in far more peaceful terms than Hobbes and Locke. Post-enlightenment thinkers developed the Hobbesian view that reasonableness consists in the qualities that dispose men to peace and the Lockeian view that it is unreasonable to be a judge in one's own cause. Where reasonableness had with Hobbes been a response to the nasty and brutish realities of the state of nature, it has, in the past two centuries, been called in to help find the philosophical common ground needed in the wake of empiricism's insistence on the uncertainty of moral and philosophical truth.[2] Its role here was to provide an attitude of openness; an attitude Popper described as that, 'which does not lightly give up hope that by such means as argument and careful observation people may reach some kind of agreement on many problems of importance' (1963, p. 225).

This philosophical reasonableness had a political corollary, for where absolute truths are denied, societies are left with individuals pursuing multiple and divergent moral ends. While in Hobbes' world (and to some extent in Locke's as well) our very lives were at stake, for Tocqueville and Mill, the central concern was to avoid social conformity, to liberate individuals from the tyranny of majority opinion. The response to such obstacles was the sort of *legalized* reasonableness seen most vividly in *On liberty's* plea for toleration.

The actual terms of that reasonableness/toleration became political philosophy's central focus in the latter half of the twentieth century, beginning with the development of Rawls' 'constructivist' theory of justice. In developing and extending Kant's basic insights, Rawls emphasized the importance of reasonableness[3] as a way to accommodate 'value pluralism,' that is, the existence of multiple and often conflicting conceptions of 'the good' (what Rawls took to be a brute fact of modern societies). His central argument was that the hallmark of just political principles would be the degree to which individuals, through a framework of constraints upon their partiality, would arrive at them in conjunction with others similarly constrained. These constraints – e.g., 'the condition of publicity, the veil of ignorance ... the stipulation that the basic structure is the first subject of justice' (1980, p. 317) – revealed principles that are *reasonable* rather than 'true' in the sense offered by rational intuitionism (1980, pp. 340–341, 355). In other words, they are principles that *reasonable* individuals, individuals 'prepared to find substantive and even intractable disagreements on basic questions' (1989, p. 478), would find *reasonable* (and thus morally binding).

The contemporary concern with reasonableness is not unique to Rawls (although its existence elsewhere clearly owes much to him). To the extent that much contemporary political philosophy seeks to derive principles of justice in abstraction from particular religious and moral perspectives, it relies on this notion of reasonableness, or its synonym, impartiality.[4] Nagel, for instance, argues that, 'the right principles to govern a practice are those which no one could *reasonably* reject' (1991, p. 36, italics added). In taking this position, he is following the lead of Scanlon, for whom 'what is fundamental to morality is the desire for reasonable agreement' (1977, p. 115 note 10). In Hampton, reasonableness is seen as a fundamental commitment of liberalism,[5] a commitment she describes as follows:

> Whatever the religious, moral or metaphysical views of the people, they are expected to deal with one another in the political arena through rational argument and reasonable attitudes, and the legitimizing arguments directed at individuals in order to procure their consent must be based on reason (1998, p. 181).

The concept reaches its high point in Gauthier, who claims that

> in certain situations involving interaction with others, an individual chooses rationally only in so far as he constrains his pursuit of his own interest or advantage to conform to principles expressing the impartiality characteristic of morality. To choose rationally, one must choose morally (1986, p. 4).

All of these theories share a basic premise, namely, that reasonableness is the necessary cure for our natural tendency to view justice through our own moral and religious lenses. People are reasonable when they recognize that the necessities of their own ends are not relevant to the subject of justice. Reasonableness, then, is not altruism or generosity; it is simply that which remains when one's own ends are taken from the equation.

These theories also share another feature: they all presume that the justice of a basic juridical structure can be determined by procedures imbued with reasonableness. There is, of course, a far more direct method of making such determinations, and that is to look not to the reasonableness of procedures but rather the reasonableness of the laws themselves. In the Natural Law tradition, for instance, positive law is judged by the degree to which it conforms to a universal and higher natural law, a law to which we gain access through our capacity for reason.[6] Martin Luther King, in response to the hypothetical question 'How can you advocate breaking some laws and obeying others?', dwells only briefly on standard Natural Law responses (e.g., 'A just law is a man-made code that squares with the moral law or the law of God') before falling back on a more pragmatic appeal to the reasonable. Hence, an unjust law is 'a code that a majority inflicts on a minority that is not binding on itself', or one that is 'inflicted upon a minority which that minority has no part in enacting', or 'when a law is just on its face and unjust in its application' (1963, pp. 293–294).

In shifting the focus from justice per se (as determined by just procedures) to the justice of this law or that, the requirements of reasonableness become less of an issue. In place of concerns about motivational states (e.g., rational self-interest, a desire for peace) or one's substantive concerns (i.e., the content of one's rational self-interest), we find far looser requirements: logical consistency or perhaps the capacity to recognize basic moral truths.[7] At a certain point, in fact, one might be tempted to say that appeals to reasonableness in deciding upon the justness of laws has less to do with 'reason' than it does with one's general intuitions, or that which we know as *conscience*.

Conscience

To argue that we rely, perhaps more than we know, on conscience is to have a clear grasp of how the concept has been understood in modern political thought. What, historically, have thinkers meant by conscience and what role has it played in their moral and political theories? It is to these questions that we now turn.

The Enlightenment's Locke

A central problem for liberal political theory is that Locke is completely Hobbesian in his philosophy, insisting on the irrationality of conscience in his *Essay concerning human understanding* (1690, I.iii.8–10), while, in his political writings, granting conscience an indispensable role. Locke asserted the inviolability of conscience in his *Letters concerning toleration* and gave conscience a crucial role in his *Two treatises of government*. In his third *Letter concerning toleration*, Locke (1823, pp. 358, 362, 532) three times referred to responsible individuals 'following the light of their own reason, and the dictates of their own consciences'. Locke did not elaborate the relationship between enlightening reason and dictatorial conscience. He emphasized that both reason and conscience have to be one's own, not a Burkean collective reason or conscience, manifest in traditions of authoritative interpretations by lawyers and clerics. Both reason and conscience are forms of individual judgment. However, the problem is that Locke, in his philosophic work, deprecated conscience as irrational, while in his practical works, championed the certainties of conscience.

The central differences between Hobbes's and Locke's political philosophy pertain to the right of private judgment, the right to property (including the individual's right to consent to taxation [Locke, 1962, pp. 138, 140]), and the right to revolution. Hobbes would have thought anarchic Locke's view that 'where the Body of the People, or any single Man, is deprived of their Right, or is under the exercise of a power without right, and have no Appeal on Earth, they have a liberty to appeal to Heaven, whenever they judge the Cause of sufficient moment' (1962, p. 168). By an appeal to heaven, Locke did not mean prayer but armed resistance to government. On the question of who judges whether the government has abused its trust, Locke urged (1962, p. 21): 'Of that I my self can only be Judge in my own Conscience, as I will answer it at the great Day, to the Supreme Judge of all Men.'

Locke's influence on the French Enlightenment was quite different from that on Anglo-American radicals. The former attended to Locke's *Essay concerning human understanding* and ignored his revolutionary politics, whereas the latter followed Locke's revolutionary teaching on conscience and natural law in *The letters on toleration* and the *Treatises of government*, however much it contradicted his position on these issues in his philosophic *Essay*. In that work (1690, I.iii.8–10), Locke repudiated the idea that conscience is an innate practical principle and adopted the Hobbesian position that conscience is, despite its claims of certainty, mere uncertain opinion; a contingent product of one's upbringing, education and social environment. The French Enlightenment espoused Locke's opposition to innate ideas and to conscience as an innate practical principle, and his presentation of the human mind as a *tabula rasa* fit to receive any ideas enlightened educators impress on it. It also admired his celebration of consciousness and deprecation of conscience. After asserting that conscience is merely opinion subject to the contingencies of education and environment, Locke wrote that (the newly coined term) consciousness constituted human identity, foreshadowing the Freudian view that conscience or superego is opposed to reason or the conscious ego. Locke's position on conscience and consciousness was extremely influential on eighteenth century continental thought (Davies 1990, p. ch. 2), since it seemed to foster a secular conception of human understanding or to distance human nature from conscience as the divine inner light. In their entry on *conscience* in *L'Encyclopédie*, Diderot and D'Alembert lamented that the French have no philosophical sense of conscience, which means 'the opinion or inner sentiment that we have ourselves of what we do; it is what the English express by the word *consciousness,* which one can render in French only by periphrasis'. The non-philosophic (theological and moral) sense of *conscience* is dangerously antinomian, and in this archaic sense, *conscience* must be strictly governed by reason (Diderot & D'Alembert 1969, p. 902).

Locke's *Essay* asserts that human beings have an innate desire for happiness and aversion to misery (1690, I.iii.3), or desire pleasure as good and pain as evil (1690, II.xx.2, II.xxi.42), but have no innate ideas of good and evil or practical principles. Conscience is not 'written on their Hearts' but is produced 'from their Education, Company, and Customs of their Country'. Conscience 'is nothing else, but our own Opinion or Judgment of the Moral Rectitude or Pravity of our own Actions' (1690 I.iii.8). Locke goes on to say that men will do any evil when 'at Liberty from Punishment and Censure' (1690 I.iii.9). He denied that there are innate principles or natural laws regulating our conduct (1690 I.iii.13). Later, he omitted natural law in his typology of law: divine law, concerned with sins and duties, civil law, concerned with criminality and innocence, and the law of opinion or reputation, concerned with virtues and vices. In the first edition of Locke's *Essay*, he divided law into the Divine Law, the Civil Law and 'The Philosophical Law, if I may so call it' (1690: II.xxvii.7, 158). Philosophic law is the rule of public opinion, being governed not by one's conscience but by social approval and censure. Natural law, which plays such a large role in Locke's political doctrine, is not an alternative to positive (divine or human) law in Locke's philosophy. The place of natural law in Locke's political doctrine is filled by philosophic law or the law of fashion.

Locke elaborated this philosophic law. 'Vertue and Vice are names pretended and supposed every where to stand for actions in their own Nature, Right and Wrong.' In reality, however, they 'are constantly attributed only to such actions, as in each Country and Society are in reputation or discredit.' Therefore the real measure of what 'is every where called and esteemed Vertue and Vice, is this approbation or dislike, praise or blame ... according to the Judgment, Maxims, or Fashions of that Place' (1690, II.xxvii.10, 158).

Locke declared that conscience is not an innate practical principle; conduct is to be regulated, for philosophers and dedicated followers of fashion, by public opinion or social approbation and disapprobation. The internal monitor is replaced by external censure in philosophic law. Locke wrote:

> I think, I may say, that he, who imagines Commendation and Disgrace, not to be strong Motives on Men, to accommodate themselves to the Opinions and Rules of those with whom they converse, seems little skill'd in the Nature, or History of Mankind, the greatest part whereof, he shall find to govern themselves chiefly, if not solely, by this Law of Fashion; and so they do that, which keeps them in Reputation with their Company, little regard the Laws of God, or the Magistrate (1690 II.xxvii.12, 159).

The *philosophes* agreed with Locke's social psychology. Baron D'Holbach's *Common sense* (1772) asked the rhetorical question: 'Does not everyone see, that he has the greatest interest in meriting the approbation, esteem and benevolence of the beings who surround him, and in abstaining from everything, by which he may incur the censure, contempt, and resentment of society?' Society, for D'Holbach, replaces God in meting out rewards and punishments. Conscience is no longer one's self-awareness, coupled to the consciousness of God's impending judgment upon one's soul, but, according to D'Holbach, 'is the internal testimony, which we bear to ourselves, of having acted so as to merit the esteem or blame of the beings, with whom we live' (1995, p. 148).

Locke's philosophic law was the law for *philosophes*; the law of changing fashion was to be set by philosophers. The *philosophes* were educators of public consciousness; they were not moral populists – such as Jean-Jacques Rousseau or William Blake – who upheld the doctrine of innate conscience and relied on the untutored judgments of common men. *Les lumières* were to govern public opinion, which is policed not by law enforcement officers as with Civil Law, or by God as with Divine Law, but by the reactions of spectators, by social approval or censure. Adam Smith's conscience as impartial spectator is individual self-awareness in the eyes of God reconstituted as self-consciousness reflected in the eyes of one's fellow members of society.

Locke was authoritative for the Enlightenment precisely because of his rejection of innate ideas, including conscience as innate awareness of good and evil. Voltaire's *Lettres philosophiques* canonized Locke, along with Bacon and Newton, as progenitors of Enlightenment and singled out Locke's rejection of innate ideas as worthy of respect (Voltaire 1961, p. 56). D'Alembert's *Preliminary discourse to the Encyclopedia* indicated that he would like to include his compatriot Descartes as one of the progenitors of Enlightenment. Unfortunately, Cartesian teaching was enmeshed in the obsolete and unproductive doctrine of innate idea, whereas Locke, by rejecting innate ideas, created an 'experimental physics of the soul' (d'Alembert 1995, pp. 80, 83).

Scottish moral sense

Locke's student, the third Earl of Shaftesbury, thought that it was 'Mr Locke that struck at all fundamentals, threw all *order* and *virtue* out of the world, and made the very *ideas* of these ... *unnatural*, and without foundation in our minds. *Innate* is a word he poorly plays upon ... Thus virtue, according to Mr. Locke, has no other measure, law, or rule, than *fashion* and *custom*' (Shaftesbury 1746, pp. 32–33). Francis Hutcheson's *An inquiry into the original of our ideas of beauty and virtue* defended Lord Shaftesbury's notions of taste and moral sense against the egoistic individualism of Hobbes, Locke and Mandeville. Hutcheson insisted that the internal moral sense does not imply innate ideas any more than the external senses, but asserted that our moral sense is as natural as the principles of self-love and is antecedent to custom, education or example (Hutcheson 1726, pp. 82, 135, 87, 134). Our moral sense is the natural conscience of a social being, our natural tendency to approve virtuous actions – and to censure vicious actions – in others, and to do so regardless of their advantage or disadvantage to us. The love and esteem of our fellow humans is as essential to our being as the air we breath. A humane and generous character is closely connected to a strong love of esteem (Hutcheson 1726, p. 256), although Hutcheson did not agree with Hobbes and Mandeville that virtuous acts are motivated by a desire for praise or social esteem. For Hutcheson, the moral sense is the conscience of a social being. Thomas Reid was later to take up Hutcheson's idea of a moral sense, but the central thinkers of the Scottish Enlightenment, David Hume and Adam Smith, rejected the idea; our moral sentiments are socially constructed from our desire to be approved or our fear of being shunned by our fellows.

David Hume defined virtue as '*whatever mental action or quality gives to a spectator the pleasing sentiment of approbation*; and vice the contrary' (1875, vol. 2, pp. 85–66). Hutcheson, and later Smith, came close to identifying what conscience dictates with what spectators approve, but neither defined virtue as what is socially approved and vice what is disapproved. Hume was also bolder than his compatriots in following up the Hobbesian equation of love of virtue with love of praise. Hume wrote:

> By our continual and earnest pursuit of a character, a name, a reputation in the world, we bring our own deportment and conduct frequently in review, and consider how they appear in the eyes of those, who approach and regard us. This constant habit of surveying ourselves, as it were, in reflection, keeps alive all the sentiments of right and wrong, and begets, in noble natures, a certain reverence for themselves as well as others; which is the surest guardian of every virtue (1998, p. 77).

We see ourselves as others see us, and keep in the path of rectitude in order to maintain a favourable reputation. Moral character is a product of our desire for a good reputation. One cannot rely on conscience as one can on the desire for social approval. In Hume's mind:

> our regard to a character with others seems to arise only from a care of preserving a character with ourselves; and in order to attain this end, we find it necessary to prop our tottering judgment on the corresponding approbation of mankind (1998, p. 77).

Hume deprecated the man of conscience who stands up for his convictions against public opinion: 'Our opinions of all kinds are strongly affected by society and sympathy, and it is almost impossible for us to support any principle or sentiment, against the universal consent of every one, with whom we have any friendship or correspondence' (1875, vol. 4, p. 15). He thought we cannot pride ourselves on anything unless the grounds of our self-satisfaction 'be also obvious to others, and engage the approbation of the spectators' (1875, vol. 4, p. 153). The universal desire for fame and applause serves individuals 'to fix and confirm their favourable opinion of themselves' (1875, vol. 4, p. 15). Self-respect depends upon social esteem.

Smith evaded the boldness of Hume's social conformism in his refusal to reduce what is praiseworthy into what is praised, the 'demigod within the breast' to the judgments of external spectators. He declared that '[t]he man without aims at praise, the man within at praise-worthiness' (Smith 1804, vol. 1, p. 264). To be sure, 'The love of praiseworthiness is by no means derived altogether from the love of praise', although 'they resemble one another, though they are connected, and often blended with one another' (Smith 1804, vol. 1, p. 233). Later he tells us that 'this demigod within the breast appears ... partly of immortal, yet partly too of mortal extraction' (Smith 1804, vol. 1, p. 266). The mortal extraction of conscience paralleled the account of his friend Hume:

> Nature, when she formed man for society, endowed him with an original desire to please, and an original aversion to offend his brethren. She taught him to feel pleasure in their favourable, and pain in their unfavourable regard. She rendered their approbation most flattering and most agreeable to him for its own sake; and their disapprobation, most mortifying and most offensive. (Smith 1804, vol. 1, pp. 239–240)

The mortal seems to take on immortality in the different phrasing of the same idea.

> The all-wise Author of Nature has ... taught man to respect the sentiments and judgments of his brethren; to be more or less pleased when they approve of his conduct, and to be more or less hurt when they disapprove of it. He has made man, if I may say so, the immediate judge of mankind; ... and appointed him his vicere-gent upon earth, to superintend the behaviour of his brethren (Smith 1804, vol. 1, p. 263).

Smith went on to say that, while we have an immediate judge in our fellow humans, we appeal 'to a much higher tribunal, to the tribunal of their own consciences, to that of the supposed impartial and well-informed spectator, to that of the man within the breast, the great judge and arbiter of their conduct' (Smith 1804, vol. 1, p. 264). Nevertheless, Smith thought that moral sentiments 'suppose the idea of some other being, who is the natural judge of the person that feels them; and it is only by sympathy with the decisions of the arbiter of his conduct, that he can conceive, either the triumph of self-applause, or the shame of self-condemnation' (Smith 1804, vol. 1, pp. 405–406). Moral agents are like actors on stage who are judged by spectators rather than themselves.

When Claude-Adrien Helvétius asked the rhetorical question, 'What in fact is that original goodness or moral sense, so much boasted of by the English?', he could not properly have included Hume or Smith in his category of the thoughtless English. 'Nothing is more absurd than this theological philosophy of Shaftesbury; and yet the greatest part of the English are as fond of it as the French are of their music.' This English blindness had infected the *anti-philosophe*, Jean-Jacques Rousseau, with his ideas on the original goodness of men and innate conscience. The Rousseauan position does not require enlightened educators of the people and 'is nothing at bottom but the system of innate ideas destroyed by Locke' (Helvétius 1969, vol. 2, p. 14).

Rousseau on conscience and law

Taking aim at *les lumières*, Rousseau juxtaposed the sway of opinion (and opinion-makers) and the dictates of innate conscience:

> What good is it to seek our happiness in the opinion of another if we can find it within ourselves. Let us leave to others the care of informing peoples of their duties, and limit ourselves to fulfilling well our own. We do not need to know more than this.

> O virtue! Sublime science of simple souls, are so many difficulties and preparations needed in all hearts, and is it not enough in order to learn your laws to commune with oneself and listen to the voice of one's conscience in the silence of the passions? That is true philosophy (1969, vol. 3, p. 30; 1964, p. 64).

In *Émile* Rousseau declared: 'Our own conscience is the most enlightened philosopher' (1969, vol. 4, p. 767; 1979, p. 408) One doesn't need Cicero or any other philosopher to be a virtuous man or woman.

In her *Vindication of the Rights of Women*, Mary Wollstonecraft, while critical of Rousseau's sexism, borrowed this idea of conscience as 'the most enlightened philosopher'. She, however, extended Rousseauan inner-directedness to women. For Rousseau stated that women ought to be governed by public opinion or a concern for their reputation in the way that his enlightened adversaries thought men are, and ought to be, regulated – namely, by a desire for social esteem and a fear of social censure. Men, according to Rousseau, can follow their inner compass; women must follow external maps. 'Opinion is the grave of virtue among men and its throne among women' (1979, p. 365; 1969, vol. 4, pp. 702–703).

In his letters to Sophie d'Houdetot, Rousseau declared his doctrine of conscience, which later appeared in his *Profession of faith to a Savoyard vicar*, as a profession of antinomian love. In writing to the lover of his friend, Rousseau stated that conscience is 'an innate principle of justice, and of moral truth anterior to all national prejudices, to all maxims of education' (1969, vol. 4, p. 1108). Such professions of conscience were put forth to celebrate his and Sophie's sensibility above reason and society, or the opinions of *les philosophes*. The vicar's celebrated panegyric to conscience was advanced first to loosen the hold of public opinion barring a fusion of Rousseau's and Sophie's souls. 'Conscience, conscience! Divine instinct, immortal and celestial voice, assured guide of an ignorant and limited, but intelligent and free, being; infallible judge of good and evil, sublime emanation of eternal substance, which makes man resemble Gods, it is you alone which makes the excellence of his nature' (1969, vol. 4, p. 1111).[8] Conscience elevates man and woman above mere law, and assures them that unlawful acts partake of divinity. Conscience cannot bear the light of publicity and the noise of public prejudice. 'Conscience is timid and fearful, it searches out solitude; the world and noise startle it' (1969, vol. 4, p. 1112).[9]

Rousseau's thinking marks a break from the rationalism of the natural law tradition. As he asserts in *Emile*, 'by reason alone, independent of conscience, no natural law can be established' (1979, p. 235; 1969, vol. 4, p. 523). Moral law is based on human freedom, it is the law we prescribe to ourselves. Our human distinctiveness derives from our faculty of choice and our perfectibility. What we are is the result of our moral choices, and thus we are equal in a fundamental respect. While we may be unequal in respect of our reasoning ability, we are equal in what most matters, our moral choices.

Richard Noble argues that Rousseau's conception of conscience, advanced in the *Profession of faith of the Savoyard vicar*, contains his 'most explicitly philosophical account of his conception of the self' (Noble 1991, p. 142). Rousseau attempted to synthesize a Cartesian subject, present to itself in reflection and unconditioned by sensation and sensibility, with a Humean empirical self, conditioned by changing sense impressions, the identity of which is loosely bound together by memory and habit (Noble 1991, pp. 144–148). Rousseau's conscientious self is neither reflection nor habit; it constitutes its identity by its moral choices. Not theoretical but practical reason reveals our self to itself. More precisely, since reason provides no common standard of right and wrong, conscience rather than reflective reason determines human conduct and, in so doing, constitutes who we, as individuals, are. That is, conscience does not simply serve the confessional goal of self-disclosure.[10] Rather, conscience is creative or constructive; it constitutes us as moral agents. Rousseau's conscience, as agent, is distinct from Adam Smith's conscience as impartial spectator. Julie (of *Julie, ou la nouvelle Héloise*) reports Wolmar saying to St Preux: 'we see nothing if we remain content with looking on; that we must act ourselves in order to judge of men's actions, and I made myself an actor in order to qualify myself as a spectator' (1969, vol. 2, p. 494). Rousseau's conscience is not merely a witness to an action or a spectator at the theatre of life; it is not simply a judge to determine whether an act accorded with law or a man of taste who judges the merit of a spectacle. Conscience is a legislator who makes the rules by which he is bound, or the author of one's life drama.

Kant grasped the novelty of the Rousseauan conscience as autonomous and, like the Rousseau of *The social contract* and *Discourse on political economy*, attempted to bind antinomian conscience to law. Against the heteronomous sensualism and utilitarianism of *les lumières*, Rousseau and Kant championed Protestant freedom of conscience. Respecting difficult moral questions, Rousseau disclosed in his fourth promenade,

> I have always found the way to resolve them by the dictation of my conscience, rather than the lights of my reason; never has the moral instinct deceived me; it has retained up to now this purity in my heart sufficiently for me to yield myself to it: and if it is silent sometimes in the fact of my passions in my conduct it resumes its power over them in my memory; it is there that I judge myself with perhaps as much severity as I shall be judged by the sovereign Judge after this life (1927, p. 85; 1969, vol. 1, p. 1028).

Conscience is the internalized eye of God, not of one's fellow men.

If, however, Rousseau's conscience were infallible, or if it served to restrain injustice when his passions were not aroused, how did it permit his disposing of his children to a probable death in a Foundling Hospital, or his betrayal of his wife and friends? Is conscience just an excuse for extraordinary conduct? In his fourth promenade, Rousseau followed Plato in praising salutary untruths: 'I have followed in practice the moral directions of my conscience rather than abstract notions of false and true' (1927, p. 100; 1969, vol. 1, p. 1038). Conscience is antinomian; it prescribes a singular standard to oneself rather than a common measure for all humans. As Wolmar says to St Preux: 'It is vain then to try to mould different minds by one common standard' (1969, vol. 2, p. 566). The Savoyard vicar avows the antinomian call of conscience: 'I know by my experience that conscience persists in following the order of nature against all the laws of man' (1979, p. 267; 1969, vol. 4, p. 566).

Conscience, like equity, is bound in relations of attraction and repulsion to law; it stands outside positive law as a standard for its correction. In his *Discourse on political economy*, Rousseau describes law in the glowing colours with which he describes conscience in *Emile*.[11] In *The social contract*, Rousseau links moral freedom to law as the general will, a will in the form of a rule that comes from all and applies to all. However, *Emile* confirms the teaching of *The discourse on inequality*; actual laws are 'always so occupied with property and so little with persons, because their object is peace not virtue' (1979, p. 37; 1969, vol. 4, p. 246). Indeed, Rousseau declared: 'The universal spirit of the laws of every country is always to favor the strong against the weak and those that have against those who have not. This difficulty is inevitable and it is without exception' (1979, p. 256; 1969, vol. 4, p. 524).

Revolutionary conscience and liberal rule of law

Wollstonecraft and her fellow friends of the American and French Revolution, such as Godwin, Paine, Price, Priestley and Blake, made the rights of conscience central to their revolutionary politics. Freedom of conscience, for them, was not confined to matters of religious belief. Nor was it limited to the realm of thought and speech, as Diderot, Kant and Bentham wished to combine free speech and obedience to law. As Godwin declared: 'There is but one power to which I can yield a heart-felt obedience, the decision of my own understanding, the dictate of my own conscience' (1946, vol. 1, p. 212). The radical republicans followed Locke's teaching, in *The second treatise of government*, on the right of revolution based on the right of individual judgment of good and evil, rather than the Enlightenment's Locke that rejected conscience as an innate practical principle.

Kant, a friend of the French Revolution but opposed to the right of revolution (Reiss 1987, pp. 145–146, 162, 175, 182–185), espoused Rousseau's principle of right, the rule that laws must come from all and apply equally to all. Rousseau was, for Kant, 'the Newton of the moral world,' the man who had vindicated the claims of the common man (Muthu 2003, pp. 135–139, 281). The crucial feature of Rousseau's teaching is, to repeat our earlier statement, that we are unequal with respect to our capacity for reason – Rousseau agreed with classical rationalists and his enlightened contemporaries; he favoured aristocratic government for this reason (1994, p. 103) – but we are equal with respect to what matters most, our moral choices. Kant's moral theory is based on Rousseau's free will and conscience (Kant 1996, pp. 218–219, 529–530, 559–562), although Kant called Rousseau's moral freedom practical reason, perhaps attempting to evade the anarchic or antinomian character of Rousseau's conscience.

If Kant developed Rousseau's conscience into the moral law, drawing together Protestant conscience and enlightened reason in the categorical imperative, radical thinkers, at the end of the eighteenth century, echoed Rousseau's defence of conscience and the common man. Godwin championed conscience above law in his anarchist doctrine: 'The universal exercise of private judgment is a doctrine so unspeakably beautiful, that the true politician will certainly feel infinite reluctance in admitting the idea of interfering with it' (1946, vol. 1, pp. 181–182). The anarchist free thinker based his doctrine of proprietary justice in Biblical teaching (1946, vol. 2, pp. 429–430, 469).

The reinstatement of conscience into moral philosophy was a reaction against the Enlightenment's position that conduct is best governed by public opinion, by social approval or disapproval. As Niklas Luhmann wrote of the decline and reappearance of conscience in the eighteenth century:

> If we drop this religious or ontological warrant of individuality, we arrive at the *homme aimable,* the sociable person of the eighteenth century ... The results were disappointing, particularly for the self-conscious individual: somehow, the individual withdrew from interaction. By the end of the century, the *homme du monde,* the *homme de bonne compagnie,* was no longer an individual (1986, p. 316).

The romantic reaction to the Enlightenment reinstated conscience into moral philosophy in stressing that individuality was threatened by social approval and disapproval or by the rise of public opinion, and the radical dissenters and revolutionaries emphasized conscience as the voice of common men and women. Conscience and reason diverge in that humans are equal with respect to their moral choices, unequal with respect to their ability to calculate consequences. Reason as prudential calculation, an instrument or servant of one's passions, interests or creature comforts, is distinct from conscience. If, however, reason is conceived to be moral not instrumental (reason as the submission of one's conduct to general rules), conscience, despite its antinomian character, converges with reason in moral autonomy or the categorical imperative. On the other hand, because of its antinomian character, conscience diverges from practical reason, or conformity to publicly accepted rules. For Rousseau and Blake, conscience is individual judgment of right and wrong (for oneself, not necessarily for others) certified by the divine within one's soul. Romantic and revolutionary conscience is neither rational, as Hume and Diderot understood rationality, nor reasonable, as Kant understood practical reason.

The anarchic and antinomian conscience of Rousseau and Blake does not sit comfortably with the practical reason of Kant. What one judges as appropriate to oneself is not necessarily the same as conformity to universally recognized rules. Conscience judges what is right for oneself; reason judges what is universally valid. The silent call of conscience cannot always be translated into publicly acceptable reasons; to avow one's stand of conscience publicly is to engage in self-advertising or self-promotion. Contemporary Kantians, such as Rawls and Habermas, overlook the silent call of conscience in their demand that reasonableness requires publicly voiced reasons to persuade one's fellow citizens of the rectitude of one's moral choices. What more is there to say to the public than one could not live with oneself if forced to do what goes against one's innermost convictions? Conscientious dissenters and objectors will always appear unreasonable to the public they address. The Levellers who refused to follow Cromwell into Ireland, the Israelis who refuse to serve militarily in the West Bank, the Americans who defect to Canada to avoid fighting in Vietnam, stand outside the overlapping consensus of their peers.

Conclusion

As suggested by the above remarks, the relationship between reason(ableness) and conscience has been fluid and, at times, antagonistic. Each has been glorified and disparaged and promoted as the preferred guide for public behaviour. Contemporary political philosophy has given appeal to the notion that conscience is simply that which is unarticulated, or worse, what is incapable of rational articulation; that in sidestepping the task of publicity and persuasion, conscience becomes nothing more than undeveloped reason, something that – by the standards of reason anyway – is *ipso facto* flawed. If we cannot persuade others of the rightness of our actions by the force of a better argument, then our convictions about those actions are deemed unworthy of political discourse.

For a number of reasons, we should not be in too great a rush to accept such a view. For one, there is a tendency here to conflate conscience not with the *a*reasonable – which it unabashedly is – but rather with the *un*reasonable; that is, with views that no one *would* reasonably hold. To be sure, conscience could be unreasonable in this sense. In that potential, however, it differs little from the community standards embodied in Smith's impartial spectator; standards that have, after all, given rise to some of history's more regrettable chapters. In fact, many *unreasonable* acts made ostensibly in the name of conscience might be more accurately described as the unconscious conformity to the standards of a depraved community. Is it, for instance, really the *conscience* of the Klansman that draws him to the lynching, or might we more soundly presume that, if anything, conscience would save him from such collective insanity? An act of conscience has to be fully transparent, done in the light of day, not at night and masked. A conscientious individual avoids the anonymity of the mob and does not protect himself, even through lawyers, against adverse legal consequences.

Moreover, it is not even clear that reasonableness itself is immune to the unreasonable. If it were, the logic of the eminently reasonable 'just following orders' would seldom be heard as a defence for *not* following the dictates of one's conscience. Neither Rousseauan conscience nor Humean community can guarantee that conscientious or reasonable agents will always act in accord with what impartial spectators outside one's own community would consider right or good.

In the final analysis, then, there is little reason to view the outcomes of either conscience or reason as leaning in the direction of any particular substantive ends. To underscore that point, consider that even on an issue where there appears clear substantive demarcations – whether or not to obey the law – the battle lines are more blurred than one might suspect. Certainly conscience has been a powerful tool against the alleged sanctity of law. Statesmen are not easily comforted by Martin Luther King's insistence that 'we cannot in all good conscience obey … unjust laws … because noncooperation with evil is as much a moral obligation as is cooperation with good' (1968, p. 74). And yet, perhaps they should be, for while King's words point to the fragility of laws, they also, ironically, might lead us to whatever security can be found for them. Indeed, if conscience is powerful enough to draw us outside our legal boundaries, it might just be our best – and only – hope of remaining within them. After all, St Paul (Romans, 13, 1–8) counselled us to obey all laws of the civil authorities 'not only for wrath, but also for conscience's sake'.

This point leads to a more compelling reason for not rejecting conscience, one that has to do with a division of labour. As we have seen, conscience and reasonableness are not necessarily in search of the same sorts of things. The more recent demand in political theory for publicly acceptable reasons has been part of a quest to understand justice *per se*, and indeed, such a demand, in this context, is reasonable enough. Yet disciples of reasonableness need a bit of humility here, for even if the nature of justice could be established, this grand finding would surely not put an end to debate over the justness of *particular* laws. What justice is, and what, *concretely*, conforms to it are two issues that are not always as inextricably linked as one might suppose. As Raz (1998) has put it, morality underdetermines law. However much, say, Reaganomics meets the criterion of Rawls' difference principle (for its 'trickle-down' effects), it seems likely that many Rawlsians will resist supporting it as a true instantiation of justice. Given that disciples of Rawls could have many similar such debates, it would appear the guidance that abstract theories of justice can offer in determining the justice of individual laws will be of a very general (e.g., a winnowing down of the possibilities) nature. In other words, we cannot simply say that differences over the legitimacy of *particular* laws reflect culture, gender, race, partiality generally, or some other sin against reasonableness; for even if all such sins were accounted for, it strains credulity to think that principles of justice will yield uniform laws. (Indeed, defenders of justice make no such claim.)

But how then should we account for debate that occurs *within* the boundaries of reasonableness? With the cliché that reasonable people can disagree? With the

Popperian plea to embrace fallibility? Precisely in their reasonableness, both responses are perhaps missing a more plausible explanation, one that begins with the realization that some differences simply cannot be explained in rational terms. It might, in other words, be the case that reasonable people may disagree not *in virtue* of their reasonableness, but rather on account of convictions for which no reasonable explanation (or justification) can be given. And if that is correct, might such convictions, might *conscience*, be the *complement* of reason rather than its adversary?

Consider an example used frequently in the case of conscience, namely an individual's decision of whether or not to fight for her nation in war. There are obviously many layers to that decision, layers in which rational deliberation is the individual's primary guide. One must know, for instance, whether the war is in itself a just one; that is, whether the cause for which her nation is fighting meets criteria commonly accepted by various just war theories. And let us suppose that this rational process renders an unequivocal judgment. Then what? If the war is deemed unjust, to what does the individual owe allegiance, her nation or justice? Lest we think that reason dictates following reason-derived justice, consider that our bonds to the nation might themselves be conceived in rational terms, terms that might explicitly preclude giving presumptive weight to abstract notions of justice. How, then, to decide?

More troublesome still is what one must do if the war is deemed just, for a rational justification might matter little if a potential soldier simply feels she could not live with herself if she killed someone who posed no threat to her life. What good is reason here? On what *rational* grounds might such an individual justify her decision not to fight?

That conscience might fill in the lacuna here should come as no surprise. Reason, after all, has always presented difficulties for moral justification, if not at the level of *what* one should do, then certainly at the level of *why* one should do it. For many accounts of what can motivate moral action, reason is too closely linked to the instrumentality of self-interest. Indeed, moral freedom, which for Rousseau and Kant depends on subduing the passions and interests, may best be thought of as doing one's duty, without recourse to prospective rational calculation and retrospective rational justification. It may, in other words, be a matter of conscience.

Acknowledgements
The authors would like to thank Shaun Young for his invaluable help with this essay.

Notes
1. Other essays in this volume will more than compensate for this necessarily general overview of reasonableness.
2. That the perspective became thoroughly liberal could be seen in Russell's claim that '[t]he genuine Liberal does not say "this is true"; he says, "I am inclined to think that under the present circumstances this opinion is probably the best"' (1947, p. 21).

3. Indeed, the idea of the reasonable was Rawls' earliest philosophical concern (see 1951, pp. 2–4, 10–11), and one he never left behind (see 1997, pp. 573–615).
4. Rawls himself uses reasonableness synonymously with impartiality. See Rawls (1951, p. 4).
5. She also sees it as part of a broader lineage: 'It is this commitment to reason that makes all traditional liberal theories ... descendents of the Enlightenment' (1998, p. 181).
6. See Kern (1948) for the definitive historical discussion of the relationship between positive law and higher law. For a contemporary defence of natural law, see Figgis (1982).
7. Or perhaps basic *reasonable* truths – as King put it: 'There is nothing wrong with a traffic law which says you have to stop for a red light. But when a fire is raging, the fire truck goes right through that red light, and normal traffic had better get out of its way' (1968, p. 65).
8. Cf., 1979, p. 290; 1969, vol. 4, p. 600. Rousseau placed the gods in capital letters – 'aux Dieux'.
9. Cf. 1979, p. 291; 1969, vol. 4, p. 601.
10. E.J. Hundert compares Diderot's *Rameau's nephew*, which demonstrates the impossibility of self-disclosure, with 'Rousseau's most compelling literary creation, the hero of *The confessions*', for whom 'the goal of self-conscious disclosure was an unrealizable project'. See Hundert (1986), p. 239.
11. Compare 'the celestial voice' of law in *Discourse on political economy* with 'the celestial voice' of conscience of the Savoyard vicar. Cf. 1969, t.3, p. 248 with 1969, t.4, p. 600.

References

Alexander, L., ed. 1998. *Constitutionalism: philosophical foundations.* Cambridge: Cambridge University Press.

Cooper, A., 3rd Earl of Shaftesbury (1746) *Letters* (London: n.p.).

D'Alembert, J., 1995. *Preliminary discourse to the Encyclopedia of Diderot,* trans R.N. Schwab. Chicago: University of Chicago Press.

Davies, C.G., 1990. *Conscience as consciousness: the idea of self-awareness in French philosophic writing from Descartes to Diderot.* Oxford: The Voltaire Society.

Diderot D. and D'Alembert, J., [1751] 1969. *L'Encyclopédie ou Dictionaire raisonné des sciences, des arts et des métiers, Tome III.* New York: Readex Microprint.

Figgis, J., 1982. *Natural law and natural rights.* Oxford: Clarendon.

Gauthier, D., 1986. *Morals by agreement.* Oxford: Oxford University Press.

Godwin, W., 1946. *Enquiry concerning political justice and its influence on morals and happiness,* ed. F.E.L. Priestley. Toronto: University of Toronto Press.

Hampton, J., 1998. *Political philosophy.* Boulder, CO: Westview Press.

Heller, T.C., Sosna, M. and Wellberg, D.E., eds, 1986. *Reconstructing individualism: autonomy, individualism and the self in western thought.* Stanford, CA: Stanford University Press.

Helvétius, 1969. *A treatise on man: his intellectual faculties and his education,* vol. 2, trans. W. Hooper. New York: Burt Franklin.

Hobbes, T., 1994. *Leviathan,* ed. and intro, E. Curley. Indianapolis, IN: Hackett Publishing.

Hume, D., 1875. *The philosophical works,* vol. 2. London: Longmans Green.

Hume, D., 1998. *An enquiry concerning the principles of morals: a critical edition,* ed. T. L. Beauchamp. Oxford: Clarendon.

Hundert, E.J., 1986. A satire of self-disclosure: from Hegel through Rameau to the Augustans. *Journal of the history of ideas,* 47, 235–248.

Hutcheson, F., 1726. *An inquiry into the original of our ideas of beauty and virtue: in two treatises.* London: J. Darby etc.

Kant, I., 1996. *Practical philosophy,* trans. and ed. M.J. Gregor. Cambridge: Cambridge University Press.

Kern, F., 1948. *Kingship and law in the middle ages.* Oxford: Blackwell.

King, M.L., 1963. Letter from Birmingham city jail. In: M. L. King, 1994. *A testament of hope: the essential writings and speeches of Martin Luther King, Jr.* San Francisco, CA: Harper Collins, 289–302.

King, M.L., 1968. *The trumpet of conscience.* New York: Harper and Row.

King, M.L., 1994. *A testament of hope: the essential writings and speeches of Martin Luther King, Jr.* San Francisco, CA: Harper Collins.

Kramnick, I., 1995. *The portable Enlightenment reader.* Harmondsworth: Penguin.

Locke, J., 1690. *An essay concerning human understanding.* London: Thomas Bassett.

Locke, J., 1823. *The works.* London: Thomas Tegg.

Locke, J., 1962. *Two treatises of government.* Cambridge: Cambridge University Press.

Luhmann, N., 1986. The individual of the individual: historical meanings and contemporary problems. In: T.C. Heller, M. Sosna, and D. Wellberg, eds. *Reconstructing individualism: autonomy, individualism and the self in western thought.* Stanford, CA: Stanford University Press, 313–325.

Muthu, S., 2003. *Enlightenment against empire.* Princeton, NJ: Princeton University Press.

Nagel, T., 1991. *Equality and partiality.* Oxford: Oxford University Press.

Noble, R., 1991. *Language, subjectivity and freedom in Rousseau's moral philosophy.* New York: Garland.

Popper, K., 1963. *Open society and its enemies,* vol. II. Princeton, NJ: Princeton University Press.

Rawls, J., 1951. Outline of a decision procedure for ethics. In: J. Rawls, 1999. *Collected papers,* ed. S. Freeman. Cambridge, MA: Harvard University Press, 1–19.

Rawls, J., 1980. Kantian constructivism in moral theory. In: J. Rawls 1999. *Collected papers,* ed. S. Freeman. Cambridge, MA: Harvard University Press, 303–358.

Rawls, J., 1989. The domain of the political and overlapping consensus. In: J. Rawls, 1999. *Collected papers,* ed. S. Freeman. Cambridge, MA: Harvard University Press, 473–498.

Rawls, J., 1997. The idea of public reason revisit. In: J. Rawls, 1999. *Collected papers,* ed. S. Freeman. Cambridge, MA: Harvard University Press, 573–615.

Rawls, J., 1999. *Collected papers,* ed. S. Freeman. Cambridge, MA: Harvard University Press.

Raz, J., 1998. On the authority and interpretations of constitutions. In: L. Alexander, ed. *Constitutionalism: philosophical foundations.* Cambridge: Cambridge University Press, 152–193.

Reiss, H., ed., 1987. *Kant's political writings.* Cambridge: Cambridge University Press.

Rousseau, J.J., 1927. *Reveries of a solitary walker,* trans. J.G. Fletcher. London: George Routledge and Sons.

Rousseau, J Jr, 1964. *The first and second discourses,* trans. R. Masters and J. Masters. New York: St Martin's Press.

Rousseau, J-J., 1969. *Oeuvres completes.* Paris: Gallimard-Pléiade.

Rousseau, J-J., 1979. *Emile, or on education,* ed. A. Bloom. New York: Basic Books.

Rousseau, J-J., 1994. *The social contract,* trans. C. Betts. Oxford: Oxford University Press.

Russell, B., 1947. *Philosophy and politics.* Cambridge: Cambridge University Press.

Scanlon, T., 1977. Contractualism and utilitarianism. In: A. Sen and B. Williams, eds. *Utilitarianism and beyond.* Cambridge: Cambridge University Press, 103–128.

Sen, B., and Williams, B., eds, 1977. *Utilitarianism and beyond.* Cambridge: Cambridge University Press.
Smith, A., 1804. *The theory of moral sentiments,* vol. 1. London: T. Cadell.
Thiry, P. H. (baron d'Holbach), 1772. Common sense, or natural ideas opposed to super-natural. In: I. Kramnick, ed. 1995. *The portable Enlightenment reader.* Harmondsworth: Penguin, 140–150.
Voltaire., 1961. *Philosophical letters,* trans. E. Dilworth. Indianapolis, IN: Bobbs-Merrill.
Wollstonecraft, M., 1993. *Political writings,* ed. J. Todd. Toronto: University of Toronto Press.

Exercising political power reasonably

Shaun P. Young

The philosophical–political project of liberalism was born out of a desire to protect individuals against the arbitrary and tyrannical exercise of political power. A liberal political framework was (and continues to be) promoted as the foundation for a society in which all citizens could be free from the fear, injustice and socio-political turmoil produced by capricious judgments and punishments enforced via the subjective use of state power.

The efforts of early liberal political philosophers such as Thomas Hobbes,[1] Baruch de Spinoza and John Locke – to name only three – were motivated by a wish to escape and avoid a recurrence of the seemingly endless cycle of intractable civil wars and subsequent political instability produced by the religious intolerance, persecution and oppression that plagued much of sixteenth- and seventeenth-century Europe. Accordingly, their principal concern was the effective resolution of the political problems generated by religious pluralism. Both for personal and practical reasons, each successive generation of liberal philosophers has tended to broaden the scope of concerns which it seeks to address. In the course of the preceding four centuries the original occupation with the political difficulties produced by religious pluralism has expanded to encompass moral and philosophical disputes about the nature of the good life in general.

Not surprisingly, the broadening of the scope of concerns of liberal political philosophers has been accompanied by a corresponding evolution in their understanding of what constitutes an abuse of political power. Whereas early liberals typically focused on abusive behaviour in the form of actions that deny to individuals the conditions necessary for self-preservation, modern and contemporary (i.e., post-1850[2]) liberals have argued that, for various reasons, such a focus is too narrow; power is also abused, for example, when it is employed to establish and maintain conditions that unreasonably prevent citizens from either pursuing or achieving 'self-fulfilment'.

Such differences aside, all liberals have agreed that securing the conditions essential to a just and stable polity requires establishing certain institutional and regulatory arrangements to control undesirable behaviour both on the part of individuals and government. In particular, if individuals are to be accorded the respect and liberty due to them as free and equal beings and thereby provided with the conditions that will enable self-preservation *and* self-fulfilment, then it is necessary to limit the power of governments to restrict individual freedom 'unreasonably'. The difficulty has been in identifying limits that not only achieve such a goal but can also be voluntarily and reliably supported by individuals who affirm a plurality of often conflicting and irreconcilable conceptions of the good.

For Hobbes, Spinoza, Locke and subsequent generations of liberal political philosophers, the notion of 'reasonableness' has provided a moral and legal standard for judging the acceptability and, by extension, legitimacy of government behaviour. In order for a government directive to constitute a legitimate obligation on citizens, it must be compatible with the dictates of reason and treat all citizens in a 'reasonable' manner.[3] Arguably, such an approach achieves its most powerful presentation (to date, at least) in the theories of 'political' liberals, who typically assert that reasonableness must be the 'final court of appeal' in relation to decisions concerning matters of public import[4] – i.e., those that place demands upon all citizens of the polity.[5] It is necessary that reasonableness be the 'litmus test' for legitimate public policy/behaviour if the governance framework[6] is to be and remain equally respectful of all citizens and their beliefs and thereby provide the conditions needed to secure and sustain socio-political justice and stability. To employ a different standard, such as a single understanding of the 'truth', would be to disrespect and degrade others' beliefs, and, in so doing, effectively preclude the achievement of a *well-ordered* – which is to say, just and stable – liberal democracy (e.g., Rawls 1996, pp. xviii, 38).

However, the ability of the concept of reasonableness to serve the function entrusted to it by political liberals is questionable, at best. Indeed, it seems equally likely that efforts to secure the sought after protection against disrespectful (i.e., abusive) public/political behaviour may actually be undermined in a number of ways if reasonableness is employed as the ultimate benchmark for acceptable government behaviour. In particular, such an approach generates what could be labelled a *paradox of reasonableness*: in demanding that the governance framework assign primacy to reasonableness, political liberalism actually facilitates the emergence of unreasonableness (i.e., abusive behaviour) to a degree that critically enfeebles the former's capacity to sustain the political justice and stability deemed necessary to establish and preserve a well-ordered polity.

The principal purpose of this essay is to offer a brief review and critique of the 'reasonableness' paradigm promoted by political liberals (in particular). In the course of doing so, I will identify and explain the fundamental components of the paradox of reasonableness and comment on the potential for its resolution.

Reasonableness in political liberalism

The notion of 'reason(ableness)' has been a central feature of liberalism since the latter first emerged as a coherent philosophical project. Indeed, arguably, reasonableness is the core value animating the liberal outlook (e.g., Moore 1996, p. 167; see also, for example, Macedo 2000). That is not to suggest that 'reasonableness' has been defined in an identical manner by all liberal philosophers. A perusal of even a portion of the vast discourse that directly engages the idea of 'reasonableness' emphasises that, like 'equality', 'respect', and 'justice' – for example – 'reasonableness' is a complex, fluid and 'essentially contested' concept; it has been understood differently not only across time and place, but also within a given epoch. Not surprisingly, then, early liberals and their successors have often differed in their conclusions regarding the specific character and demands of reason(ableness). Despite such variations, liberal political philosophers have typically argued that establishing the conditions needed to enable all individuals to achieve a secure and meaningful life (however that might be understood) requires that the governance framework embody reason and allow for the pursuit and possible realisation of all 'reasonable' conceptions of the good.

Though the idea of reasonableness is a fundamental feature of all forms of liberalism, it exerts an unparalleled degree of influence on the character of conceptions of political liberalism. In essence, political liberals are concerned to offer a *reasonable* governance framework that can accommodate the demands of *reasonable* people situated in an environment of *reasonable* pluralism and *reasonable* disagreement. The importance of reasonableness for political liberalism is perhaps best exemplified by the fact that reasonableness is the supreme standard against which the citizens of a polity guided by the principles of political liberalism must judge the acceptability and, by extension, legitimacy of the governance framework and all claims and decisions concerning its validity. Political liberals argue that the diversity of 'reasonable' moral, religious, and philosophical beliefs – i.e., the 'fact of reasonable pluralism' (e.g., Rawls 1996, p. 36) – that characterises contemporary liberal democracies renders such an approach necessary if one wishes to treat all individuals with the respect they deserve as free and equal beings, and, subsequently, secure the type of widespread, voluntary public agreement (i.e., an *overlapping consensus*) on a single governance framework needed to establish and preserve a just and stable liberal democracy.[7]

The notion of 'reasonableness' is thus an indispensable component of political liberalism. Indeed, the capacity of political liberalism to achieve its stated goal is a measure of the 'reasonableness' of the governance framework it promotes, which is understood to be a direct reflection of the reasonableness of the citizens who must live under its constraints. Essentially, political liberals define 'reasonable' citizens as those who not only exercise the basic capacities of reason and converse with others in good faith, but also embrace an overarching moral commitment to the principle of equal respect (e.g., Larmore 1999, p. 602). Such individuals will voluntarily agree to seek 'a social world in which they ... can cooperate with others on terms all can accept' (Rawls 1996, p. 50); they will recognise that in contemporary liberal societies a plurality of competing, conflicting, often incommensurable and irreconcilable views is an ineliminable fact of life, and such being the case, adequately respecting the human dignity of one's fellow citizens will necessitate accepting the continued existence and public accommodation of views with which one disagrees. In turn, reasonable citizens also agree that it is unreasonable to use state power to enforce adherence to the dictates of a single understanding of the good; any attempt to do so necessarily requires the *excessive* use of state coercion to secure obedience, and the use of such force is both an unacceptable insult to the human dignity of reasonable persons and incompatible with liberal ideals – as such are understood by political liberals (e.g., Rawls 1989, p. 242; see also Larmore 1999, p. 607; Shklar 1989, p. 29). In other words, 'reasonable' citizens freely and willingly accept the notion of *reasonable disagreement* and its associated demands and recognise the need to endorse a governance framework that embodies such an acceptance.

The extent to which a governance framework possesses the necessary 'character of acceptance' will determine its capacity to secure an environment in which all reasonable individuals will have the opportunity to realise the personal freedom needed to pursue a conception of the good of their own choosing and design – the only type of freedom that adequately respects human dignity (Shklar 1989, p. 30; similarly, see Larmore 1996, pp. 123–124; Larmore 1999, pp. 607–608; and Rawls 1996, pp. 48–50, 53–54). According to political liberals, such freedom can be achieved only if the governance framework restricts its concerns to matters of public import and embodies only those values that all 'reasonable' people can 'reasonably' be expected to endorse voluntarily and faithfully – i.e., *political values* (e.g., Rawls 1996, pp. 139–140). Such values include 'equal political and civil liberty; fair equality of opportunity; [and] the values of economic reciprocity' (Rawls 1996, p. 139).

Maintaining a 'respectful' degree of accommodation and freedom requires that in the case of a conflict between the values animating the governance framework and those populating citizens' comprehensive doctrines,[8] the former always be assigned primacy. Political liberals contend that, provided the governance framework guarantees certain basic liberties (e.g., freedom of thought, freedom of expression, freedom of association, etc.) which enable all reasonable individuals to pursue their chosen way of life without undue interference from either the state or their fellow citizens,[9] it can be assumed that in those instances when it is necessary to do so, reasonable citizens will voluntarily assign primacy to the values that comprise the public conception of justice. That conclusion is based upon the following assumptions: 1) all reasonable people will want to secure a just and stable society; 2) all reasonable people affirm reasonable comprehensive doctrines; 3) all reasonable comprehensive doctrines are compatible with a political conception of justice; 4) each person's 'overall view' consists of two distinct yet related views – a 'public' view and a 'nonpublic' view – thus enabling all individuals to assign primacy to the values comprising the conception of justice[10] without having to compromise adherence to the values animating their own comprehensive doctrines (Rawls 1996, pp. 38, 140; Larmore 1987, pp. 71, 74, 76; Shklar 1989, 24–25, 31); and 5) only those values that conflict with 'the very conditions that make fair social cooperation possible on a footing of mutual respect' will conflict with the values guiding the conception of justice (Rawls 1996, p. 157). Such 'facts' are complemented by the knowledge that 'reasonable' citizens will freely and willingly support and faithfully adhere to what John Rawls has labelled the *precept of avoidance*. In doing so, citizens are agreeing to refrain from publicly asserting or denying the validity of 'any particular comprehensive religious, philosophical, or moral view, or its associated theory of truth and the status of values' (Rawls 1996, p. 150); they are agreeing to apply 'the principle of toleration to philosophy itself' (Rawls 1996, p. 10).

Political liberals argue that a conception of justice premised upon the notion of reasonable disagreement and embodying the precept of avoidance is able to reduce divisive conflict significantly because such a conception purposely avoids passing judgment as to the truth of religious, philosophical, and moral views. By incorporating the precept of avoidance into its governance framework and securing certain basic rights and liberties and assigning them 'a special priority' (Rawls 1996, p. 157; see also p. 161), a political conception of justice 'removes from the political agenda the most divisive issues, serious contention about which must undermine the bases of social cooperation' (Rawls 1996, p. 157) – such issues include, for example, the provision of 'equal liberty of conscience and the rejection of slavery and serfdom' (Rawls 1996, p. 151, n. 16). When issues are taken off the political agenda, they cease to be 'appropriate subjects for political decision by majority or other plurality voting ... [such issues are to be considered] as correctly settled once and for all' (Rawls 1996, p. 151, n. 16). While political liberals do not propose that all potentially controversial or divisive issues will or can be resolved in such a manner, they do suggest that those that remain will, for the most part, be related to less controversial matters that are much less likely to generate any problematic degree of socio-political division or instability (e.g., Rawls 1996, pp. 151–152).

Combined, the above-noted 'facts' are claimed to make it possible for all reasonable citizens to defer freely and willingly to the values animating the conception of justice when such deference is necessary. Moreover, the conditions secured by the presence of such facts are sufficiently fair and beneficial to convince all reasonable people that 'no conflict of values is likely to arise that justifies their opposing the political conception as a whole, or on such matters as liberty of conscience, or equal political liberties, or basic civil rights' (Rawls 1996, p. 155). Importantly, such a situation enables the adherents of the various comprehensive doctrines that are *likely* to survive in a *just* constitutional democracy to agree voluntarily on a single conception of justice to regulate society's *basic structure* – i.e., its main political and social institutions (Rawls 1996, p. 15; see also Rawls 2001, pp. 4, 7–8, 32). Political liberals contend that only by securing such an 'overlapping consensus' is it possible to obtain a stable political environment, which, in turn, is necessary if all reasonable individuals are to be given a meaningful opportunity to realise freely chosen goals. Without political stability, there can be no reasonable assurance that existing circumstances which allow the pursuit and achievement of particular interests and ends will not suddenly and unexpectedly change, producing a drastically different situation that is much less hospitable or even antagonistic to those interests and ends. Recognising that fact, reasonable citizens will understand the need to develop and support a governance framework that facilitates the establishment and preservation of an overlapping consensus, and, in so doing, secures the requisite political stability.

According to political liberals, a governance framework that embodies both the notion of reasonable disagreement and the precept of avoidance and, consequently, assigns primacy to reasonableness, is best suited to achieve an overlapping consensus. In turn, the conditions that enable the achievement of an overlapping consensus substantially reduce the need to employ coercive state power in order to secure obedience to government directives, and thus minimise to the greatest extent possible the likelihood of 'abusive' behaviour by government. Indeed, only by adopting and maintaining a governance framework that secures such conditions is it possible to obtain and preserve the desired protection against the unreasonable use (i.e., abuse) of political power.

Political power in political liberalism

Political liberalism embraces a very specific understanding of what constitutes the legitimate (i.e., reasonable) exercise of political power. According to political liberals, if we are to ensure that all citizens are treated with the respect they deserve as free and equal beings, then the conditions regulating the use of coercive political power must be acceptable to all those subject to that power.[11] To forsake such a requirement would be to treat individuals 'merely as means, as the objects of coercion, and not also as ends', and in so doing unacceptably disrespect individuals' distinctive capacity as persons (Larmore 1999, p. 607). Only by demanding that the principles informing the coercive use of political power be the object of 'reasonable agreement' among those they are to govern is it realistic to expect 'reasonable' people to support the governance framework voluntarily and reliably. Political liberals contend that such support is necessary if one is to secure the political stability required to establish and maintain the safeguards that will enable all reasonable individuals to pursue and (hopefully) realise a life-plan of their own design.

If the governance framework is to exhibit the respect needed to obtain and sustain the necessary support, all reasonable citizens must believe that the political process – i.e., not only the right to vote, but also the 'opportunity to hold public office and influence political decisions' (Rawls 1996, p. 327) – is fair to the adherents of *all* reasonable comprehensive doctrines, that it is not merely an 'account of how those who hold political power can satisfy themselves, in light of their own convictions, ... that they are acting properly' (Rawls 1989, p. 247; see also, for example, Rawls 1996, pp. 143–44).

Political liberals argue that the governance framework they promote is 'fair' insofar as it is *neutral* among the plurality of reasonable conceptions of the good likely to be present at anytime in contemporary liberal democracies. It is important to note that political liberals generally distinguish between three different understandings of 'neutrality' – namely, *procedural neutrality, neutrality of aim*, and *neutrality of effect* or *influence* – and contend that political liberalism achieves and need only maintain a certain degree of procedural neutrality and neutrality of aim in order to be correctly considered neutral. Essentially, what that means is that the public conception of justice must refrain from purposely favouring a particular comprehensive doctrine that contains any controversial view(s) concerning the nature and content of the good life;[12] to act otherwise would be to fail to provide the equal respect due to all reasonable persons and thus preclude the achievement of an overlapping consensus. Political liberals argue that a 'properly laid out' (e.g., Rawls 1996, p. 386) political conception of justice will ensure, to the greatest extent possible, that the political process remains equally accessible to all. By doing so, political liberalism is claimed to protect against such things as the adoption of illiberal policies and the emergence of a tyranny of the majority. Such protection will be secured insofar as the conception of justice guarantees to all individuals certain basic rights, liberties and opportunities.[13] Proponents of political liberalism contend that it offers a governance framework that embodies the necessary neutrality and, by extension, exhibits the type of fairness required to secure adequate protection against abusive behaviour and, subsequently, establish and preserve a just and stable liberal democracy.

However, the arguments employed by political liberals to justify their conclusions regarding the neutrality of their understanding of the proper exercise of coercive political power are premised upon a number of extremely questionable claims and demands. In turn, the dubiousness of those claims and demands brings into serious doubt the ability of liberals' proposed governance framework to achieve and preserve the type of neutrality it requires if it is to offer the desired protection against 'abusive' behaviour and thus secure and maintain the support essential to a well-ordered society.

A particularly problematic claim concerns the suggested effect – or, more correctly, lack thereof – of a public denial of the acceptability of certain beliefs. Political liberals acknowledge that there may be instances when it is publicly necessary 'to assert [the primacy of] at least certain aspects of … [their] own comprehensive religious or philosophical doctrine' and, in so doing, deny the acceptability of beliefs that conflict with the political conception of justice (e.g., Rawls 1996, p. 152; Larmore 1996, p. 139; Shklar 1989, p. 24). Basically, such an assertion will be required when holders of a conflicting belief also deems it acceptable to use political power to force all citizens to act in a manner that is consistent with the demands associated with that belief. Such a situation will arise 'whenever someone insists that certain questions are so fundamental that to ensure their being rightly settled justifies civil strife' (Rawls 1996, p. 152). In such instances, there may be 'no alternative but to deny this, or to imply its denial and hence to maintain the kind of thing … [political liberals hope] to avoid' (Rawls 1996, p. 152).[14] Somewhat amazingly, though, political liberals do not believe that such a public denial unacceptably violates or undermines the neutrality of the political conception of justice; they contend that so long as such public assertions deny only what is necessary to maintain the overlapping consensus, the conception of justice remains sufficiently neutral and, by extension, 'reasonable' (e.g., Rawls 1996, p. 153; Larmore 1987, p. 68).

However, political liberals essentially remain silent with respect to identifying precisely who is to determine *what* aspects of *which* doctrine(s) are to be asserted, exactly how much of said doctrine(s) need be advanced to maintain the overlapping consensus, and under what circumstances it is both necessary and just to initiate such an action. In the absence of any explicit declaration as to who will make such decisions, it seems logical to assume that they will be the strict domain of those who hold political power. In turn, in a polity governed by the principles of political liberalism, only those who satisfy the corresponding definition of 'reasonable' will have the opportunity to obtain any noteworthy degree of political power. Yet, such restrictions would seem to undermine the neutrality/ reasonableness of the governance framework and knowingly permit 'abusive' behaviour insofar as they purposely allow for inequality in terms of access to political power and opportunity to influence public policy.[15]

Nevertheless, political liberals argue that it is quite acceptable to place such 'reasonable' restrictions on the access to political power and influence. Though such an approach has the effect of requiring that all who wish to obtain political power affirm comprehensive doctrines that are considered 'reasonable' according to political liberalism, that stipulation is presented as being unproblematic. Given that there is 'no social world that does not exclude some ways of life that realize in special ways certain fundamental values' (Rawls 1996, p. 197; see also, Rawls 2001, p. 36, n. 26, p. 154, p. 55 n. 30; and Larmore 1999, p. 624, n. 27), the fact that the governance framework promoted by political liberalism is unable to accommodate equally the totality of views that will exist in a contemporary liberal democracy is not, it is argued, proof of an unacceptable degree of bias or exclusion. Indeed, by making 'reasonableness' the standard of inclusion and access, political liberalism is claimed to provide for the greatest degree of accommodation and equality of access to political power, and thus represents what is arguably the least 'abusive' regulatory framework possible under conditions of extreme diversity like those found in contemporary liberal democracies.

Not surprisingly, then, political liberals insist that a governance framework may legitimately promote 'reasonable' beliefs and values and in so doing 'shape' other doctrines (and, indeed, transgress the precept of avoidance!) without violating or undermining its neutrality or engaging in an 'unreasonable' use of state power (e.g., Rawls 1996, pp. 194, 246; see also Larmore 1987, pp. 44–46, 54, 67; 1996, pp. 139–141, 145; Shklar 1989, p. 29). It is therefore not an abuse of political power when it is exercised 'reasonably' (which is to say, legitimately) over those who refuse to adopt or maintain 'reasonable' comprehensive doctrines (e.g., Rawls 1996, p. xix; Larmore 1987, pp. 60, 66–68). Thus it would seem that political liberals accept as legitimate a bias in favour of 'reasonable' doctrines.

Inequality and the fair value of political liberties

According to political liberals, the political inequality that they tolerate is an unfortunate but unavoidable fact of life in contemporary liberal democracies. Hence, so long as political liberalism minimises such inequality to the degree humanly possible, it does nothing to jeopardise its neutrality, or 'reasonableness'. One of the principal ways in which the governance framework secures the necessary degree of equality is by providing the same political liberties to all individuals and ensuring the 'fair value' of those liberties. What that means is that, regardless of an individual's socio-economic status, the 'basic liberties'[16] secured by the conception of justice will be of 'approximately equal, or at least sufficiently equal' worth to all citizens (Rawls 1996, p. 327). It is argued that guaranteeing such 'fair value' prevents '[t]hose with greater responsibility and wealth … [from controlling] the course of legislation to their advantage' (Rawls 1996, p. 325; see also p. 360).

However, though political liberals recognise the need to guarantee the fair value of the basic liberties secured by the conception of justice, they fail to provide any suggestions as to how such an assurance might be concretely realised. Lacking such a guarantee, it does not seem unreasonable to believe that those who affirm a comprehensive doctrine/conception of the good that embodies the notion of 'reasonableness' promoted by political liberalism will be better able than others to both capitalise on the basic liberties provided by the governance framework and, consequently, secure political power and influence. So while it is supposed that all citizens will have 'a fair opportunity to hold public office and influence political decisions' (Rawls 1996, p. 327), there is no clearly identified mechanism to ensure the realisation of that goal, and, subsequently, no effective way to guarantee that political power will not become primarily the domain of those citizens who are best able to take advantage of the basic liberties secured by the conception of justice – i.e., 'those with greater responsibility and wealth'. In turn, those possessing such an advantage 'can combine together and exclude [from political influence] those who have less' (Rawls 1996, p. 328). Given the history of politics in modern democratic regimes, it does not seem overly pessimistic or unduly sceptical to fear that a group which finds itself comprising the political majority will seek to dominate the legislative process and shape public policies and practices to better accommodate its particular comprehensive view(s), with little or no meaningful concern for how such actions might detrimentally affect others. And, as Rawls notes, 'in the long run a strong majority of the electorate can eventually make the *constitution* conform to its political will' (Rawls 1996, p. 233, emphasis added).

Political liberals try to allay such fears by arguing that so long as citizens and (especially) decision-makers continue to respect the demands of reasonable disagreement and adhere to the precept of avoidance, 'the political conception will still be supported regardless of shifts in the distribution of political power' (Rawls 1996, p. 148; see also, for example, Larmore 1996, pp. 132–133), and under such circumstances there will be, in effect, little inclination to abuse political power (e.g., Rawls 1996, p. 252). According to political liberals, the observed character and behaviour of the citizens of existing contemporary liberal democracies makes it reasonable to expect the continued satisfaction of such conditions.[17] However, to accept the possibility that a group may withdraw its support for the principle of reasonable disagreement when it found itself in a position where to do so would (seemingly) be to its advantage, does not necessitate any misrepresentation of current empirical reality. As Bruce Ackerman has noted, 'It is remarkably easy for men and women to forget their political principles in their eagerness to use state power for their own aggrandizement – and then write up fancy pieces of paper proclaiming their public virtue' (Ackerman 1994, p. 377).

The belief that one can effectively minimise or manage such problems by limiting the scope of what can be legitimately 'denied' publicly – i.e., only those claims that jeopardise the security of the overlapping consensus – is itself based upon an extremely debatable and fragile presumption: namely, that in a well-ordered society political power will not be intentionally perverted for partisan purposes. Such a constraint on government authority offers an effective means for reducing or controlling both 'unreasonable' exclusion from the means of political influence and, subsequently, the illegitimate use of coercive state power, only insofar as one assumes that in those instances in which certain beliefs or values must publicly be given primacy over conflicting beliefs or values, those who are assigned the task of determining exactly what needs to be done will not use the opportunity to promote certain beliefs unnecessarily or in a manner that extends beyond that which is required to maintain an overlapping consensus. Yet, surely an individual will be motivated to behave in such a manner only to the extent that she values reasonableness more than she values the 'truth', and there exists no persuasive evidence to suggest that many individuals will voluntarily embrace and faithfully maintain such a disposition, even if requests to do so are restricted to 'political' enterprises. If anything, empirical research would seem to suggest that it is at least equally as likely that in instances of conflict between the pursuit of one's fundamental 'truths' and the realisation of publicly 'reasonable' goals, individuals will opt to act in a way that supports the former, regardless of the consequences for the latter.[18] Regrettably, throughout the course of the twentieth century and continuing into the twenty-first century, 'liberal democratic' governments have been quite willing, when they deemed it expedient, desirable or necessary, to transgress or suspend various of the basic liberties promoted by political liberals, if doing so might help to facilitate the advancement of a particular (i.e., partisan) goal.

In essence, political liberals respond to the above-noted concerns and criticisms by suggesting that '[w]e must accept the facts of commonsense political sociology' (Rawls 1996, p. 193); the potential for the perversion of political power 'is simply a fact about political power as such' (Rawls 1996, p. 33; see also, for example, Shklar 1989, p. 28). Such a concession, however, seems to acknowledge the inability of political liberalism to offer adequate assurance that those who hold political power will not use it to promote and entrench their own beliefs and values, regardless of the consequences for others who affirm different views. Hence, in practical terms, political liberalism would seem knowingly to allow for the *political ghettoisation*[19] of the least advantaged.

Importantly, even if one accepts political liberals' justifications for allowing unequal access to political power, and disregards the potential questions and concerns stimulated by the associated exclusions, problems remain. In particular, the belief that the governance framework promoted by political liberalism can secure the type and degree of voluntary support deemed essential for the establishment and preservation of a well-ordered society is itself premised upon an unrealistic assumption: namely, the presence of a universal agreement among reasonable people as to the precise character and proper application of 'reasonable' values and principles, including the reasonable use of political power. If reasonableness is the benchmark for determining what constitutes acceptable public behaviour, then each citizen's interpretation of what qualifies as the legitimate exercise of coercive political power will be intimately and inextricably connected to her understanding of the demands of reasonableness. Consequently, creating and preserving the sought after socio-political conditions (e.g., 'reasonable' individual liberty and equal respect) will require that the majority of citizens affirm and maintain an identical definition of 'reasonable', including what constitutes both the reasonable exercise of coercive political power and a reasonable inequality of access to such power.

Yet, surely it is implausible to suggest, as do political liberals, that such a prerequisite could ever be effectively satisfied, even among 'reasonable' people. Ineliminable 'reasonable' differences of opinion will exist concerning the political culture's 'most salient elements' (Klosko 1993, p. 352; see also Klosko 2000; Bohman 1995, p. 268; Neal 1995; and Young 2001) and, subsequently, the definition of what constitutes a 'reasonable' demand will itself be a noteworthy source of controversy and conflict among 'reasonable' people. While it *might* be possible to secure a broad, voluntary public agreement on what constitutes the *general* character of a reasonable 'political' demand – in this case, the acceptable exercise of coercive political power – such an agreement becomes much more difficult to maintain once one is forced to apply general principles to specific questions of political justice, especially when said questions concern matters of 'the first significance' (e.g., basic liberties). To illustrate: both my neighbour and I may agree that the right to freedom of expression is an essential component of a 'reasonable' governance framework. However, while I may believe that such a right does not include the right to publish pornography or racist literature, my neighbour may deem any censorship an unreasonable restriction upon her freedom of expression. Hence, though both my neighbour and I endorse the concept of freedom of expression, we nevertheless significantly disagree about its 'reasonable' application. Political liberals acknowledge the inevitability of such disagreement, conceding that it is 'unreasonable' not to recognise 'the practical certainty' of irreconcilable disagreements between 'reasonable' people (e.g., Rawls 1996, p. 240, 57–64; see also Rawls 2001, pp. 35–36; Larmore 1987, p. 52; 1996, p. 169; Shklar 1984, pp. 8, 227; 1989, p. 35).

In the final analysis, the unavoidably contestable character of reasonableness makes it unrealistic to presume that all 'reasonable' people will freely and willingly endorse and *remain faithful to* any single definition of 'reasonable' and its associated demands. However, only by ensuring such a homogeneity can one be 'reasonably' assured of securing the type of reliable protection against 'unreasonable' (i.e., abusive) behaviour and, subsequently, the unwavering voluntary support required to guarantee the continuation of the overlapping consensus and, by extension, the maintenance of a well-ordered society.

Conclusion

The approach advocated by political liberals (and, indeed, liberals in general) effectively renders one's ability to follow and realise a life-plan of her own design dependent upon the reasonableness of both the governance framework and her fellow citizens. In particular, providing a 'reasonable' opportunity for all citizens to adopt and pursue self-chosen interests and ends requires that the capacity of government to restrict individual freedom be subjected to 'reasonable' limitations, and the opportunity to abuse political power be minimised to the extent humanly possible. Only by instituting and preserving a governance framework that embodies such constraints and thereby safeguards against the arbitrary violation of certain fundamental individual rights and liberties can one hope to establish and sustain a just and stable liberal democracy. Accordingly, from the perspective of political liberalism, the crucial consideration for all concerned is the *reasonableness* of the restrictions on 'public' behaviour. Essentially, political liberals suggest that if individuals reject the principles of political liberalism 'unreasonably', that is a problem for those individuals, not a problem for political liberalism (Holmes 1993, p. 46); the governance framework promoted by political liberals is not 'unreasonable', or 'abusive', merely because it refuses to accommodate unreasonable expectations (e.g., Rawls 1996, p. 189).

However, if one *must* affirm a 'reasonable' comprehensive doctrine in order to have even the hope of securing any meaningful degree of political power or influence, then how politically neutral is political liberalism? Further, if only those affirming 'reasonable' comprehensive doctrines are, in effect, able to obtain any noteworthy degree of political efficacy, then why should those who are excluded from the sphere of political power consider the political conception of justice to be anything other than the unreasonable and *unjust* enforcement of the comprehensive views of those who affirm (certain) reasonable comprehensive doctrines? (e.g., Rawls 1996, p. 153–155) Contra the suggestions (or hopes) of political liberals, the number of individuals likely to suffer such 'exclusion' is significant. As Patrick Neal (among others) has noted, 'there are, have been, and will be many people (millions and millions!) who are at least as reasonable as John Rawls and ... who do not believe in the values of political liberalism or the liberal version of tolerance' (Neal 1995, p. 25). Indeed, it has been suggested that somewhere between 20% and 40% of the US population (approximately 50–100 million people!), for example, affirms doctrines that would be incompatible with the demands of political liberalism (e.g., Klosko 1996, pp. 258–259; see also Klosko 2000).[20]

While it is undoubtedly true that most individuals would prefer to prevent certain people or groups from acquiring any 'dangerous' degree of political power or influence (however that might be defined), surely, if *all* citizens are to be treated as free and equal beings able to exercise the basic capacities of reason, then the decision as to who should be allowed to acquire political power cannot be predetermined and, in effect, isolated from public debate. In other words, treating people in the manner advocated by political liberalism would seem to render invalid any *a priori* attempt to limit access to political power and influence. At minimum, by restricting the acquisition of political power to those who affirm 'reasonable' comprehensive doctrines, political liberalism generates what amounts to a *forced* doctrinal homogeneity necessitated and legitimated by the political conception of justice[21] – precisely the type of outcome that political liberalism is meant to prevent. And, as Rawls observes, 'a comprehensive doctrine, whenever widely, if not universally shared in society, tends to become oppressive and stifling' (Rawls 1992, p. 597, n. 3).[22] Hence, whether doctrinal homogeneity emerges as a consequence of explicit coercion or reasonable 'shaping', the result is the same: an 'oppressive and stifling' environment.

In the final analysis, the ability of political liberalism to protect citizens against the 'abuse' of political power is sabotaged significantly by what might be called the 'paradox of reasonableness'. Such protection is possible only if the governance framework equally respects the reasonableness of all those subject to its demands; however, insofar as it does so and relies upon the reasonableness of those involved to secure and sustain the necessary environment, it allows for the emergence and rule of unreasonableness, and in so doing impedes its ability to accomplish the task for which it has been developed.

Particularly problematic is the failure of political liberals to either seriously consider or adequately respond to the possibility that 'reasonable' people in possession of political power will, when the opportunity presents itself, use the mechanisms of state coercion to further a partisan agenda – whether their own or that of a particular group or segment of the citizenry – with little meaningful concern for how their actions might detrimentally affect those who affirm different or conflicting beliefs and values (reasonable or otherwise). Though different formulations of political liberalism acknowledge to varying degrees the problem of the potential perversion of political power, all fail to protect adequately against the abuse of political power by 'reasonable' people. Even in those instances when the problem of the abuse of political power is given centre stage – such as in Shklarian political liberalism – the resulting conception still neglects to engage more than the most blatant difficulties, and in so doing leaves problematic gaps which critically undermine the ability of political liberalism to both ensure the 'neutral' exercise of coercive political power and, subsequently, secure the type of protection against 'unreasonable' public behaviour required to establish and sustain an overlapping consensus and, by extension, a well-ordered polity (as such is generally defined by political liberals). Despite assumptions or hopes to the contrary, 'reasonable' people, too, pose a threat against which citizens need to be protected. In underestimating the threat posed by 'reasonable' people, political liberals fail to respond to the entire range of potential significant dilemmas associated with the possible abuse of political power. That failure unnecessarily leaves citizens vulnerable to such abuse.

The above remarks are not meant to suggest that it is possible to eliminate completely the threat of the abuse of political power. Rather, it is hoped that the preceding critique will help to demonstrate and emphasise the need for political philosophers to consider seriously the practical constraints within which they necessarily must operate if they wish to effect meaningful concrete change. Admittedly, many political philosophers are quite satisfied engaging in utopian theorising; indeed, for some, it represents the only 'true' form of political philosophy.[23] Arguably, however, liberalism is animated by greater (practical) ambitions. Insofar as such a conclusion is valid, liberal political philosophers must avoid convenient conjecture and utopian theorising and confront the often unpalatable socio-political realities that are the offspring of contemporary liberal-democratic capitalist societies. Such an approach does not require that liberals abandon their emphasis on 'reasonableness', but it does demand that they unqualifiedly accept and more forthrightly acknowledge and respond to the ineliminable (and seemingly increasing) practical limitations that impede the realisation of the ideally 'reasonable' liberal polity.

Acknowledgements

I would like to thank George Crowder, Janet McIntyre, George Klosko, Leah Bradshaw, Murray Faure, and Phil Triadafilopoulos for their helpful comments on earlier versions of this paper.

Notes

1. It is, perhaps, worth noting that such a characterisation of Hobbes is not universally endorsed. Whereas numerous eminent political philosophers, including Leo Strauss, Michael Oakeshott, C.B. Macpherson, and Ian Shapiro – to name only a few – have argued that Hobbes is (in one sense or another) the progenitor of liberalism, others, such as Judith Shklar and Stephen Holmes, contend that it is a gross misinterpretation to label Hobbes a liberal (e.g., Shklar 1989, Holmes 1995). Thankfully, the resolution of that debate is not required for the purpose of this essay.
2. I am here using the chronological categories employed by Bramsted and Melhuish (1978) in their detailed survey of the history of Western liberalism.
3. Briefly stated, the understanding of the relationship between 'reason' and 'reasonableness' that informs the arguments contained herein is as follows: the proper exercise of reason generates 'reasonable' results. Of course, the same results can be produced in the absence of such circumstances (e.g., purely unintentionally).
4. In the vernacular of political liberals, matters of 'public' import are also referred to as 'political' matters. Accordingly, unless specifically noted otherwise, I shall use the terms 'public' and 'political' interchangeably.
5. It might be protested that Judith Shklar, for example, not only makes no such claim but, indeed, she explicitly eschews such an approach (e.g., Shklar 1989). However, as I have elsewhere argued (e.g., Young 2002, esp. chap. 5), I believe that, despite her assertions to the contrary, her conception of political liberalism cannot help but embrace such an approach. I would suggest that the same holds true – to varying degrees – for all liberal theories of justice.
6. By 'governance framework' I mean the system of moral and legal principles and values that regulate behaviour in the public realm – i.e., what John Rawls labels the 'political conception of justice'. Unless specified otherwise, I will use the terms 'governance framework' and 'political conception of justice' interchangeably.
7. Simply put, an *overlapping consensus* is a free and willing agreement among the adherents of the various competing, conflicting and often irreconcilable comprehensive doctrines that are *likely* to survive in a *just* contemporary liberal democracy (e.g., Rawls 1996, pp. 133–172).
8. A 'comprehensive doctrine' is one that 'applies to all subjects and its virtues cover all parts of life [e.g., public and nonpublic]' (Rawls 1996, p. xxxviii, n. 4) – it is 'a moral ideal to govern all of life' (Rawls 1985, p. 245).
9. 'Basic liberties' are the 'institutional rights and duties that entitle citizens to do various things, if they wish, and that forbid others to interfere' (Rawls 1996, p. 325). Such liberties include 'freedom of thought and liberty of conscience; the political liberties and freedom of association, as well as the freedoms specified by the liberty and the integrity of the person; and finally, the rights and liberties covered by the rule of law' (Rawls 1996, p. 291).
10. Unless specified otherwise, I will use the terms 'conception of justice' and 'political conception of justice' interchangeably.
11. More specifically, coercive political power is exercised legitimately when it is employed 'in accordance with a constitution the essentials of which all citizens as free and equal may reasonably be expected to endorse in the light of principles and ideals

acceptable to their common human reason' (Rawls 1996, p. 137; see also, for example, Larmore 1999, p. 606; and Shklar 1989, p. 37).

12. For a detailed description of the notions of *procedural neutrality, neutrality of aim,* and *neutrality of effect* or *influence* see Rawls (1996, pp. 191–193).

13. For a partial general list of those rights please refer to note 9.

14. Rawls, for example, uses the concept of *rationalist believers* to illustrate the type of individuals who may necessitate such denials (Rawls 1996, p. 153, n. 18). Rationalist believers are individuals who contend that the beliefs contained within their respective comprehensive doctrines 'are open to and can be fully established by reason', and therefore it is quite proper to use state power to enforce those beliefs (Rawls 1996, pp. 152–153; see also Shklar 1989, p. 25; and Larmore 1987, p. 66). The suggestion is that rationalist believers and others like them will comprise a small minority of the population, at most.

15. Recall, political power is 'abused' not only when it is intentionally used to further the goals or values of a particular comprehensive doctrine or conception of the good to the detriment of others, but also when its employment 'unreasonably' prevents any person or group from having an equal opportunity to secure political influence/ efficacy.

16. There is an ambiguous relationship between *basic liberties* and *political liberties*: Despite some suggestions seemingly to the contrary (e.g., Rawls 1996, p. 291), it remains unclear whether the two are one and the same, if one contains the other, or if there is a distinctive difference in terms of the composition of the two (e.g., Rawls 1996, pp. 289–371). The most persuasive interpretation, and the one used in this essay, denies the latter proposition.

17. This is not to suggest that political liberals believe that the citizens of existing liberal democracies completely satisfy the requirements of the political liberal understanding of 'reasonableness' (though I believe that the arguments of political liberals often allow for such an interpretation). However, at minimum, political liberals typically suggest that the *observed* character and behaviour of said citizens is sufficiently 'reasonable' and consistent (and promising) to justify the claim that it is not unrealistic, or 'utopian', to imagine a society that is populated primarily by citizens who are completely 'reasonable' in the necessary sense.

18. For example, see Stouffer (1955); Prothro and Grigg (1960); McClosky and Brill (1983); McClosky and Zaller (1984); Gibson (1986; 1989); Sniderman, Fletcher, Russell, and Tetlock (1989, 1996); and Abu-Laban and Stasiulis (1992).

19. By *political ghettoisation* I am referring to the marginalisation of individuals who would be relegated to the fringes of political existence as a consequence of their political inefficacy. Even if political liberals could provide a viable plan by which the ideal of 'fair value' could be formally institutionalised, it is debatable as to whether any such formal entrenchment would or could eliminate, or even substantially alleviate, the problem of political ghettoisation. As Katherine Fierlbeck has noted: 'Despite the success of most Western democracies in providing formal institutions of political justice for their citizens, it remains distressingly clear that some groups within these polities have not experienced the same level of social or material (and sometimes even political) benefits enjoyed by dominant groups within the same societies' (Fierlbeck 1996, p. 3). For a recent, instructive examination of the problem of political marginalisation in the US, see Jacobs and Skocpol (2005).

20. Equally interesting, it has been argued that while anywhere from 60% to 80% of the US population affirms what could be labelled 'moderate' doctrines – that is, doctrines that do not generate 'unbridgeable gaps' among the citizenry (e.g., Klosko 1996, pp. 258–259; see also Klosko 2000) – when trying to resolve contentious political questions, the general ignorance of the members of that cohort 'allows extremists and special interest groups to play on their emotions and so to manipulate them' (Klosko

1996, p. 259), thereby enabling (purportedly) 'rational' but 'unreasonable' objectives to win the day.

21. For more on this point see Shaun Young (2002), esp. chap. 6.

22. It might be argued that such a criticism is here inapplicable or ineffective given that political liberalism is not a 'comprehensive' doctrine. However, such a characterization of political liberalism is certainly not universally accepted. Indeed, even political liberals seem to concede that it is not necessarily unreasonable to identify political liberalism as a 'partially comprehensive doctrine' (e.g., Rawls 1996, p. 29, n. 31 and p. 154, n. 20). For more on this claim see Young (1999, p. 183).

23. For example, Ronald Beiner has argued that 'true' political philosophy does not seek 'to offer sensible guidance on the conduct of social life, but rather to probe the normative adequacy of a given vision of social order by pushing that particular vision as far as it will go' (Beiner 1997, p. ix). According to Beiner, true political philosophy is 'radical, extravagant, probing, biting, and immoderate' (Beiner 1997, p. x), and it is impossible to achieve those qualities and simultaneously seek to address practical questions.

References

Abu-Laban, Y. and Stasiulis, D., 1992. Ethnic pluralism under siege: popular and partisan opposition to multiculturalism. *Canadian public policy,* 18(4), 365–386.

Ackerman, B., 1994. Political liberalisms. *Journal of philosophy,* 91(7), 364–386.

Beiner, R., 1997. *Philosophy in a time of lost spirit: essays on contemporary theory.* Toronto: University of Toronto Press.

Bohman, J., 1995. Public reason and cultural pluralism: political liberalism and the problem of moral conflict. *Political theory,* 23(2), 253–279.

Bramsted, E. and Melhuish, K., eds, 1978. *Western liberalism: a history in documents from Locke to Croce.* London and New York: Longman Group Ltd.

Fierlbeck, K., 1996. The ambivalent potential of cultural identity. *Canadian journal of political science,* 29(1), 3–22.

Gibson, J., 1986. Pluralistic intolerance in America. *American politics quarterly,* 14(2), 267–293.

Gibson, J., 1989. The structure of attitudinal tolerance in the United States. *British journal of political science,* 19(4), 562–570.

Holmes, S., 1993. The gatekeeper. *The new republic,* 209(15), 39–47.

Holmes, S., 1995. *Passions and constraint: on the theory of liberal democracy.* Chicago: University of Chicago Press.

Jacobs, L. and Skocpol, T., eds, 2005. *Inequality and American democracy: what we know and what we need to know.* New York: Russell Sage.

Klosko, G., 1993. Rawls's 'political' philosophy and American democracy. *American political science review,* 87(2), 348–359.

Klosko, G., 1996. Liberalism and pluralism. *Social theory and practice,* 22(2), 251–269.

Klosko, G., 2000. *Democratic procedures and liberal consensus.* Oxford: Oxford University Press.

Larmore, C., 1987. *Patterns of moral complexity.* Cambridge: Cambridge University Press.

Larmore, C., 1996. *The morals of modernity.* New York: Cambridge University Press.

Larmore, C., 1999. The moral basis of political liberalism. *Journal of philosophy,* 96(12), 599–625.

Macedo, S., 2000. In defense of liberal public reason: are slavery and abortion hard cases? *In:* R. George and C. Wolfe, eds. *Natural law and public reason.* Washington, DC: Georgetown University Press, 11–49.

McClosky, H. and Brill, A., 1983. *Dimensions of tolerance.* New York: Russell Sage Foundation.

McClosky, H. and Zaller, J., 1984. *The American ethos.* Cambridge, MA: Harvard University Press.

Moore, M., 1996. On reasonableness. *Journal of applied philosophy,* 13(2), 167–178.

Neal, P., 1995. Against liberal public reason. Paper presented at the annual general meeting of the Canadian Political Science Association. Unpublished.

Prothro, J. and Grigg, C., 1960. Fundamental principles of democracy: bases of agreement and disagreement. *Journal of politics,* 22(1), 276–294.

Rawls, J., 1982. The basic liberties and their priority. *In:* S. McMurrin, ed. *The Tanner lectures on human values.* Salt Lake City: Utah University Press, 4–87.

Rawls, J. (1985) Justice as fairness: political not metaphysical. *Philosophy and public affairs,* 14(3), 223–251.

Rawls, J., 1989. The domain of the political and overlapping consensus. *New York university law review,* 64(2), 233–255.

Rawls, J., 1992. The idea of an overlapping consensus. *In:* J. Arthur and W. Shaw, eds, *Social and political philosophy,* Englewood Cliffs: Prentice-Hall, 593–608.

Rawls, J., 1996. *Political liberalism.* New York: Columbia University Press.

Rawls, J., 2001. *Justice as fairness: a restatement,* ed. E. Kelly. Cambridge, MA: Belknap Press.

Shklar, J., 1984. *Ordinary vices.* Cambridge, MA: Harvard University Press.

Shklar, J., 1989. The liberalism of fear. *In:* N. Rosenblum, ed. *Liberalism and the moral life.* Cambridge, MA: Harvard University Press, 21–38.

Sniderman, P., Fletcher, J., Russell, P., and Tetlock, P. 1989. Political culture and the problem of double standards: mass and elite attitudes toward language rights in the Canadian Charter of Rights and Freedoms. *Canadian journal of political science,* 22(2), 259–284.

Sniderman, P., Fletcher, J., Russell, P., and Tetlock, P. 1996. *The clash of rights: liberty, equality, and legitimacy in pluralist democracy.* New Haven, CT: Yale University Press.

Stouffer, S., 1955. *Communism, conformity, and civil liberties.* New York: Doubleday.

Young, S., 1999. A utopian fallacy? Political power in Rawls's *Political liberalism. Journal of social philosophy,* 30(1), 174–193.

Young, S., 2001. Divide and conquer: separating the reasonable from the unreasonable. *Journal of social philosophy,* 32(1), 53–69.

Young, S., 2002. The viability of the concept of political liberalism. DLitt et Phil thesis, Department of Political Sciences, University of South Africa.

INDEX

For Product Safety Concerns and Information please contact our EU
representative GPSR@taylorandfrancis.com
Taylor & Francis Verlag GmbH, Kaufingerstraße 24, 80331 München, Germany